T0336544

Supply Chain Costing and Performance Management

Supply Chain Costing and Performance Management

SECOND EDITION

GARY COKINS
TERRANCE POHLEN
THOMAS KLAMMER

WILEY

Library of Congress Cataloging-in-Publication Data

Names: Cokins, Gary, author. | Pohlen, Terrance, author. | Klammer, Thomas P., 1944- author.
Title: Supply chain costing and performance management / Gary Cokins, Terrance Pohlen, Thomas Klammer.
Description: Second edition. | Hoboken, New Jersey : Wiley, [2021] | Includes index.
Identifiers: LCCN 2021018152 (print) | LCCN 2021018153 (ebook) | ISBN 9781119793632 (cloth) | ISBN 9781119793656 (adobe pdf) | ISBN 9781119793649 (epub) | ISBN 9781119793663 (obook)
Subjects: LCSH: Business logistics. | Cost allocation.
Classification: LCC HD38.5 .C6455 2021 (print) | LCC HD38.5 (ebook) | DDC 658.7—dc23
LC record available at https://lccn.loc.gov/2021018152
LC ebook record available at https://lccn.loc.gov/2021018153

Cover Design: Wiley
Cover Image: © Hernan4429/Getty Images

SKY10027095_051721

From Gary Cokins: I am grateful to my wife, Pam Tower, for tolerating my challenge to balance my work and family life. I would also like to dedicate this book to the late Robert S. Bonsack as a mentor and friend, under whom I worked at both Deloitte consulting and Electronic Data Systems (now part of Hewlett Packard).

From Tom Klammer: In memory of my late wife, Pat, who put up for 50-plus years with my being on the road or wrapped up in research or teaching. Also, a thank-you to the University of North Texas (UNT) for the ongoing support they provided me for many years.

From Terry Pohlen: A special thank-you to my wife, Susan, for her tremendous and enduring support during my military and academic careers. I also wish to thank the University of North Texas and the Ryan College of Business for enabling me to perform this research and to participate in the writing of this book.

Contents

Preface

DOES YOUR FIRM
- Know its supply chain costs?
- Effectively manage these costs?
- Understand how process or strategy changes impact supply chain costs?
- Have cost information adequate to support supply chain decisions?
- Understand who is responsible for (causes) supply chain costs?
- Know how much supply chain costs are unidentified?
  The answers for most firms are "Probably not!"

Supply Chain Costing and Performance Management was developed to assist supply chain executives, managers, and teams in expanding their visibility and management of cost and profit information. Supply chain management offers tremendous potential to increase performance and decrease costs while substantially improving the value proposition experienced by the end user and other key stakeholders. Despite major strides forward in integrating their supply chains, executives have achieved only the tip of the iceberg in terms of the potential savings available through supply chain management.

To achieve the full potential of supply chain management, executives require a much broader view of costs than is currently available from their firms' cost management systems. They need to improve their internal cost information and extend their "line of sight" to include how their trading partners drive costs and performance of key supply chain processes—both upstream and downstream. Without a broader perspective of cost and performance, supply chains and their associated costs cannot be effectively managed since many costs incurred within a firm are driven by the business practices of external trading partners. Extending visibility across the supply chain coupled with interfirm cost management can reveal new and potentially greater opportunities for cost reduction and performance improvements than can be achieved by a single firm.

Numerous challenges confront executives attempting to extend their visibility and control over costs and performance beyond the boundaries of their firms. Existing cost systems largely have an internal focus—within their "four walls." They do not possess the capability to portray cost information as required to support supply chain decision-making: by product, service, supply chain process, customer, and distribution channel or supply chain. Trading partners often refuse to share their cost information due to the possibility of opportunistic action with the supply chain, reduced leverage during price negotiations, release of sensitive competitive information, or simply the inability of their costs systems to produce the necessary information. An effective mechanism for fairly sharing the benefits and burdens resulting from collaborative action is missing in many supply chain relationships. Although collaborative action frequently creates value for the participating firms, executives lack the cost and financial tools to measure and demonstrate the value created.

The purpose of *Supply Chain Costing and Performance Management* is to assist executives, managers, and teams in their pursuit of supply chain costing. The implementation process is described as a journey. Many firms have a clear vision of what they are seeking to achieve, but none have fully completed the process. The journey that leading firms have followed can serve as a roadmap for others to follow. The journey taken by a firm may differ depending on the cost information required, the strategy the firm employs, and its position in the supply chains in which it participates. In many instances, firms will need to iterate through the process after having developed a foundation internally that would support the development of supply chain costing. Based on research we have defined supply chain costing as:

> the collection, expense assignment, and analysis of cost information across all of the work activities comprising a supply chain for the purpose of identifying opportunities to obtain a competitive advantage through a combination of reduced costs or improved performance.

The management of supply chain costs and performance has never been as important as it is now. The COVID-19 outbreak in 2020 and 2021 has wreaked havoc on many supply chains by creating tremendous volatility in demand and supply. Companies have experienced rapid and abrupt changes in consumer demand or sudden shifts in distribution channels as individuals worked from home and no longer dined out. Trade wars have resulted in many firms shifting the manufacture or sourcing of their products to other regions, nearshoring, or developing new domestic sources. Electronic commerce continues to rapidly expand as many consumers have changed their purchasing habits and prefer to shop online to take advantage of a wider array of goods and competitive prices. These factors and many others have accentuated the need to understand how activity and process changes occurring across the entire supply chain drive costs and performance, both internally and externally, for all trading partners. This information is essential for not only identifying opportunities to reduce cost or improve performance but most importantly for determining how to obtain and sustain a competitive marketplace advantage.

Implementation of supply chain costing and performance management can provide the next major breakthrough in supply chain management that can propel firms and their upstream suppliers and downstream customers to a much higher plateau of value creation.

The authors wish you the greatest success as you explore and move forward in your journey to implement supply chain costing and performance. We believe the many tools and concepts provided here can assist you in your journey and that it will serve as an invaluable reference during your efforts.

About the Authors

GARY COKINS IS AN internationally recognized expert, speaker, and author in enterprise and corporate performance management (EPM/CPM) improvement methods and business analytics. He is the founder of Analytics-Based Performance Management, an advisory firm located in Cary, North Carolina (www.garycokins.com). Gary received his BS degree with honors in Industrial Engineering/Operations Research from Cornell University and his MBA with honors from Northwestern University's Kellogg School of Management.

He began his career as a strategic planner with FMC's Link-Belt Division and then served as financial controller and operations manager. In 1981 Gary began his management consulting career, first with Deloitte consulting, and then in 1988 with KPMG consulting. In 1992 he headed the National Cost Management Consulting Services for Electronic Data Systems (EDS), now part of HP. From 1997 until 2013 he was a principal consultant with SAS, a leading provider of business analytics software.

Gary is active with professional institutes including the Institute of Management Accountants (IMA), the Association for Supply Chain Management (ASCM), and the Institute of Management Science and Operations Research (INFORMS). He was honored to be selected as the inaugural 2013 IMA Distinguished Member Award. One interesting honor that few know about Gary is that he is in the Cooperstown, New York, Baseball Hall of Fame for the "Oldest Computer Baseball Game," which was result of his 1970 junior year operations research game theory course project at Cornell University. Contact Gary at gcokins@garycokins.com.

Terrance Pohlen, PhD, is a professor of logistics and the senior associate dean at the G. Brint Ryan College of Business, University of North Texas. He also currently serves as the director of the Jim McNatt Institute for Logistics. Terry retired from the United States Air Force as a lieutenant colonel with 20 years of experience in logistics. *D CEO* magazine identified him as one of the 500 most influential businesspeople in Dallas–Fort Worth in 2015.

Prior to joining UNT, he served on the graduate faculty at the Air Force Institute of Technology, as an adjunct faculty member at The Ohio State University, and on the faculty at the University of North Florida. Terry received an MABA and a PhD in Business from The Ohio State University, an MS in Logistics from the Air Force Institute of Technology, and a BS in Marketing from Moorhead State University.

His research focuses on the interrelationship between the economy and the transportation system; interorganizational and supply chain learning; and the financial and performance management of logistics and supply chain systems. He co-authored CSCMP's *The Handbook of Supply Chain Costing*. His research has been published in the *Journal of Business Logistics, International Journal of Logistics Management, International Journal of Physical Distribution and Logistics Management*, and the *Transportation Journal*.

Terry chaired the professional certification in transportation and logistics (CTL) and was an American Society of Transportation and Logistics (AST&L merged with APICS) board member for eight years. He has participated in executive education programs at Northwestern University, Georgia Tech, Massachusetts Institute of Technology, The Ohio State University, the University of North Florida, and the University of North Texas. He routinely participates in the annual Supply Chain Leaders in Action (SCLA) conferences as a speaker and facilitator. Contact Terry at terrance.pohlen@unt.edu.

Thomas Klammer, PhD, CPA, is a Regents Professor Emeritus at the University of North Texas, and retired after teaching accounting at UNT for nearly four decades. Tom's PhD is from the University of Wisconsin and he has an MBA and BBA from Western Michigan University. He is a Texas CPA, a past president of the AAA Management Accounting Section, and remains active in professional organizations. His interests are cross-functional and he continues to research and write in the managerial accounting area as well as carefully monitoring presentation changes related to the statement of cash flows.

Tom's Regents Professor Emeritus designation acknowledges his teaching and research contributions. He has developed and taught web-based instructional material. He is also internationally recognized for his work in capital investment decision methods and cash flow reporting. His publications include co-authoring a modular text series, *Management Accounting: A Strategic Focus*, monographs on capital investment, capacity management, supply chain costing, and several nationally used continuing education texts. He has published numerous articles in premier academic and professional journals such as: *Journal of Business, The Accounting Review, California Management Review, Journal of Accountancy, Management Accountant,* and *Journal of Management Accounting Research.*

He has made presentations at regional and national academic and practitioner conferences, served on the editorial board of several accounting journals, and was a long time associate editor of IMA's case journal. Tom's practical experience includes extensive work with CAM-I, experience with oil and gas and CPA firms, and as a research consultant for the Financial Accounting Standards Board. He has been active in writing and presenting continuing education seminars for many years and has been named as an AICPA Outstanding Discussion Leader. Contact him at tklammer@my.unt.edu.

CHAPTER 1

The Supply Chain Costing Journey: Why You Need to Take It

Understanding the supply chain's role in the profitability of your company, and the ability to use that knowledge to your company's advantage, can be your best weapon in the economic battles ahead.[1]

COST VISIBILITY ACROSS A supply chain can open new opportunities for driving cost reductions and improving performance. Many internal costs are driven by external trading partners' behavior and business practices. Improved cost visibility enables managers and executives to better understand how supply chain relationships drive costs within their firm and with each trading partner. Visibility would also facilitate more effective cost trade-offs and optimized networks within the firm and across a firm's network of trading partners. Despite the importance of externally driven supply chain costs, managers and executives currently have very limited visibility of their trading partners' costs and little insight into what actually drives their costs. Tremendous potential exists to achieve significant cost reductions and higher levels of performance within the supply chain. The visibility and management of costs across trading partners can take supply chain management to a higher plateau of value creation.

Many companies may find it near impossible to track supply chain costs, but it is a requirement for properly tracking, reporting, and measuring item performance. And it is a true prerequisite for advance supply chain and retail optimization.[2]

To complicate matters, many managers and executives do not trust the profit and cost information reported by their CFO and accountants. We are not referring to the *external financial statutory and compliance accounting and reporting* for government regulatory agencies and for investors. We are referring to *internal management accounting* providing insights and cost information to help managers make better decisions. An example of the lack of trust involves cost allocations of indirect expenses, commonly called "overhead." Managers recognize that simplistic cost allocations with basis, such as the number of direct labor hours or number of units produced, do not have a cause-and-effect relationship in most situations. They are like spreading peanut butter across bread. Hence, the reported costs are inaccurate, flawed, and misleading.

To further complicate matters, managers observe that the internal managerial accounting information is incomplete. It does not provide a full picture of their firm's costs. The accountants stop at simply calculating and reporting the costs of product and standard service lines. They do not calculate costs *below* the gross profit margin line in an income statement. Managers need to also have visibility regarding how much their customers consume of distribution channel, selling, marketing, customer service, and administrative expenses. Managers desire seeing a profit-and-loss report for *each* customer.

Some executives may believe that they know their own internal supply chain costs and are not suspicious of the accuracy of those costs. Leaving that problem aside, research reveals a different problem, that most firms have limited knowledge of their trading partners' costs and the influence of the partners' actions on the firm's cost. Think about how you would respond to the following questions about your firm's knowledge of its supply chain costs.

- How good are your firm's measures of supply chain costs?
- Do you know, with confidence, which products and service lines are truly making or losing money—and by how much?
- How good is your understanding of your trading partners' supply chain costs?
- Do you know what costs to your firm are caused by your suppliers, aside from the purchase price to them?
- Does your firm calculate and report customer profitability?

- Do you know which types of customers are more attractive to retain, to grow, and to acquire as new ones—and which types are not?
- Does your analysis enable accurate predictions of how changes in customer behavior will drive costs within your firm and the supply chain?
- Does your firm exchange cost information with key trading partners to help effectively manage these external costs?
- Is available cost information adequate to support supply chain decisions and understand how these decisions drive costs within the firm, its trading partners, and the entire supply chain?
- Are you measuring the correct key performance indicators (KPIs) to align the priorities and actions of managers with the executive team's formulated strategy?
- Do managers even understand what the executive team's strategy is? *The answer of most firms is "Probably not!"*

Volatility in the global economy and fluctuations in transportation costs have increased the importance of having cost knowledge within and across the supply chain. Supply chain cost professionals are operating in a dynamic business environment: increased globalization, expanding product and service variety, growing end-user demands, rapidly changing technology, volatile transportation costs including fuel prices, periodic pandemics, and sustainability requirements. This environment has altered end-user demand and is changing how organizations function and interact with their trading partners. Measuring and managing existing and prospective supply chain costs is essential for sustaining profitability and remaining competitive in this increasingly complex environment.

Supply chain costing in this dynamic environment poses a significant management dilemma. Executives require targeted, precise cost information by product, service line, distribution channel, and customer and supply chain. However, the general ledger cost accounting systems firms use does not provide this information. Traditional cost systems provide detailed information about the *input* expenses incurred with labor, material, freight, or other natural expense accounts, but they fail to provide the *output* cost information most needed by management. For example, managers seeking to improve their supply chain processes, such as order fulfillment, need information on the total cost of the end-to-end business processes, the cost of the individual activities performed within those processes (internally and the cost of the activities performed by external trading partners), and estimates of how these costs will change in response to any process changes.

COMMONLY ACCEPTED OBSERVATIONS

Executives and their managers will agree that the visibility and management of costs across trading partners offers tremendous potential for value creation within the supply chain. However, few firms today have cost visibility beyond their own four walls and far fewer have visibility of their immediate upstream supplier and downstream customer trading partners' costs. The external visibility of cost information is very limited and does not produce the transparency required to achieve the full potential from an effective supply chain

---

EXHIBIT 1.1 Common Observations

- Common definition of supply chain management missing
- Costing considered an essential supply chain competency
- Level of trust and dependency affect the exchange of cost information
- Limited focus on the suppliers' indirect costs
- Management perceptions of cost influenced by the information provided
- Standard cost systems being adapted to reflect supply chain complexity
- Cost estimation models used to overcome trading partners' reluctance to exchange cost information
- Cost information requirements vary by position within the supply chain
- Very limited two-way sharing of cost information
- Supply chain costing increases the complexity of cost systems
- Supply chain costing includes a wide range of costing tools employed to support supply chain management
- Firms at multiple steps along the journey toward supply chain costing

---

management system. Exhibit 1.1 displays what most supply managers observe about supply chain management.

The adoption of supply chain management and a process view requires a much different perspective regarding cost management than exists in most firms. A supply chain perspective shifts the focus from determining and analyzing only the costs incurred within a single firm to the total costs incurred by all trading partners in delivering the final product or service line to the end customer. Based on the need for a broader costing perspective, supply chain costing can be defined as:

> Supply chain costing is the collection, expense assignment, and analysis of cost information across all of the work activities comprising a supply chain for the purpose of identifying opportunities to

obtain a competitive advantage through a combination of reduced costs, increased revenues, and improved performance.

This definition recognizes that supply chain executives require an extended view of costs. Companies do not operate in isolation and many costs incurred by the firm are driven by the business practices of external trading partners. The cost incurred by the end-user customers represents the sum of the activity costs performed by all the trading partners plus their profit margins. Supply chain managers need a better understanding of these costs and their root causes to manage and control the final cost experienced by the end user. Without additional cost visibility, managers cannot take advantage of potential opportunities to further reduce costs or optimize costs at a more strategic level through interfirm cost trade-offs. Supply chain costing and its supporting framework are described in Chapter 3.

Few, if any, organizations can be described as having fully implemented supply chain costing as described in this book. The varying levels of cost visibility span a spectrum, ranging from firms actively working with trading partners to obtain costs across several supply chain tiers to those firms still struggling to obtain a better understanding of their own internal costs. Despite the differences in their progress, management teams recognize that there is a need to obtain better cost information internally and regarding their trading partners. Most firms are actively working to gain control over supply chain costs and performance.

Several common themes keep resurfacing with senior executives. These themes include the need for greater cost knowledge within the supply chain, that many costs are driven by the behavior of trading partners, and that by managing supply chain costs a competitive advantage can be obtained. Different costing techniques will need to be used because the problems being addressed or a firm's position in the supply chain can differ between types of firms.

 ## THE JOURNEY TO IMPLEMENTING SUPPLY CHAIN COSTING

The need for a different supply chain perspective has led supply chain managers in many firms to embark on a journey toward improved supply chain costing. While the journey remains somewhat unrefined and as yet untraveled by many firms, it is inevitable that managers who begin to implement progressive supply chain costing methods will obtain greater insight and understanding of how their own internal costs and the activities and processes performed by each trading partner contribute to overall supply chain costs.

The firms that begin the supply chain costing journey—and some have begun the journey—will initiate efforts that capture expense information and calculate costs from the end user across and through the ultimate source of supply. The resulting cost knowledge allows supply chain professionals to report the magnitude and types of supply chain costs, get senior management's attention, and focus on key cost drivers across the supply chain. The process, or journey, for implementing supply chain costing consists of five steps displayed in Exhibit 1.2.

EXHIBIT 1.2 The Process, or Journey, for Implementing Supply Chain Costing

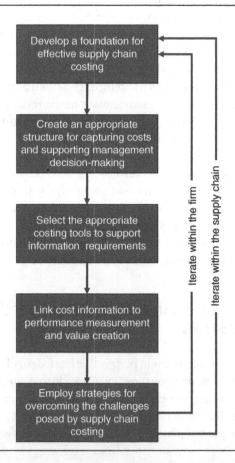

Develop a Foundation for Effective Supply Chain Costing

First executives need to develop a foundation for effective supply chain costing. Essential elements of this foundation include a shared vision of supply chain management and determining what cost information is needed to gain insights and support management decision making based on the firm's strategy, its production methods, and its operating environment. Without this foundation, the pursuit of supply chain costing may produce insightful information but not the type of information that managers need to appropriately act.

EXHIBIT 1.3 A Typical Supply Chain

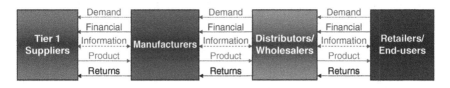

Source: Adapted from Douglas M. Lambert and Mark L. Bennion, "New Channel Strategies for the 1980s," in *Marketing Channels: Domestics and International Perspectives,* ed. Michael G. Harvey and Robert L. Lusch (Norman: Center for Economic Management Research, School of Business Administration, University of Oklahoma, 1982), p. 127.

Identifying when and how to capture, measure, calculate, and use supply chain cost information presents major challenges and tremendous opportunities for supply chain professionals. To effectively manage supply chain costs, decision makers must agree on what constitutes a supply chain and supply chain process. A supply chain perspective requires a firm to capture and analyze costs across multiple trading partners (Exhibit 1.3). The importance of measuring supply chain costs must be recognized, and decision makers must be cognizant of the factors that are fundamental to managing these costs. Decision makers must refine their understanding of what drives supply chain costs and of the measurement methodologies and tools that are available to help manage these costs. Without this type of information, supply chain professionals cannot effectively implement the changes needed to improve supply chain decisions. For these change initiatives to be successful, it is necessary to change behavior, modify culture, and realign performance measurements within the organization and throughout the supply chain. The issues and actions required to develop a foundation for effective supply chain costing are presented in Chapters 3 and 4.

Create an Appropriate Structure for Capturing Costs and Supporting Management Decision Making

The second journey step is where management creates an appropriate structure for capturing costs and supporting management decision making. A tremendous amount of complexity exists in most supply chains, and supply chain costing needs to capture costs in a manner that enables managers to view and portray costs in many different ways. This step means giving careful consideration to the classification and assignment of costs. Most firms continue to rely on traditional general ledger cost accounting systems. Chapter 5 compares traditional cost systems with supply chain costing and explains why general ledger accounting systems need to be adapted to support supply chain decision making. Chapter 6 then describes the different views of cost information and alternative ways costs can be classified.

Effective supply chain management requires multiple views of cost and the use of cost classifications that permit the isolation of costs by product, customer, or supply chain. This information supports the application of supply chain costing tools such as customer profitability analysis and target costing as well as linking supply chain costs to performance and value creation by using economic value-added or balanced score card models. Chapter 7 addresses the key issues associated with indirect costs and cost assignments. Indirect costs represent a significant portion of overall supply chain costs, and these costs must be appropriately assigned to activities and cost objects (products, service lines, distribution channels, and customers, or supply chains). Inaccurate or inappropriate expenses-to-costs assignments will send misleading signals to management. Accurate expenses-to-costs assignments provide greater clarity regarding exactly what is driving supply chain costs and where management focus should be concentrated. Many supply chain executives stress the importance of the cost assignment process. Cost assignments drive behavior, and managers need to ensure that the techniques and cost drivers used in their costing drive the right behaviors and send the right signals to management and the firm's trading partners. Chapter 10 will describe activity-based costing (ABC) as an accepted way to trace and assign resource expenses into calculated costs.

Select the Appropriate Tools to Support Information Requirements

Firms use many costing methods and tools to increase the visibility and management of internal and external costs. As a result, supply chain costing encompasses a wide variety of tools and software technologies (Exhibit 1.4). The most appropriate method often depends on the management question being asked or the position of the firm in the supply chain. Some costing techniques work better than others for different circumstances. Certain cost tools are particularly useful for improving the supply chain cost structure while

EXHIBIT 1.4 Frequently Employed Supply Chain Costing Tools

- Activity-based costing (ABC)
- Balanced scorecard (BSC)
- Cost estimation
- Cost-to-serve
- Customer profitability analysis (CPA)
- Economic Value Added (EVA)
- Kaizen costing
- Landed costing
- Life-cycle costing
- Open books costing
- Standard costing
- Target costing
- Value chain analysis

others are more valuable for cost planning or as part of a strategic analysis of supply chain costs. Some tools work well in mass production environments while others better support lean production methods.

Chapters 8 through 11 provide information regarding the costing techniques shown in Exhibit 1.4 and should assist managers in selecting the most appropriate method(s). Chapter 8 covers a uniquely important costing tool, value chain analysis. After working on the first two implementation steps, firms can use a value chain analysis to increase their understanding of the different components of their supply chains and to obtain a high-level view of where costs are being generated. Chapter 9 addresses customer profitability analysis and the information requirements needed to assign costs by customer or channel. Customer profitability often follows value chain analysis as the next tool used in supply chain costing. Organizations are increasingly developing customer profitability analysis or cost-to-serve models. Upstream suppliers recognize that not all customers are equal or equally profitable, and they need to understand how their customers' behavior drive costs and profit within their firms.

Chapter 10 describes four tools that can help managers in their cost reduction efforts. Standard costing, activity-based costing (ABC), landed costs, and kaizen costing can expand management's cost visibility outside the firm and over broader segments of the supply chain. Chapter 11 turns to the *predictive* view of supply chain costing. This chapter examines cost estimation, budgeting, rolling financial forecasts, capital budgeting, and target costing. These tools provide powerful "what-if" capabilities, and, in the case of target costing for new products, can transmit cost reduction pressure within the firm and to its upstream trading partners.

Link Cost Information to Performance Measurement and Value Creation

Performance measurement poses several unique challenges for supply chain management due to the breadth and complexity of most supply chains. Despite the challenge, executives need to understand how the supply chain affects performance within their firm. Supply chain costing offers the capability to translate supply chain performance into financial performance. Although cost reduction is often the focus of supply chain costing efforts, effective supply chain management can create value by increasing sales, gaining additional market share, reducing inventory, accelerating throughput cycle time, or improving asset productivity for multiple trading partners. The ability to persuade trading partners to change their business practices will largely depend on the ability to demonstrate how the change creates value in the trading partner's organization.

Executives often strongly emphasize that supply chain costing must be linked to the performance measurement system. Supply chain costing should not be implemented in isolation but should be part of the firm's performance measurement system. Performance should be evaluated based on the ability to achieve corporate strategic objectives and the effect on intra- and interfirm cost. By linking cost to performance measures, managers across the supply chain will take a much greater interest in understanding their costs and what drives cost in their firms. *A key observation is that the integration of cost and performance represents a major step forward in cultivating a cost-conscious culture within the firm.*

Chapter 12 describes the linkage between supply chain costing, strategy, value creation, and performance measures. The linkage is accomplished by using several additional costing techniques, including activity-based management, economic value-added (EVA), and the balanced scorecard. The combination of these tools permits the translation of nonfinancial, operational measures into financial (cost) measures. EVA provides the capability to demonstrate how changes in supply chain performance drive value, not only in the firm but across trading partners. In this chapter, costs and performance are evaluated across a supplier–customer link in the supply chain. Most firms pursue supply chain costing and process improvements by identifying a key link in their supply chain and then working with that customer or supplier to obtain a desired outcome.

Strategies for Overcoming the Challenges Posed by Supply Chain Costing

The book concludes by identifying and describing the key challenges supply chain professionals will need to overcome during the journey to supply chain costing. Chapter 13 begins by describing the challenges and their significance to supply chain costing (Exhibit 1.5). The remainder of the chapter presents the strategies for overcoming challenges the firms face (Exhibit 1.6). The challenges encountered during supply chain costing implementation range from a lack of trust between trading partners to accounting systems failing to capture needed information. Although these challenges pose significant obstacles, supply chain managers can apply strategies employed by other firms that have successfully overcome these challenges and made major strides forward along their journey.

EXHIBIT 1.5 Challenges to Implementing Supply Chain Costing

- Behavioral
  - Lack of trust
  - One-way flow or exchange of cost information
- Perceptions of an inequitable sharing of benefits and burdens
- Technical
  - Limited cost knowledge
  - Prevalence of traditional, general ledger cost systems
  - Limited cost estimation capability
  - Multiple definitions of cost

EXHIBIT 1.6 Strategies for Overcoming the Challenges Confronting Firms Implementing Supply Chain Costing

- Adopting a supply chain process perspective for costing
- Developing a cost estimation capability
- Leveraging information sharing requirements
- Pilot projects as a catalyst for fostering collaboration and trust
- Focusing on trading partners for exchange of cost information
- Implementing a value-based strategy

NOTES

1. Rick Blasgen, "Supply Chain Managers and CFOs: Unlikely—But Important Allies," *Logistics Quarterly* 14, no. 2 (2008): 56.
2. Robert Bruce, VCC Associates Inc., retired vice-president, Supply Chain Strategies, Walmart.

CHAPTER 2

Key Observations That Support the Development of the Book

T HE NEED TO MANAGE and control supply chain costs is more important than ever. Senior executives face pressure from multiple fronts to continually reduce supply chain costs. Value-conscious end users and competitors who achieve cost reductions by integrating portions of their supply chains are increasing management awareness of the importance of reassessing supply chain management. This is an issue the firm and its trading partners need to jointly address. Significant progress has been made regarding the exchange of demand and planning information and in the integration of key processes within the supply chain. However, the exchange and management of cost information across firms' boundaries lags far behind and remains largely unexplored as an opportunity to further integrate the supply chain. As a result, supply chain managers are often ill-equipped to understand how they or their trading partners affect overall supply chain costs or profitability.

The research the authors conducted to write this book focused on how many different firms are attempting to expand their visibility and integrate cost management within their supply chains. The book is structured to assist supply chain professionals in their implementation of supply chain costing and in obtaining the cost information necessary to effect cost reductions and improve performance within their supply chains. The firms researched spanned multiple industries, from manufacturing to retailing, as well as from multiple tiers in a supply chain. The authors also conducted exhaustive analysis and review of supply chain management research.

This chapter summarizes key findings that address several topics, including supply chain management, costing supply chain processes, management decision making, the relationship of supply chain cost information to performance, and the challenges of supply chain costing.

 ## KEY FINDINGS

The authors learned that firms approach supply chain costing in many different ways, use a variety of costing methods and tools, and are aware that they still have much to learn about supply chain costing. A common definition of supply chain management and costing does not currently exist among managers or across trading partners. The lack of a shared vision of supply chain management affects the collection, assignment, and exchange of cost information within and between firms. Although most firms do not possess good information on the costs of their processes that span the internal and external supply chain, senior managers believe that increased cost visibility will significantly improve their decision making and ability to make more effective trade-offs to lower total supply chain costs. As a result, firms have embarked on a journey toward obtaining greater cost visibility within their supply chains. How far firms have progressed on the journey depends on their experience and the resources applied to the costing effort. As the level of internal cost knowledge increases in firms, cost-based performance measures are developed as leading management indicators and to align activity behavior with strategic objectives.

The segments that follow in this chapter elaborate on the key findings shown here:

- Firms are at multiple stages in the supply chain costing journey.
- Common supply chain definitions are missing.
- Costing is an essential supply chain competency.
- There is limited two-way sharing of cost information.
- Trust issues influence cost information exchanges.
- Supply chain costing increases the complexity of cost systems.
- Cost transparency is essential but unlikely for supply chain costing.

Subsequent chapters incorporate findings that are specific to the use of particular costing tools or approaches to supply chain costing. Examples are woven into the discussion of the foundational elements, cost structure, cost management tools, performance measurement issues, and major segments of the book.

Firms Are at Multiple Stages in the Supply Chain Costing Journey

No firms that have fully implemented supply chain costing were identified by the authors. Some firms have achieved varying levels of proficiency in obtaining and using supply chain cost information. The levels range from firms that are actively working to obtain cost information across supply chain tiers to those focused on obtaining a better understanding of how the supply chain affects costs within their firm. However, management teams recognize that obtaining better cost information about their trading partners is essential for gaining greater control over overall supply chain costs and performance.

The firms with the greatest cost knowledge are actively seeking cost information across several tiers in the supply chain. Their suppliers generally do not provide this information on a voluntary basis, but firms are frequently able to leverage their purchasing power to extract this information from suppliers. When the customer cannot leverage the supplier, modeling techniques are often used to estimate the supplier's costs.

The cost information obtained by leading-edge firms allows them to map costs to the key *inbound* supply chain processes for their firms. This effort focuses on obtaining cost information on natural expense accounts such as labor, materials, equipment, overhead, and freight. Managers recognize the importance of understanding the nature of both fixed, step-fixed, and variable costs, the factors driving these costs, and how these costs would change when processes change within the supply chain and across trading partners. Currently, managers use the information primarily to lower landed costs by working with suppliers to streamline their processes, improve sourcing, leverage the purchasing power of multiple suppliers, and optimize transportation, or by shifting functions across trading partners to the lowest cost provider.

Similar to firms at the forefront of supply chain costing, managers of other firms also focus primarily on their upstream suppliers where they can leverage their purchasing power. They also express reluctance to share cost information with any of their customers to avoid eroding their profit margins. However, many do engage in selective collaborative efforts where some cost information is exchanged on a limited basis.

Despite these differences, most management teams recognize the need for greater cost knowledge, understand that many costs are driven by the behavior of their trading partners, and acknowledge that managing supply chain costs can lead to competitive advantages. Supply chain costing initiatives are all moving in the same direction, but they take different approaches and are at different stages in their level of cost knowledge. The processes followed are similar, although the tools they employ frequently differ based on the problems being addressed or the firm's position in the supply chain. These stages became the basis for the steps in the supply chain costing journey described in this book.

Common Supply Chain Definitions Are Missing

The managers interviewed did not possess a common definition of the supply chain or supply chain management. The lack of a common definition inhibits communication and action across the supply chain. This situation limits managers' ability to exchange cost information and to align performance measures across the supply chain.

Managers generally define the supply chain as ranging from "dirt to dirt." However, their attention and actions focus on managing either the internal supply (value) chain or limited segments of the overall supply chain, such as inbound flows (supply management) or outbound flows (distribution or customer service). Functions or positions containing "supply chain" in the title rarely encompass the management activities beyond transactions or relationships with immediate upstream or downstream trading partners. *A key point made by managers is that they and their trading partners continue to view supply chain management very differently.* This issue is developed further in Chapter 3.

Communication in the supply chains occurs primarily between trading partners while they are planning operations or when they are performing transactions. The information exchanged depends on the firms' respective upstream or downstream location in the supply chain and the products or commodities being bought or sold. Processes involving manufacturing or assembling tend to exchange a wider range of information that includes product design, specifications, and demand information. Consumer product supply chains tend to exchange a narrower range of information such as forecasts, shipping, and/or demand and inventory information. Information exchange generally occurs between management teams attempting to use the supply chain to obtain a marketplace advantage or with trading partners that have growth strategies. Even among firms recognized as being at the forefront in supply chain management, these relationships represent a relatively small proportion of their trading partners.

Costing Is an Essential Supply Chain Competency

An explicit supply chain costing focus is typically found in firms with a strong cost management culture. Senior managers in these firms consider cost knowledge to be a source of competitive advantage and costing to be an essential competency for managing their firm and supply chain costs. They argue that an understanding of how decisions and performance, within and across firms, drive costs is essential to managing their operations. They note that this knowledge has enabled them to obtain significant and sustainable cost reductions for their firm. These managers collect extensive cost information about all facets of their firm's operations, and they employ a range of sophisticated tools to capture, model, and simulate the effect of process changes on total cost. Costing and the use of cost information has become part of their day-to-day culture.

The need to understand how performance and decisions across all firms in the supply chain drive costs has made supply chain costing a core competency in leading-edge firms. Senior executives adamantly assert that their firms have obtained a competitive advantage through having a better understanding of supply chain costs than their competitors. They believe their firms have far greater cost "intelligence" and can make better and more informed decisions. Having greater visibility of cost information enables them to make effective cost trade-offs—within and across firms—and to reoptimize (restructure) their supply chains to become more efficient. These firms dedicate the resources required to obtain needed cost information, incorporate supply chain cost management into their strategic plans, and integrate cost management into their performance measures and supply chain objectives. These management teams regard themselves as being very numbers-driven and analytical in their planning and execution. Cost knowledge plays a key role, but is not necessarily the determining factor, in their decision-making process.

Supply chain costing for these firms entails the collection of extensive amounts of cost information. Senior executives indicate that collecting and maintaining this information represents a significant investment in time, people, and funding, but they consider the investment necessary and more than worthwhile for managing their businesses.

Two-Way Sharing of Cost Information Is Limited

The authors' investigation identified few instances of a two-way exchange of cost information between trading partners. Many impediments preclude the exchange of cost information, and these barriers to supply chain costing are discussed later in this chapter. The sensitivity of cost information and the lack of detailed internal costs represent an obstacle that firms must overcome. However, examples of firms exchanging cost information do exist, and managers' interest in two-way exchange of cost information is increasing.

Currently the exchange of cost information generally flows in one direction—from supplier to customer—and is precipitated by customer requirements for information. Customers request the cost breakout as part of their purchasing process, and suppliers either produce the information or risk losing the sale. Only suppliers with a large, diverse customer base or those selling bulk commodity items have sufficient negotiating leverage to refuse. The customers' buyers use this information to analyze their suppliers' business and cost structure, to drill down and determine where process improvements could yield a potential cost (price) reduction. However, they acknowledge that the quality and accuracy of this information depends on a supplier's cost knowledge and cost management system.

Major manufacturers are expanding their current requirements for suppliers to provide a detailed breakout of the costs for producing a product or delivering a service. However, as customers, they typically do not share or plan to share any of their firm's information with their suppliers. When asked about this practice, managers indicate that releasing any cost information would reduce their negotiating leverage and not lead to any meaningful cost reductions.

Larger manufacturers have adopted processes requiring their suppliers to generate additional cost savings each year. The processes provide a target price or cost reduction for the supplier to achieve. As an alternative to a price reduction, a supplier can achieve its objective by reducing the customer's costs in areas such as receiving, production, material handling, returns, or product complexity. Since the customer does not provide any cost information, the supplier develops a business case based on operational data obtained from the customer, such as the labor hours required for each activity performed. The manufacturer (customer) evaluates supplier proposals to determine whether any "hard" savings would likely result from the proposal. If accepted, performance measures are established to ensure the supplier's actions produce the projected cost savings.

When two-way cost exchanges between trading partners do exist, they share several characteristics: (1) the firms believe they mutually benefit by exchanging cost information, (2) cost data is needed to justify the process change, and (3) the cost information firms exchange is limited to the direct costs affected by the process change. For example, a supplier delivers products employing a direct store delivery (DSD) model. The trading partners incur a significant amount of costs due to delivering, receiving, and in-checking deliveries at the retail level. By mapping the process and assigning costs to the process steps, the trading partners can determine how eliminating several receiving activities would affect costs in both firms. Since both firms would experience an overall reduction in total costs, the process change would be implemented.

A two-way exchange of cost information is more likely with new trading partners or with those partners seeking to increase their market share. In most longstanding relationships, existing suppliers have little incentive to share costs. These suppliers do not want to disclose any information that might provide negotiating leverage to their customers and result in lower margins. When the requesting firm represents only a small proportion of a supplier's volume, it has little leverage to obtain the cost information and only limited opportunity to help the supplier obtain major cost savings.

TRUST ISSUES INFLUENCE COST INFORMATION EXCHANGE

A major concern about sharing cost information is that the other party may act opportunistically and take advantage of this information. Most firms exhibit a great deal of sensitivity regarding their costs. Releasing information about cost structure may reveal how a particular company achieves a competitive advantage by eliminating process steps, employing new technologies, allocating funds to product development, or adopting innovative business practices. Managers are reluctant to disclose any information that could possibly provide information to their competitors or negotiating leverage to their customers. For example, firms using customer profitability analyses carefully protect this information and attempt to prevent their trading partners from even being aware of this capability. Managers contend that their customers would seek this information and attempt to negotiate a price reduction. Firms with limited cost information hold similar concerns, believing the lack of cost information would place them at a disadvantage during price negotiations.

Despite the sensitivity attached to cost information, some firms have begun to exchange a limited amount of cost data to promote and develop trust in their supply chain relationships.

Suppliers sometimes provide detailed product manufacturing costs to customers as a defense mechanism where adversarial price negotiations prevail. The release of cost information provides support for a current price or is used to justify a price increase. The supplier's supporting rationale may indicate that the price is based on material and operations costs, higher service-level agreements, quality requests by the customer, or the risk and investment incurred by the supplier.

Companies exchanging information report that the exchange of cost information has led to greater trust. These firms are able to collaborate on initiatives, leading to cost reductions for both trading partners. They explore additional ways to create value and exchange supporting cost information. They learn to trust each other as the relationship expands and neither firm abuses the shared information. Trust results from the exchange rather than being a prerequisite. Even in instances where information flows only one way, managers believe the exchange fosters additional trust. They gain a greater understanding of their supplier's manufacturing costs and how their behavior and performance affect upstream costs.

Supply Chain Costing Increases the Complexity of Cost Systems

Cost management becomes significantly more complex as management pursues improved supply chain costing. Managers discover that multiple cost classifications are required to analyze costs from different perspectives to support supply chain decision making. For example, costs often need to be classified by behavior (fixed, step-fixed, or variable), product, customer, or supply chain. The broader scope necessitates additional activities and cost drivers being incorporated into their analyses.

Classifying costs by customer occurs where there are customer differences that have a significant effect on cost. Those differences often include product or packaging customization, order placement, cycle time, and delivery. In some instances, a firm will extensively collaborate with a customer and other process costs are affected such as research and development or manufacturing costs. Depending on the size and uniqueness of the customer, the cost-to-serve (customer profitability) analysis can break out costs separately for very large or key accounts and aggregates smaller customers by class of trade. However, if warranted, accounts profitability can be obtained even for small accounts.

The firms at the forefront of supply chain costing have begun classifying costs by distribution channel or supply chain. Multiple supply chains pass through these firms and they use several channels to reach different market segments. Each supply chain comprises a unique set of trading partners and employs different business practices. As a result, each supply chain or distribution channel drives costs differently. Additional cost classifications are necessary to capture and understand these differences.

Cost Transparency Is Essential but Unlikely for Supply Chain Costing

Supply chain costing incorporates the concept of cost transparency between trading partners. Cost transparency can be defined as follows.

> A practice in which the customer and supplier share detailed confidential information about their in-house activities, pertinent to the supply of goods and services which links them. It can be seen as an extension of open book negotiation, the only difference being that the customer shares information on its activities with the supplier, in addition to the flow of information in the other direction. The objective of practicing cost transparency is to reduce costs through the joint development of good ideas thereby improving the mutual competitive position of both organizations.[1]

Several premises support the incorporation of cost transparency within supply chain costing.

- First, supply chain optimization cannot occur without trading partners sharing cost information regarding their activities and processes.[2]
- Second, supply chain managers must explain their reasoning for joint improvements in terms of the effect on each trading partner's costs and financial performance.[3]
- Third, firms seeking to reduce costs or improve the competitiveness of their supply chains will increasingly seek greater cost transparency.[4]
- Fourth, supply chain managers need to understand how costs accumulate through the supply chain to determine what to change and how to prioritize such changes.[5]
- And last, intense pressure from competitive supply chains will drive the requirement to continually reduce costs through new opportunities made available only through closer collaboration and the sharing of cost information.[6]

Closely linked to the concept of cost transparency is the practice of open book costing. However, the use of this concept differs greatly in practice. Conceptually, open books refer to situations in which suppliers open their books to customers. The intent is for the supplier and customer to work together to reduce costs and to improve other factors.[7] Practically, open books generally represents a one-way flow of cost information, from supplier to customer. Firms generally find it easier to ask another party to assume the risk associated with exchanging cost information than to assume the risk themselves. Consequently, most managers infer that cost transparency equates to open books—the transfer of sensitive cost information from supplier to the customer.

The concept of cost transparency across an entire supply chain does not currently exist in practice. Research studies have not detected any instances of supply chain cost transparency. A two-way exchange of cost information occurs only on a very limited basis and only within dyads representing significant value to the participating firms. Research by Hines et al.[8] and Kajuter and Kulmala[9] reveals that managers perceive that the risks associated with exchanging cost information outweigh any potential benefits. They contend that cost transparency entails the dangers of revealing sensitive information and strategic plans, leading to the loss of competitive advantage and the loss of independence for suppliers.[10] This situation presents a unique paradox. The same managers who contend that cost transparency and the exchange of cost information across the supply chain will lead to tremendous opportunities also believe that the release of cost information will pose a significant danger to their firms. This paradox may indicate that although cost transparency is currently not being practiced, it does not necessarily mean that it is impractical or will not be pursued in the future.[11]

Companies are much more willing to share operational data to achieve the outcomes of reduced cost or improved performance. They do not attach the same sensitivity to operational performance data as to cost information. Operational measures frequently serve as surrogates for cost-based measures. Managers recognize that if the operational measures move in previously determined directions, the costs will move in the same directions. These managers have essentially substituted cost drivers for the costs in their exchange. Hines et al. noted a similar situation regarding the willingness of firms to share technical and operational data.[12]

There is an overarching need for increased cost transparency in supply chain management. Unfortunately, the research supports other research findings that there are significant inhibitors to achieving cost transparency in supply chain management (see Exhibit 2.1).

EXHIBIT 2.1 Inhibitors to Cost Transparency

Inhibitor	Actions
Supplier guile	Suppliers may report inaccurate information or create a second set of books to misrepresent costs during open books exchange. The intent is to mask margins or to keep the customer from seeking an alternative source of supply.[13]
Cost exchange as recent phenomenon	Many managers have little to no previous experience with exchanging sensitive cost information with their trading partners.[14]
Need for a long-term view	A greater potential exists for cost exchange in longer-term projects or relationships. This potential stems not only from the opportunity to obtain cost reductions but from the levels of dependence and trust perceived in the relationship.[15]
Weaknesses in cost information	Managers are aware of the weaknesses in their cost systems and do not want to make their trading partners aware of this potential vulnerability.[16]
Cost management viewed as an internal affair	Managers contend cost management and reduction is an internal company affair and not an issue for the network [supply chain] to pursue.[17]
Disagreement on reporting	Supply chain members cannot agree on what costs should be reported or how.[18]
Reliance on traditional cost systems	Many trading partners continue to rely on archaic and poor cost allocation processes. Cost disclosures originating from these systems will provide misleading and erroneous cost information to the other trading partners in the supply chain.[19]
Differences in overhead cost allocation	Firms employ different definitions of what constitutes overhead and how to allocate these costs.[20] These differences highlight the need for an activity-based approach for assigning costs which identifies the resource and activity drivers used for making cost assignments.
Management culture	Management culture plays an important role in developing cost information and providing the resources to obtain the more accurate information needed to support supply chain decision-making. In many firms, managers are not held accountable for nonfinancial measures and budget execution. The culture focuses on achieving operational performance measures rather than a disciplined, continuous focus on cost reduction. The development of accurate cost information at the activity-level is perceived as too difficult and not worth the resources expended.

Source: Kajüter et al. 2005; Cokins and Gray 2001 and Munday 1992.

Other Findings

Several additional research findings are summarized below and discussed in subsequent chapters of this book.

- The limited cost sharing that occurs is focused primarily on direct costs. There is little focus on indirect costs that relate to supply chain processes. An important element of supply chain costing is first understanding and then more effectively managing indirect costs.
- The lack of clear cost definitions makes communication and collaboration challenging. Managers interviewed were asked how well they knew their costs. Almost everyone responded that they knew costs down to the penny. However, further investigation revealed that although managers may know labor, material, and other direct costs, they lack detailed information regarding the costs associated with performing specific activities or processes, or the cost to serve different customers. The lack of accurate and timely cost data is seen as the Achilles heel of supply chain costing.
- Many managers lack confidence in the cost information that is available in their firm. There is considerable unease with cost information that appears to be "soft," imprecise, or unreliable. Information that improves managers' understanding of different types of costs and how that cost information can be used is essential, particularly as supply chain processes must deal with an increasing variety of activities.
- Many firms continue to track most costs by responsibility center rather than by activity or process. Tracking costs by responsibility center provides little, if any, management insight into how business practices drive internal costs or how the firm contributes to overall supply chain costs. Tracking costs by responsibility center reports what amounts were spent but provides no context or insight into what causes or influences the costs incurred.
- Accounting and cost management systems often send misleading signals to managers by using arbitrary cost allocations based on broad averages (e.g., number of units produced, labor hours) rather than assigning costs based on actual consumption. For example, allocating costs based on sales dollars suggests that customers who generate the same revenue have identical costs—as if these customers have no variation in how they place service demands on the supplier. Such cost allocations violate a key principle of managerial accounting: the causality principle, which relates a cost to what caused that cost.

■ A wide range of costing techniques are being used to support supply chain management. The majority of these tools remain rooted in traditional cost management, but a growing number of firms are experimenting with tools that support the informational needs and process complexity associated with supply chain management.

NOTES

1. Richard Lamming, Owen Jones, and David Nicol, "Transparency in the Value Stream From Open-Book Negotiation to Cost Transparency," in *Value Stream Management*, ed. Peter Hines, Richard Lamming, Dan Jones, Paul Cousins, and Nick Rich (Harlow, UK: Pearson Education Limited, 2000).

2. Ibid., p. 297.

3. Gary Cokins, "Managing Effective Supply Chains" (presentation given at Pennsylvania State University, November 13, 2007).

4. Max Munday, "Buyer-Supplier Partnerships and Cost Data Disclosure," *Management Accounting* 70, no. 6 (1992): 28, 35.

5. Alan Braithwaite and Edouard Samakh, "The Cost-to-Serve Method," *International Journal of Logistics Management* 9, no. 1 (1998): 75.

6. Peter Kajuter and Harri I. Kulmala, "Open-Book Accounting in Networks Potential Achievements and Reasons for Failures," *Management Accounting Research* 16 (2005): 179.

7. T. Berry, A. Ahmed, J. Cullen, A. Dunlop, W. Seal, S. Johnston, and M. Holmes, "The Consequences of Inter-Firm Supply Chains for Management Accounting," *Management Accounting* 75, no. 10 (1997): 74.

8. Lamming, Jones, and Nicol, "Transparency in the Value Stream," pp. 281 and 299.

9. Kajuter and Kulmala, "Open-Book Accounting."

10. Lamming, Jones, and Nicol, "Transparency in the Value Stream," pp. 281, 299.

11. Ibid., p. 299.

12. Ibid., p. 277.

13. Ibid, 275.

14. Ibid.

15. Kajüter, Peter and Harri I. Kulmala (2005), "Open-Book Accounting in Networks Potential Achievements and Reasons for Failures," *Management Accounting Research*, Vol. 16, page 199.

16. Ibid., page 198.

17. Ibid., page 196.

18. Ibid,, pages 195–197.

19. Cokins, Gary (2001), *Activity-Based Cost Management: An Executive's Guide*, New York, NY: John Wiley & Sons, Inc., page 170.

20. Munday, Max (1992), "Buyer-Supplier Partnerships and Cost Data Disclosure," *Management Accounting*, Vol. 70, No. 6, pp. 28 and 35.

CHAPTER 3

The Nature of Supply Chain Costing

S UPPLY CHAIN MANAGEMENT REQUIRES a much broader view of profits, costs, and cost management than most firms currently possess. Senior executives across industries and at different levels in the supply chain have observed that their firms need to extend their "line of sight" to include their upstream and downstream trading partners' costs of performing different activities within key processes. The firms need this information to effectively manage and reduce supply chain costs, make effective cost trade-offs, and know where the greatest opportunities exist in their supply chain to reduce costs, increase profits, and improve performance.

Several formidable challenges confront managers attempting to expand cost visibility beyond their firms' boundaries. Despite the focus most firms place on supply chain management, managers in many small suppliers and customers are not familiar with the concept or how their interactions with other trading partners drive costs and performance throughout the supply chain. The cost systems most firms use continue to focus internally, emphasize direct costs, and use traditional costing methods and tools to support supply chain decision making.

NATURE OF SUPPLY CHAIN MANAGEMENT

Considerable confusion continues to exist regarding the term *supply chain management*. Everyone has a somewhat different perspective or definition of this concept. Many logistics professionals and academics have suggested that *logistics* refers to those activities involved with material flows within the firm while supply chain management encompasses those material flows that span multiple firms. Others refer to supply chain management as the management of vendors or inbound supply.

The lack of a common definition inhibits communication and management across the supply chain. This situation limits managers' ability to exchange profit margin and cost information and to align operational and financial performance measures across the supply chain. Managers must ensure that they and their trading partners share a common definition to permit effective communication of information across the functions within the firm and among the firms that make up the supply chain. Otherwise, situations can easily arise where firms focus on different parts of the supply chain and have conflicting objectives. For example, one trading partner may view the supply chain as the internal value chain, another may equate supply chain management with logistics, while a third trading partner may adopt a much broader view. Unless these differences are resolved, the ability to capture cost information and align performance with supply chain objectives will be extremely difficult.[1]

To ensure consistency and to support a broader perspective of supply chain costs, the following definition can be used for supply chain management:

> Supply chain management is the management of relationships in the network of organizations, from end customers through original suppliers, using key cross-functional business processes to create value for customers and other stakeholders.[2]

This definition represents an end-to-end process view of supply chain management. Supply chain costs can be most effectively managed when they are captured at the process level. There are eight commonly identified supply chain processes that span the supply chain from end user through the original sources of supply. Executives often speak in terms of these processes when describing their supply chains and interactions with their trading partners.

These processes exist in all supply chains and extend back from the end user across multiple firms to the ultimate supplier. As shown in Exhibit 3.1, each process bisects the functional silos found within the trading partners comprising a supply chain.[3] The activities that comprise these processes transform material and information into value for the end user. Each of these activities drives cost and affects performance within the supply chain.

EXHIBIT 3.1   Supply Chain Framework and Processes

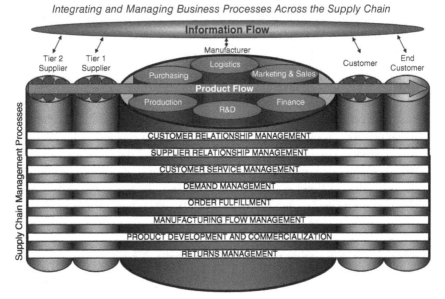

Integrating and Managing Business Processes Across the Supply Chain

Source: Douglas M. Lambert, ed., *Supply Chain Management: Processes, Partnerships, Performance,* fourth edition (Ponte Vedra Beach, FL: Supply Chain Management Institute, 2014), p. 3. © Copyright Douglas M. Lambert. Used with permission. For more information about the SCM Framework, see drdouglaslambert.com.

These processes can and should be a focus of supply chain cost management. Depending on the supply chain, trading partners, and strategies employed, firms may have defined these processes differently. However, when a firm uses a standard set of processes, it obtains more effective communication and a shared understanding between managers from different firms in the supply chain. It also enables benchmarking with comparative "apples-to-apples" definitions.

Managing these eight processes to create the greatest value for the end user, at the lowest total cost, is an essential part of supply chain management. It requires integration of these processes internally and externally across multiple trading partners in the supply chain. These processes directly affect the value delivered to the end user and to key stakeholders throughout the supply chain. To improve the value proposition, managers need to understand how their decisions affect cost and performance both within their firm and in each of the trading partners comprising the supply chain. The timing and nature of these decisions affect costs differently and must be reflected in the costing approach to improve accuracy and support management decision making.

Supply chain management requires a level of understanding of cost and what causes cost beyond that which currently exists in most firms. For example, a retailer's decision to implement vendor-managed inventory (VMI) focuses on obtaining high product availability while simultaneously reducing the costs associated with holding inventory, forecasting, and order placement. The supplier assumes responsibility for these activities. If the supplier can perform these activities at a lower cost than the retailer, the supply chain can become more competitive by offering lower costs and higher availability to the end user. However, companies typically have limited control over the activities performed by supply chain partners and usually lack knowledge of what their activities cost. By analyzing these activities and how each firm contributes to overall performance and costs, managers can identify new opportunities to increase competitiveness and profitability.

A Need for a Broader View of a Supply Chain

Although most managers understand the supply chain concept defined here, in practice their focus remains narrow in scope. Managers generally define the supply chain as ranging from "dirt to dirt"; however, attention and action focus on managing the internal supply chain or limited segments of the supply chain such as inbound flows (supply management) or outbound flows (distribution or customer service). Functions or positions containing "supply chain" in the title rarely include the management of activities beyond transactions with immediate upstream or downstream trading partners.

A key premise of this book is that supply chain management (strategy, operations, and processes) drives the costing process. Executives need to understand the key features of their supply chain. These features include the operational processes and activities comprising the supply chain; how interactions occurring between firms drive differences in processes and activities (which drive costs); and how the role of the firm in the supply chain affects the interaction, processes performed, and supply chain cost.

SUPPLY CHAIN COSTING FRAMEWORK

Supply chain costing remains a work in process, and most firms have taken the first steps toward supply chain cost visibility. Cost management has long been a topic of significant discussion, first in physical distribution, then in logistics management, and now in supply chain management. Yet, most managers continue to rely on traditional general ledger accounting systems and simplistic (and flawed) cost allocation methods for the cost information needed to manage their operations. The purpose of that information is for external financial reporting and for compliance with government regulatory agencies. What is needed is internal managerial accounting that uses better and more valid assumptions to calculate costs.

Despite the tremendous effort expended in developing costing tools such as distribution costing, total cost management, direct product profitability, activity-based costing, and cost to serve (customer profitability analyses), this narrow focus persists.

Faced with factors such as globalization, technology changes, intense competitiveness, and a well-informed and price-conscious end user, supply chain managers are putting a renewed focus on cost management. Cost increases, such as rising transportation costs, have forced managers to seek new opportunities to reduce costs in order to maintain prices without eroding profit margins.

Unfortunately, most managers focus their efforts on managing only those activities under their direct control. They view their responsibilities as beginning with the acquisition of inbound material and ending with delivery to the customer. In many instances, these managers work with their suppliers or customers to improve performance or reduce costs, but they generally do not attempt to examine or actively manage the processes and business practices of their trading partners. Instead, the focus is on obtaining the inputs or outputs necessary for achieving specific objectives for their internal value chain and leaving decisions on how these objectives are to be obtained to their trading partners.

Several leading-edge firms have moved forward to advance their cost management systems and the cost and performance "intelligence" available to support the decisions managers make. These firms have made substantial gains in their ability to reduce costs, improve production, and increase profitability. They have applied technology to eliminate labor-intensive and "non-value-adding" activities from their operations. Timely and more accurate information has enabled them to reduce forecasting error, inventory levels, and cycle times. The coupling of technology, information, and more accurate costs has allowed these firms to optimize their entire internal network and to incorporate several formerly disconnected processes into a systemic whole. These include order processing, order fulfillment, manufacturing flow, purchasing, returns management, and new product development and commercialization. Despite these tremendous advances, supply chain executives in these firms recognize that they have largely attacked only the "low-hanging fruit" or those portions of the supply chain and related processes that lie under their direct control.

The Next Frontier in Supply Chain Cost Management

Supply chain managers recognize that the next frontier in supply chain cost management lies in the portions of the supply chain beyond their direct control. These executives have long recognized that many of their costs and business processes are driven by the behavior and practices of their trading partners. To address these factors, these executives are attempting to implement practices that focus on management throughout and across the supply chain. In a sense, they are attempting to influence the performance of activities and achieve outcomes from processes in which they exert little direct control or ownership. They also realize that their firms lack the cost and performance intelligence necessary for making informed business decisions that affect the supply chain. To date, supply chain managers have combated this situation largely by exchanging operational performance data. Cost information is rarely exchanged due to the sensitivity associated with financial data and concerns regarding the release of competitive information. In most instances, managers perceive the exchange of operational data as having significantly less risk than exchanging cost and financial information. Compounding this situation, existing cost management systems frequently preclude the exchange of the needed cost information. Traditional general ledger cost systems do not possess the capability to provide the accurate cost information needed for managing products, services, and information flows through complex supply chains.

Conventional cost systems fail to support supply chain decision making. To demonstrate why, divide the value chain into two segments—internal and external. The internal value chain represents the firm. Conventional approaches view the firm as a group of functions that perform tasks, produce costs, and create value. The profit margin represents the difference between what the firm's customers are willing to pay for the product or service minus the firm's costs. Multiple processes link the internal value chain to the external value chain, which is made up of a network of trading partners. As goods or services move through the supply chain, they pass through other firms in the supply chain where value and costs are created. However, conventional cost systems fail to capture how these interactions drive costs within the firm or the trading partners in the external supply chain. The portrayal of the supply chain as a network of internal value chains is useful for understanding why a broader view of costs is required so that managers can better manage the linkages and interrelationships to affect the costs and profits of each trading partner.

Many of the costs incurred with a firm's internal value chain are driven by business practices occurring in the external supply chain (see Exhibit 3.2). The figure illustrates that a company must think beyond its four walls. For example, the manufacturer's purchasing, receiving, inventory, and manufacturing process costs are driven by how well external suppliers make and deliver components. A decision by a supplier to employ a low-cost motor carrier to reduce transportation costs may increase the manufacturer's costs through increased variability in order cycle time. The result may be higher inventory levels or work stoppages on the manufacturing line. A supplier's business practices also have a direct effect on the cost of raw materials or components acquired by the manufacturer.

EXHIBIT 3.2 Intrafirm Costs Largely Driven by Trading Partners' Business Practices

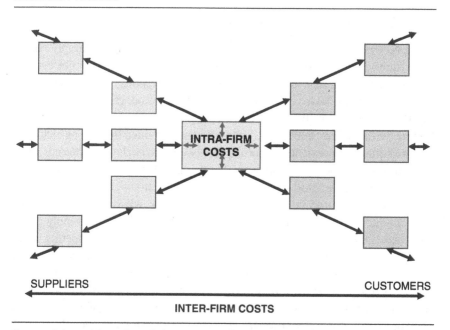

SUPPLIERS

CUSTOMERS

INTER-FIRM COSTS

Source: Adapted from Gary Cokins, *Activity-Based Cost Management: An Executive's Guide* (New York: John Wiley & Sons, 2001), p. 164. Copyright Gary Cokins. Used with permission of the author.

Downstream customers can also have a major effect on upstream suppliers' internal costs. A key retailer may unilaterally decide to reduce inventory levels and order more frequently. This decision may result in higher costs for the manufacturer, who now needs to hold more inventory and has a higher frequency of deliveries. The tailoring of supply chains to meet end-user needs drives many different costs within the upstream trading partners. Suppliers increasingly go to market through several distribution channels and have shifted functions across trading partners to best meet these needs. Supply chain managers have begun to employ tools such as customer profitability and total landed cost analyses to understand the implications of going to market through multiple channels.

Likewise, external costs incurred by trading partners can be driven by the firm's internal business practices. If a retailer chooses not to exchange demand data, upstream suppliers will consequently experience the "bullwhip" effect. In the bullwhip effect, wide swings in demand result in higher costs for suppliers due to increased forecast error and inventory levels, greater use of expedited transportation, and changing production levels and schedules. The retailer experiences higher costs as well because fewer products are available and suppliers pass along their costs in the form of higher prices.

Supply Chain Management Is Complex

By its very nature, supply chain management is very complex. Supply chains are frequently described as an interlinked set of trading partners that convert raw materials or data into products or services in response to end-user needs. These descriptions fail to capture the many different products and services flowing through the firm, the variety of trading partners and relationships that interact with the firm, and the multiple processes in which the firm participates. Firms frequently operate in numerous supply chains, each with different strategies, trading partners, and end users. This complexity makes supply chain cost management challenging and difficult. In addition, managers often are reluctant to exchange information, especially about costs, when their trading partners conduct business with competitors. Exhibit 3.3 illustrates supply chain complexity and the relationship between trading partners and competing firms.

Supply chain professionals must recognize that they cannot apply a one-size-fits-all strategy when managing their business relationships or the processes that support these relationships. As business practices are tailored to meet the needs of these relationships, so must the performance measures and cost information be tailored so managers can determine how the relationship is performing and affecting the firms.

EXHIBIT 3.3   Complexity Driven by Participation in Multiple Supply Chains

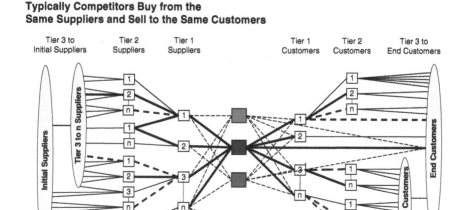

Source: Douglas M. Lambert, ed., *Supply Chain Management: Processes, Partnerships, Performance*, fourth edition (Ponte Vedra Beach, FL: Supply Chain Management Institute, 2014), p. 7. © Copyright Douglas M. Lambert. Used with permission. For more information about the SCM Framework, see drdouglaslambert.com.

The nature of supply chain decision making requires a different approach for capturing and analyzing cost data across multiple firms. Decisions made within a single firm can have a ripple effect across the supply chain, driving costs in a manner totally unanticipated by the decision maker. In some instances, a decision made with the intent to improve a firm's profitability may have severe consequences elsewhere in the supply chain and decrease the marketplace competitiveness of the end product or service. This situation results from the lack of cost visibility and knowledge within the supply chain.

Arraying Costs Along Three Dimensions

Supply chain costing extends the focus of cost management across the firm's boundaries. Traditional systems are constrained by design to capturing cost information within the four walls of the firm and to satisfy the requirements for external financial reporting. Supply chain costing broadens managers' perspectives by providing cost visibility at the activity level from the ultimate source of supply to the end user. Activity-level information further expands managers' views by identifying the cost drivers for these activities and by providing the capability to portray costs along the *supply chain resources, supply chain cost objects, and supply chain process dimensions* (see Exhibit 3.4).[4]

EXHIBIT 3.4　Dimensions of Supply Chain Cost Information

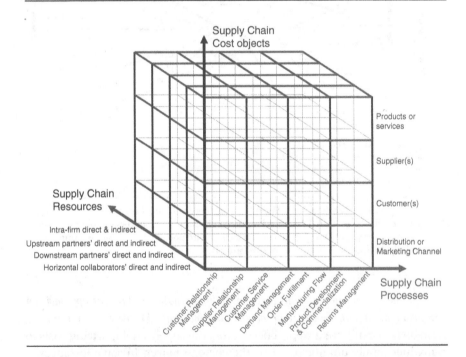

- The *supply chain resources dimension* addresses not only the direct and indirect costs within the firm but expands these categories to include the resource costs of trading partners spanning the entire supply chain. This dimension portrays costs based on the behavior of these costs and the decisions that create them. These cost categories include the direct and indirect costs for the firm and its upstream and downstream trading partners. Direct costs can be directly traced to an activity and are caused by the performance of the activity. Direct costs would include the direct labor and materials consumed in production in a traditional cost management system. Indirect costs include those costs not directly incurred in production. However, many indirect costs can be assigned to activities performed by other functions in the firm such as marketing, logistics, or research and development. Since indirect costs are not directly consumed by production activities, traditional cost systems arbitrarily allocate indirect costs to production activities such as direct labor hours.

■ The *supply chain processes dimension* captures costs driven by activities performed within each supply chain process[5] by trading partners spanning the supply chain. Process costs encompass the cost of the activities comprising the process across all firms in the supply chain (Exhibit 3.5). This view enables supply managers to determine how each firm's performance contributes to the overall cost of performing each process, or how the behavior of upstream suppliers or downstream customers drives activity performance costs. Supply chain managers can use this information to more effectively determine how to improve the overall performance or total cost of performing the process. Process improvement efforts can focus on high-cost activities, functions, or activities that can be shifted to other trading partners who can perform them more efficiently, or cost trade-offs can be performed between activities and other processes to lower the overall total cost achieved by the supply chain.

EXHIBIT 3.5   Process View of Cost Information in a Supply Chain

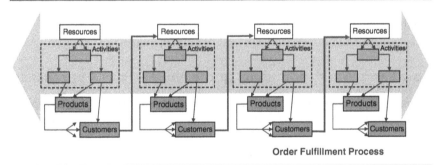

Order Fulfillment Process

Source: Adapted from Gary Cokins, *Activity-Based Cost Management: An Executive's Guide* (New York: John Wiley & Sons, 2001), p. 169. Copyright Gary Cokins. Used with permission of the author.

■ The *supply chain cost object dimension* classifies costs by customer, supplier, product, or service, and by distribution or marketing channel to support a cost or profitability analysis by any of these cost objects. This dimension breaks out costs by customer or supplier relationships and distribution channels within the supply chain. Costs are traced to specific trading partners or channels based on how their behavior, business practices, or transactions incur costs within the supply chain. Transaction costs include the costs of conducting activities between the firm and its upstream suppliers or downstream customers. The supply chain view includes the portion of each trading partner's costs associated with participating in a specific supply chain. The supply chain cost differs from the sum of the trading partners' costs since any trading partner may simultaneously participate in multiple supply chains. This dimension captures the costs incurred by employing a specific strategy across the supply chain. Product costs include those costs, direct and indirect, associated with the product. Product characteristics are used to classify or categorize costs. Product design captures all the supply chain costs associated with the research and development of a product, or product category, across the supply chain. Production costs incorporate all the production costs, including raw materials, components, and subassemblies. The life-cycle category encompasses all the costs incurred by the supply chain during the lifespan of the product, from initial concept and design through to disposal and recycling.

These three dimensions act as a kaleidoscope, allowing managers to view costs in different ways simultaneously. Cost information can be portrayed as needed by product, process, or trading partner/channel to support decisions managers make. Within the supply chain, all costs need to be identified to be effectively analyzed and controlled. These dimensions encompass a wider array of costs than incorporated in traditional cost systems.

How Firms Are Responding to the Need—Four Approaches

We can categorize how managers have responded to the need for a more sophisticated and expanded view of cost management into four different approaches:

■ *The first approach* includes those firms that have developed sophisticated and detailed cost management systems. These firms have begun to expand their line of sight regarding performance and cost information in the supply chain. They do this by requiring their suppliers to provide cost information, estimating their trading partners' costs, or engaging in limited exchanges of cost information with select trading partners.

■ *The second approach* consists of those firms that have held back from attempting to exchange cost information. They hold back because their cost systems cannot provide the needed information; development of a more sophisticated system appears impractical; managers believe the investment to obtain better cost information may not be worth the effort; they anticipate that impending ERP implementations will produce the needed capability; or they have major operational issues to address before being able to commit resources to obtain better cost information.

■ *The third approach* includes many small suppliers and customers that lack an understanding of supply chain management or costing techniques. Despite their size, these firms represent a large proportion of many supply chains and have a significant effect on process performance (time, quality, functionality, and flexibility) and costs.

■ *The fourth approach* encompasses managers who understand how interactions between and across the supply chain drive cost and performance both within their firms and in their trading partners. These managers and their firms have embarked on a journey toward having end-to-end visibility across the entire supply chain, or what we refer to as supply chain costing. Some firms are much further along this journey than others; however, no firm has yet completed the journey. Due to the complexity of the process, participation in multiple supply chains, the varying capabilities of other trading partners, and ongoing changes occurring in the supply chain, few firms will ever fully complete this journey. Managers recognize that the journey may never be fully completed, but the knowledge and insight available to managers and the potential to achieve sustainable cost reductions and performance improvements makes the journey a worthwhile pursuit.

Integrating Supply Chain Activities

Integration of supply chain activities offers significant opportunities for cost reduction. Although the costs, complexities, and risks of managing a highly integrated supply chain can be as substantial, they are not significantly different from the costs of integrating and operating a corporation of comparable size.[6] In many instances, how costs will change due to integration is not well understood or recognized. As a result, most supply chain integration efforts have, to date, been limited in scope.

Supply chain costing is fundamental to the concept of supply chain management. Cost reduction is one of the most frequently stated objectives of executives employing supply chain management. Few supply chain executives currently have the cost visibility necessary to understand how each trading partner drives cost and performance. Having this understanding coupled with the ability to effectively make cost trade-offs across the entire supply chain can lead to the identification of opportunities to achieve a sustainable competitive advantage.

Executives across all tiers in a supply chain require a framework for costing and analyzing key business processes. They need to share cost information in a consistent and understandable format to promote trust across multiple trading partners. It is essential to measure and sell the benefits of collaborative action in the supply chain. This means identifying opportunities to lower costs and improve performance, demonstrating the value created for key stakeholders, and translating process improvements into financial performance in the firms' financial statements. It requires determining how each trading partner is contributing to value creation, measuring the progress of the supply chain toward achieving performance targets, and ensuring that the benefits and burdens resulting from supply chain initiatives are equitably allocated among the participating trading partners.

Later sections of this book expand on these ideas by developing the conceptual foundation required for cost management and developing cost information. Supply chain costing tools are summarized and, when appropriate, discussed. There is an emphasis on the importance of aligning performance measures with supply chain management practices and articulating the challenges to reaching the supply chain cost management goals firms are seeking.

 ## SUPPLY CHAIN COSTING DEFINITION

The adoption of supply chain management and a process view results in a different perspective regarding cost management than exists in most firms. The focus shifts from determining and analyzing only the costs incurred within a single firm when producing goods or services to one of determining the costs incurred by the entire supply chain in providing the final product or service to the end user. To improve the value proposition presented to the end user, supply chain managers must look across the entire supply chain for new ways to enhance product or service quality while reducing costs. The need and concept for supply chain costing has been discussed; however, the literature has not previously defined supply chain costing.

Based on the research performed for this book, the following definition of supply chain costing was developed:

> Supply chain costing is the collection, expense assignment, and analysis of cost information across all of the work activities comprising a supply chain for the purpose of identifying opportunities to obtain a competitive advantage through a combination of reduced costs or improved performance.

Supply chain managers require an extended view of costs. Companies do not operate in isolation, and many of the costs incurred by a firm are driven by activities and processes performed by external trading partners. As products or services move forward in the supply chain, more and more costs are accumulated. The marketplace cost experienced by the end user is the sum of the activity costs performed by all the trading partners.

Supply chain managers require visibility of costs, and what causes costs, from dirt to dirt to have the ability to control the final cost experienced by the end user (Exhibit 3.6). The exhibit represents at a high level an activity-based costing (ABC) cost assignment and tracing flow. The "resource" expenses are consumed by the work activities of people and assets. The work activities are in turn consumed by the products and customers. Then, like circus elephants in a line with each one's trunk holding onto the tail of the elephant in front of it, the upstream tier customer's purchase price and volume becomes a "resource" expense to its next tier as a buyer. Without this visibility, managers will miss opportunities to reduce costs or the ability to optimize costs at a more strategic level through interfirm cost trade-offs.

The process view incorporated in this definition of supply chain costing enhances strategic management by breaking out direct and indirect product costs as well as the transaction and process costs occurring across the supply chain. It involves tracing all types of costs to the products, customers, or channels and measuring their contribution to the firm's profitability. Managers can target the supply chain relationships that yield or show the potential to yield the greatest contributions and act to minimize high cost/low value-added relationships.

EXHIBIT 3.6 Visibility of Cost Information Provided by Supply Chain Costing

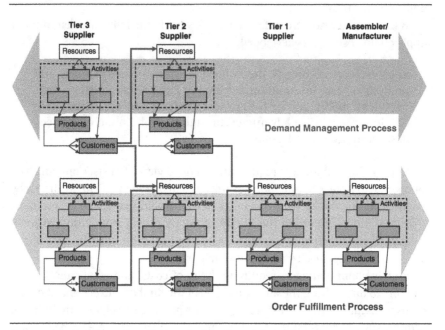

Source: Adapted from Gary Cokins, *Activity-Based Cost Management: An Executive's Guide* (New York: John Wiley & Sons, 2001), p. 169. Copyright Gary Cokins. Used with permission of the author.

The combination of activity-level information and the cost, product, and relationship dimensions enables supply chain costing to categorize costs as needed to support the decisions managers make at the operational, tactical, and strategic levels. Operational decisions will require detailed information involving directly assignable costs and transaction costs by product and trading partner. For example, a purchasing supervisor may be deciding whether to source a product from two competing vendors based on the landed cost or total cost of ownership. In contrast, a tactical decision may involve a different view of costs at a higher level. Supply chain managers may be determining whether to outsource functions and will need to determine how supply chain, interface, trading partner, product, production, and process costs will vary. Strategic decisions would require cost information at a different level. Senior executives would require information regarding how different network designs would drive process costs with each trading partner across an entire supply chain over the entire life cycle of the products being distributed. Supply chain costing can support these different decision-making levels by having visibility of activity costs and cost drivers.

NOTES

1. Douglas M. Lambert and Terrance L. Pohlen, "Supply Chain Metrics," *International Journal of Logistics Management* 12, no. 1 (2001): 1–19.
2. Douglas M. Lambert, ed., *Supply Chain Management: Processes, Partnerships, Performance*, Fourth Edition, Ponte Vedra Beach, FL: Supply Chain Management Institute, 2014, p. 2.
3. A complete and thorough discussion of this framework, the eight supply chain processes, and the application of these processes to integrate and manage the supply chain can be obtained at drdouglaslambert.com.
4. The following section expands on Seuring's framework of cost, product, and relationship dimensions based on the results of the research and review of the literature related to supply chain costing. See Stefan Seuring, "Supply Chain Costing," in *Cost Management in Supply Chains*, ed. Stefan Seuring and Maria Goldbach (Heidelberg, Germany: Physica-Verlag), p. 24.
5. Refer to Figure 3.1 for the eight major supply chain management processes.
6. National Research Council, *Surviving Supply Chain Integration: Strategies for Small Manufacturers* (Washington, DC: National Academy of Sciences, 2000), p. 31.

CHAPTER 4

Developing a Foundational Understanding of Strategic Supply Chain Cost Management

A
GREEING ON THE DEFINITION of the supply chain, its processes, supply chain management, and supply chain costing is a critical first step in the supply chain cost management journey. Progress through this costing journey requires that several obvious, but too often overlooked, foundational elements be in place. This chapter discusses the need to establish the importance of supply chain costing and supply chain decisions. It emphasizes the need for a common understanding of the environment in which the firm operates and where the firm is currently positioned strategically, operationally, and within the supply chain.

Each of these elements represents foundational understandings that are essential to strategic supply chain costing. Without these elements in place, firms do not have an appropriate commitment to or direction for their supply chain costing efforts. Managers in the firms that have progressed furthest on the supply chain costing journey generally understand these foundational elements rather well. However, many of their trading partners currently do not "get it," and there is a need to educate them on the foundational elements summarized in this chapter.

IMPORTANCE OF SUPPLY CHAIN COSTING

Supply chain professionals reading this book almost certainly already understand the importance of supply chain costing for their firms. *The key question is whether top management, other key internal decision makers, and your supply chain trading partners adequately understand the importance.*

Events such as a dramatic fluctuation in transportation costs should make selling decision makers on the importance of supply chain costing seem unnecessary. However, many firms and departments within firms are not yet focused on finding ways to better manage supply chain costs. This lack of focus is understandable given the numerous management issues and business challenges that compete for managers' attention. Thus, it may be necessary to sell managers who oversee portions of the supply chain processes and/or supply chain trading partners on the importance of devoting resources to improving supply chain costing.

Major categories of costs within firms are easily overlooked when the costs are not explicitly identified or grow from relatively small to much more significant amounts. The literature is replete with examples of what happens when firms fail to adequately monitor, measure, and manage a large pool of costs. The following are just a few of the many areas from which the literature draws its examples: indirect manufacturing costs, administrative costs, quality costs, and environmental costs. Cost leaders recognize the importance of documenting the magnitude of supply chain costs. Their objective is to ensure that the importance of managing these costs is understood at all levels of the organization and throughout the supply chain. They also recognize that it is going to take some significant educational efforts to bring certain trading partners within their supply chains up to speed.

Magnitude of Supply Chain Costs

The literature is surprisingly silent on the magnitude of total supply chain costs. This measurement dearth may result from the lack of a shared definition of the supply chain and supply chain processes, or from an inability to obtain good supply chain cost information with the measurement tools firms currently have in place. Yet there is common agreement that supply chain costs are significant and represent a fruitful area for cost management. While there is limited information available on the magnitude of total supply chain costs, Exhibit 4.1 provides a few examples of the magnitude of costs in selected supply chain areas such as logistics.

EXHIBIT 4.1 How Large Are Elements of Supply Chain Costs?

Companies engaged in ecommerce confront substantial logistics costs. For example, Amazon's annual shipping and fulfillment cost was $78.1 billion in 2019,[1] or approximately 27.9% of net sales.

Supply chain costs as a percent of sales range from approximately 5.7% for best in class supply chains with an overall average of approximately 9.8% of sales.[2]

The total cost to serve for the health care supply chain averages 37.3% of the total cost of patient care.[3]

"Logistics costs can make the difference between a product customer, or channel that is profitable and one that is less profitable . . . or even unprofitable. Yet companies often are surprised to learn how great an impact logistics costs can have."[4]

United States business logistics costs were estimated to be $1.6 trillion or 7.6 % of nominal GDP in 2019.[5]

---

1 Statista, https://www.statista.com/chart/17207/amazon-shipping-and-fulfillment-costs/#.~:text=Last%20 year%20alone%2C%20the%20company's,to%20a%20hefty%20logistics%20bill, accessed November 2020.
2 Benchmarking Success quoted in Logistics Bureau, Reducing Supply Chain Costs. https:www. logisticsbureau.com/reducing-supply-chain-costs/, April 9, 2016, accessed November 2020.
3 Gartner, https://www.gartner.com/en/supply-chain/insights/healthcare-supply-chain-management, accessed November 2020.
4 William C. Copacino, "A Cost-to-Serve Analysis Can Be an Eye-Opener," *Logistics Management and Distribution Report* 38, no. 4(1999): 33.
5 A.T. Kearney, *CSCMP's State of Logistics Report (2020)*.

Importance of Measuring and Managing Supply Chain Costs

Quantifying the size of the supply chain costs an organization or supply chain process incurs is one approach to selling skeptical managers on the importance of measuring and managing supply chain costs. Unfortunately, accounting systems typically do not separately identify all the supply chain costs associated with a particular process, even within a single firm. Many supply chain costs are subsumed within other functional and departmental cost categories. For example, the cost of inbound freight may not be a separate component of inventory purchases. Wages for delivery schedulers may be aggregated into a broader salary classification. The cost of billing and collecting from transport customers may be grouped with administrative costs.

To the extent that supply chain costs are combined with other costs, managers cannot assess the total supply chain costs currently incurred by the firm. When supply chain costs are not separately identified, managers have difficulty knowing what the firm is spending on its supply chain processes and even more difficulty assessing the effectiveness of a firm's supply chain spending. Are supply chain dollars being focused on the right items? Are they yielding the highest benefits? Because traditional cost classifications systems may mask the scope of supply chain costs, documenting the magnitude of these costs within the organization can make the cost more visible.

Despite the limitations of existing cost systems many firms are attempting to actively manage supply chain costs. This management has been primarily for local optimization. Large firms have often lowered inventory levels and increased delivery reliability by moving responsibility for these items to suppliers—who then often move the responsibility to their suppliers. The supply chain costs for the individual firm appears lower, but total supply chain costs often increase. The result is that customers pay more. However, the fact that customers pay more is not immediately transparent from existing cost measurement systems.

Even within existing data constraints, by many measures the supply chain sector has successfully reduced costs. Logistics costs as a percentage of GDP have been steadily declining since 1980, from nearly 16% of U.S. gross domestic product to 7.6% in 2019.[1] However, substantial reductions have not occurred since 2010, and the pressure to further reduce costs is likely to continue as firms attempt to obtain a cost advantage in the marketplace. Many firms are in the early stages of partnering with other supply chain members in an effort to increase efficiency and lower the overall cost of supply chain processes. It is in these cooperative efforts that future cost reductions are most likely to be successful.

To date, many firms have not changed how they manage the supply chain. Many company executives lack a supply chain background and may not understand why supply chain costs are so high. They often wonder, how hard can it be to get products to the right place at the right time? Competitive pressures to keep reducing costs make it essential to get both top managers' attention and supply chain partners focused on supply chain costs. Supply chain cost management is made more difficult by several factors,[2] including: fragmented demand for products and services with shorter life cycles, less predictable demand patterns, increased complexity from outsourcing, new technology, and complicated distribution models.

Firms share little information about their supply chain performance, and this area has typically been off-limits to researchers. However, one study shows that "when a supply chain malfunction is announced, stock prices plunge an average of 8.62% and shareholder wealth decreases by \$120 million or more per company."[3] This finding is a dramatic indicator of the importance of supply chain cost issues. A failure to carefully monitor and manage supply chain costs is likely to have a crippling financial effect on the firm. Supply chain costs result from a wide variety of strategic and operational decisions. As part of the analysis conducted before making these decisions, managers must estimate what supply chain costs will be incurred and how supply chain costs are expected to change.

IDENTIFYING THE DETERMINATES OF SUPPLY CHAIN COST SYSTEMS

Many factors influence supply chain costs. Understanding these determinate factors is fundamental for managing supply chain costs and selecting appropriate costing systems. Every organization and supply chain decision maker is positioned within a supply chain structure, is influenced by dynamic environmental factors, makes strategic and operational product and service choices, and selects or uses production processes. Together these interactive factors influence the type of cost information managers need in order to make decisions that affect supply chain costs.

Structure of the Supply Chain

Managers must carefully document the firm's position in the total supply chain. This positions them to develop firm and supply chain strategies and to select appropriate production and service approaches for supply chain processes. The firm's position in the supply chain directly influences which supply chain costs it can effectively manage, especially where there is little joint sharing of cost information across the value chain.

Organizational size and scope directly influence the type of supply chain cost information that is available internally and how much choice the firm has in the way it structures supply chain processes. To illustrate:

- A firm spanning most of the supply chain, such as Exxon in the oil and gas industry, has access to internal information on nearly all its supply chain costs. Theoretically, top management can dictate what information is accumulated and shared internally or externally. They can make decisions that fundamentally alter supply chain processes. Even in this type of firm it is often difficult to obtain key supply chain information because of the functional and responsibility focus of existing cost and performance measurement systems.

▪ A large firm, such as Walmart, can control many aspects of the supply chain. The firm can dictate how and when suppliers deliver to warehouses or stores, the way goods are packaged, how billing occurs, and when suppliers are paid. Large firms may even have the clout to compel a certain amount of cost sharing by suppliers or customers. This power can also be misused and lead to long-term problems with trading partners.

▪ Conversely, smaller firms have direct access to cost information for only a small segment of the supply chain and are less able to control many aspects of supply chain processes. This position can make them particularly distrustful of sharing information.

Strategic and production decisions that affect current and future supply chain costs are made at many levels in the firm. An understanding of how the firm's position in the supply chain and what type of decision is being made (operational, tactical, or strategic) helps decision makers evaluate what cost information they need and what costs the decision will affect. A strategic decision to acquire a fleet of delivery vehicles or to outsource customer billing fundamentally changes the firm's long-term cost structure. A warehouse manager evaluating whether to make a special delivery requested by the customer is making an operational decision that influences only a limited number of short-term costs. Supply chain professionals must understand who their firm's trading partners are, both internally and externally, and document how these partners influence costs.

Operating Environment

All organizations function in a dynamic environmental setting. Understanding the nature of this environment and how it is changing is essential because environmental factors constrain and influence strategic, production, and supply chain process choices. Exhibit 4.2 is a depiction of these relationships. Key *operating environment* elements are shown on the right side of the outer ring. These elements directly influence and constrain how the firm operates. The operating environment elements include: the level of *competition* for the firm's products and services, *customer* and *supplier* expectations, the quantity and type of *labor* available, access to *capital* investment funds, and the nature of available *technology*. Each of these operating elements helps identify the threats and opportunities the firm faces and scope the resources it needs.

EXHIBIT 4.2 The Organization and Its Environment

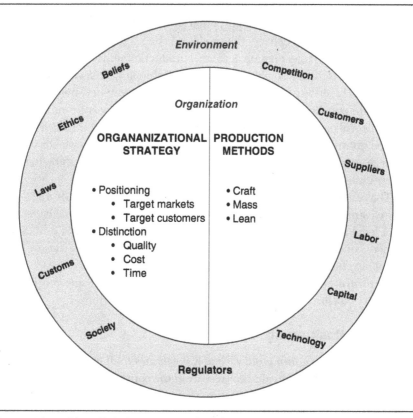

Source: Adapted from Shahid Ansari, Jan Bell, and Thomas Klammer, unpublished working material, 2005.

The left side of the outer ring consists of the *cultural environment* factors. Every organization operates within the constraints imposed by legal and regulatory rules; political influences; and cultural norms, beliefs, and values. As the environment changes, strategies are modified and choices of production and logistical processes are rethought.

Consider the following examples of the influence of environmental elements and how these factors impact a firm's strategy, production processes, and supply chain cost:

▪ Advances in tracking technology permit shippers to monitor truck location and speed, facilitate on-time delivery, and increase routing flexibility. An investment in this technology may alter fuel costs, improve regulatory compliance, and upgrade customer perceptions of delivery quality and timing.
▪ The size of the market for a particular product directly influences how the firm produces and delivers the product. When the market for a product is large, the firm may operate dedicated production and shipping facilities. If the market is small, flexible production and shipping processes are essential.
▪ Effectively serving big box stores (as opposed to mom-and-pop stores) may require suppliers to use different distribution channels to minimize cost while still providing appropriate levels of quality and on time delivery.
▪ The quantity of labor available, its cost, and whether that labor is union or nonunion influences decisions on what labor to utilize and whether to automate processes.
▪ The amount of financial capital available to add capacity or meet other investment needs influences how products and services are delivered.
▪ A legal requirement that certain goods can be shipped only on U.S. carriers constrains shipping flexibility and changes the cost structure of the supply chain.
▪ A cultural bias against sharing information with other firms may limit the ability of a firm to function as a lean producer or distributor.

Strategic Positioning

Strategy is the way a firm positions and distinguishes itself from its competitors.[4] Organizations make strategic choices within the context of their environment. Strategic positioning encompasses the selection of the firm's target markets or customers and its place in the overall supply chain. Strategic distinction delineates the organizational approach a firm uses to differentiate itself from other firms. Variations in quality, cost, and time are the three primary elements the firm employs for making product and service strategy distinctions.

▪ *Quality* is characterized as the customer's total experience with the product or service. It encompasses features such as accurate shipment quantities and after-sales support. The reliability of each product or service feature is another dimension of quality.

▪ *Cost* includes all the resources expended throughout the supply chain from product or service initiation to final disposal. Administrative selling and product costs are all part of the costs of interest.

▪ *Time* means providing the product or service when it is needed, quickly developing new features or functions, moving these innovations to market, and considering how long it takes to cycle through the production (delivery) process.

Decisions related to the supply chain are directly influenced by the firm's strategic distinctions. The specific meanings of quality, cost, and time vary by product and type of organization. But focusing on only a single dimension of strategy represents an unsustainable option for the firm in today's competitive environment. If the "cheapest" shipper is chronically late or regularly delivers the wrong quantity or type of goods, the customer is unlikely to be retained by the customer. If a retail store does not have the product a customer wants when they are ready to buy, the store gains no advantage from advertising that they have the lowest price.

Production Methods

The term *production method* as used here represents the set of activities that occur when providing a service or producing a product. *Production is much broader than manufacturing.* It includes the activities that are part of each supply chain process. The level of flexibility is directly linked to decisions made about physical production, delivery, and other support processes.

Mass and lean are the basic production methods firms use to transform resources into products or services. *Mass production* is making or delivering large quantities of identical products or services using standardized methods. The manufacture of canned goods or household appliances as well as mining and shipping trainloads of coal to large utilities are examples of mass production and mass delivery processes.

Lean production is a flexible manufacturing or delivery approach that permits firms to provide small quantities of customized products or services to customers. Examples of lean manufacturing include Class 8 truck manufacturers that custom-build tractors to the unique specifications of their customers. These firms employ lean processes to enable the manufacture of customized products with quick changeover while also minimizing inventory levels.

While the majority of writings on lean methods focus on the manufacturing area, the attributes of a lean system have enormous implications throughout supply chain processes. Which method or combination of production methods is most effective varies with the characteristics of the supply chain process environment. A fundamental part of supply chain management is making decisions about when and where in the supply chain processes to apply lean and mass production methods.

Most firms are going to use a combination of mass and lean techniques based on the characteristics that are most appropriate in particular situations. To illustrate, a mass production approach may be appropriate for a distribution channel that delivers truckload quantities of the same product to the same customer distribution centers each week. The same firm may need a distribution channel with lean production characteristics when products are being delivered to a changing group of customers, in varying and uncertain quantities every week.

The characteristics of mass and lean can be quite different. Exhibit 4.3 provides an *extreme contrast* of mass and lean production characteristics to emphasize the potential implications of these differences. Several attribute categories, noted below, are listed in the first column.

- *Structural elements* refer to how labor, technology, and capital assets are employed.
- *Work processes* are how the firm organizes work relationships.
- *Management accounting* refers to the focus of costing systems for particular production processes.
- *Technical* attributes focus on the primary decision focus and process emphases in the organization.
- *Behavioral* attributes are characterized as assumptions and consequences.
- *Cultural* attributes refer to the underlying beliefs and values.

Generally, the characteristics listed in the lean column of the figure are more consistent with reaching the supply chain costing goals that are the basis of the costing journey described in this book. The process focus, close relationships with suppliers, a customer focus, flexible equipment, and other factors are all elements of modern supply chain management and supply chain costing. Practically, firms can restructure mass production systems to feature many of the characteristics of lean production approaches. Mass production methods are still appropriate as part of many supply chain processes, but they can be improved if firms can learn different ways to focus on information.

EXHIBIT 4.3 Characteristics of Mass and Lean Production Methods

Attribute	Mass	Lean
Structural elements		
	Inflexible single purpose equipment	Flexible multi-use equipment
	High setup time for equipment	Low setup time for equipment
	Simple tasks and low-skilled labor	Complex tasks and skilled labor
Work processes		
	Top-down control of employees	Empowered workers
	Supplier relationships at arm's length	Cooperative relationship with suppliers
	Limited relationships with customers	Continuous customer focused organization
	Linear design process	Concurrent design of product and process
Management accounting		
	Relationship of volume to cost	Relating "drivers" to cost
	Responsibility accounting – unit focus	Process accounting – value chain focus
	Inventory driven – reporting and control	No inventory reporting
	Labor reporting	Indirect cost reporting
Technical		
	Short-run decisions	Long-run cost structures
	Internal efficiency	External environmental focus
	Single responsibility unit focus	Cross-functional and value-chain focus
	Little process emphasis	Primary emphasis on process
Behavioral		
	Assumptions	*Assumptions*
	Strong control of workers, suppliers	Empowered responsible workers, suppliers
	Individual accountability	Team responsibility
	Monetary motivations	Multiple motivational factors
	Accountant as control agent	Accountant as team player
	Consequences	*Consequences*
	Quality problems	Quality commitment
	Local optimization	Global optimization
	Less employee burnout	Pressure and employee burnout
Culture		
	Individual responsibility	Team responsibility
	Competition and market efficiency	Cooperation
	Pro-capital and management	Work for common good
	Management power	Knowledge-based power

Source: Adapted from multiple figures: Shahid Ansari, Jan Bell, and Thomas Klammer, "Management Accounting in the Age of Lean Production," in the modular series *Management Accounting: A Strategic Focus* (Ansari, Bell, Klammer: Lulu.com). A more detailed explanation of lean characteristics can be found in this module.

DOCUMENTING SUPPLY CHAIN DECISIONS AND PRODUCTION PROCESSES

A final element of the foundational information structure that supply chain professionals need in place to make better decisions is adequate documentation of the different types of decisions that relate to the eight supply chain processes (Exhibit 3.1). The variety of decisions related to supply chain processes is virtually unlimited. Categorizing decisions by their nature and type helps supply chain professionals identify and select appropriate tools to use for supply chain costing.

The influence of a decision varies in both scope and time. Some decisions have long-term implications for the entire supply chain. Others have only a short-term effect on a small segment of an organization. Three decision categories that relate to time and scope are long-term strategic, tactical, and short-term operational.

- *Strategic decisions* have a long-term effect on the supply chain and the decision outcomes often have far-reaching effects. Because of their complexity and far-reaching effect on both the firm and the supply chain, these decisions involve considerable uncertainty and risk. They can fundamentally alter the cost structure of the individual firm and potentially all firms in the supply chain. Most costs related to strategic decisions are controllable until the decision is finalized. The costing techniques currently employed by most firms often fail to identify how these decisions affect costs over time for the decision maker and particularly for other trading partners.
- *Tactical decisions* are made to achieve a short-to-medium-term objective. By definition, tactical decisions involve a shorter time horizon and fewer resources than strategic decisions. They carry less risk and typically have only moderate long-term consequences for the firm and the supply chain. Tactical decisions should be made within the constraints resulting from strategic decisions. However, supply chain professionals often make tactical and operating decisions that are inconsistent with the strategic plans and objectives of the organization. Incongruent decisions raise costs. The failure to share strategic information throughout the firm, much less the full supply chain, is often why decisions inconsistent with strategy are made.
- *Operational decisions* focus on the day-to-day activities within the supply chain. They are made frequently by operating managers or teams. There

is little time for careful thought and analysis, so simple decision rules are structured to facilitate decision efficiency and consistency, hopefully within the constraints established by strategic and tactical decisions. The consequences of individual decisions are minimal, but a series of judgment errors can quickly accumulate and have a detrimental effect on supply chain performance.

Understanding the type of production process that a supply chain decision is intended to support is also important. An organization may find it useful to subdivide operating, tactical, and perhaps even strategic decisions into smaller subclassifications that highlight key differences that might influence data needs or decision rules. The integrated nature of the extended supply chain decision means that ultimately decision makers need to adopt different approaches for capturing and analyzing data across multiple firms. An awareness of how decisions made within a single firm can have a ripple effect across the supply chain and drive costs in unanticipated ways is important for decision makers. Documenting and classifying supply chain decisions is one step in developing this multiple firm focus.

NOTES

1. Trend developed from the Council of Supply Chain Management's Annual State of Logistics Reports, 1980 through 2020.
2. Steve Matthesen, cited in "You Can't Manage What You Can't Measure: Maximizing Supply Chain Value" from Boston Consulting Group, Knowledge@Wharton, September 2006.
3. Vinod Singhal and Kevin Hendricks, "Putting a Price on Supply Chain Problems: Study Links Supply Chain Glitches with Falling Stock Prices," *Georgia Research Tech News*, December 2000.
4. Shahid Ansari, Jan Bell, and Thomas Klammer, "Strategy and Management Accounting," in the modular series *Management Accounting: A Strategic Focus* (Ansari, Bell, Klammer: Lulu.com).

CHAPTER 5

Why Supply Chain Cost Systems Differ from Traditional Cost Systems

S UPPLY CHAIN COST SYSTEMS should support a firm's strategic and production choices as well as the broad variety of decisions related to supply chain processes that executives and managers need to make. The importance of restructuring cost systems so the information they provide more effectively supports supply chain management is made repeatedly by supply chain executives. Information needs should drive the design of supply chain cost systems, and the information should provide insights and support the decisions managers make at the strategic, tactical, and operational levels.

Supply chain costing is complex and many choices exist to assist firms in better managing supply chain processes. The identification of what cost information is needed and the selection of the appropriate tools for measuring, reporting, and analyzing supply chain costs are key challenges. The next several chapters can assist executives in making these choices. This chapter provides a structural foundation for the more explicit discussion of the costing tools. Modern supply chain cost information must match costing methods and tools with the time frame and nature of the decision, while thinking outside the box of functional and internal costs to include costs across trading partners in the supply chain. Firms must adopt a strategic perspective for managing supply chain costs and managers must understand how modern supply chain costing differs from traditional costing.

COST DATA NEEDS

Responsibility cost center–based cost systems are in place in almost every orga-nization. They are reported in the general ledger accounting system. These systems collect data by the department, division, or functional area where a manager has spending responsibility. While useful for safeguarding assets, responsibility cost center expense data is of limited value for strategic analysis or decision making because the focus is on who incurred a cost rather than on whether the right activities are being supported. Responsibility cost center–based systems lack the characteristics needed to properly support the variety of activities that are inherent in increasingly lean supply chain processes. How-ever, they can, in some situations, be adapted to capture cost data that is useful in this changing environment.

Consider standard costing, a tool that is widely used. When a firm routinely fills the same types of orders for the same customers, the cost factors involved in providing this service are easy to identify. Standards for each cost factor are developed and cost systems routinely collect information on the small number of cost factors that drive costs in this type of mass production process. Actual costs are compared with expected costs in each category and area. The rea-sons for cost deviations, commonly referred to as cost variances, are analyzed as part of an ongoing effort to maintain costs at a predetermined level and to evaluate manager performance.

Change to Reflect Modern Data Needs

When the order fulfillment activities in the firm vary widely, a more complex system is needed to accumulate the cost of these activities. The nature of costs incurred broadens, costs do not recur with as much frequency, and they are more difficult to predict. To attempt to develop standards for these changing activities, different or modified costing tools are required. Firms are adapting their standard costing systems to focus on activities that recur. There is analysis of differences in actual and standard costs of activities to find ways to improve processes such as order fulfillment or demand management.

The boundaries of the firm represent the limit for data collection when the focus is on financial reporting. Strategically, decisions must be made about which activities in a supply chain process the organization will con-duct internally and which it will leave for other members of the supply chain. Consideration should be given to the costs and profits of other trading partners in the supply chain. Supply chain executives emphasize the importance of supply chain cost managers having this external focus. There are numerous examples of how and why their supply chain costing systems attempt to measure how much the decisions made by other members of the supply chain influence their firm's costs. Knowledge of these externally driven upstream and downstream costs help manage these costs more effectively.

Lean product or service providers typically need to use more sophisticated cost analysis tools to handle the increased level of costing complexity. When a firm produces or delivers a single product using mass production methods, cost (price) is the primary strategic emphasis. Understanding how changes in volume influence costs is essential. If a firm produces many specialized products or customizes delivery service to various customers, there is more complexity. Cost data is needed to analyze how costs change with a wider variety of cost drivers. Other factors, such as quality and time, also continue to increase in importance.

 ## MANAGEMENT PERCEPTION OF COSTS

Managers frequently express frustration with a lack of confidence in the cost information used within their firms. They are typically looking for accurate and stable cost information to plan, budget, and evaluate the performance for their operations and the cost information provided to them appeared "soft," imprecise, or, in some instances, unreliable. This situation appears to result from the ambiguous nature of cost and expectations that may be unrealistic in an increasingly lean environment where change rather than stability is the norm.

There are many ways to define cost, and the lack of clear and consistent understanding of the many ways cost can be defined and used will jeopardize actions to implement supply chain costing. Management accountants across a supply chain assign costs in different ways depending on the focus of their costing efforts. A product and service costing approach produces quite different results than those derived from a customer-oriented costing approach. One firm's standard costing system may assign only direct costs and use an arbitrary scheme for assigning indirect costs (commonly referred to as overhead). Another firm in the supply chain may use an activity-based costing (ABC) approach that attempts to trace and assign costs more accurately. ABC will be discussed in Chapter 10.

Why Allocation Matters

How a firm allocates indirect or overhead costs has a major influence on supply chain costs and thus on supply chain management. The majority of firms' overhead costs are still arbitrarily assigned to work centers or activities using single allocation bases such as unit volume, labor hours, headcount, or revenue. These do not have cause-and-effect relationships. Managers who have little to no control over the overhead costs allocated to their responsibility center are still expected to continually reduce costs by a fixed percentage or generate sufficient returns to recover these allocated costs. The allocation (assignment) techniques are an important influence of managers' behavior. Since performance is evaluated against these costs, they attempt to find means to avoid or minimize these allocations. The cost allocation process drives what they do. In some instances, it drives them in directions contrary to what is best for the firm or the customer. *Effective cost allocations should align with the firm's objectives. Performance measures should support those objectives to ensure the desired outcome.* Cost allocation is an area of such importance that it is addressed in Chapter 10.

Not having clear cost definitions makes communication and collaboration within the supply chain very challenging. Most firms use accounting systems that provide detailed information regarding labor, material, and other direct expenses. If asked about the influence of indirect costs, the costs of processes, or the cost to serve specific customers, managers generally indicate that their cost systems do not provide this information. However, they recognize that knowing these costs is needed to manage their supply chains. Even in firms with intricate standard cost systems, managers have difficulty determining what it costs to produce a custom product or service. This is primarily due to the cost averaging that occurs at some level. Measuring customer profitability is discussed in Chapter 9.

A lack of accurate and timely data is the "Achilles heel" of costing. Data issues and data structure can prevent effective and accurate cost allocation in some firms.

One firm cited the need to get their arms around the cost drivers for total load (TL) and less than total load (LTL) deliveries to control their transportation costs. The firm's prior cost system did not capture or break out the cost differences when deliveries were multistop and did not differentiate between brokered, commercial, or private deliveries. The firm developed an allocation system that provided cost information for the different types of deliveries and pallets delivered. When they were able to capture this information, accurately assign costs, and understand exactly what was driving their costs, the doors opened for them to really drive supply chain costs in the right direction. The senior executive responsible for this process stated that their firm was able to take millions of dollars out of their supply chain costs and that they have been able to keep transportation costs stable despite fluctuating fuel costs and other factors occurring in the economy.

Senior managers find their subordinate managers feel discomfort and frustration with the cost data. They frequently distrust the cost information in the accounting system. Many executives state that they routinely question the results of cost study teams due to the many assumptions made to derive costs and the inability to reconcile these special studies with the corporate cost management system. In some instances, they have mandated that all cost studies be coordinated with the CFO to ensure some degree of consistency. As a result, these managers consider it difficult to communicate internally in cost-based terms and even more difficult to communicate externally with their trading partners.

An approach some firms use to overcome inconsistencies in costs is to assign a financial analyst, or sometimes a financial controller, to the supply chain function. The analyst typically fills a matrix position within supply chain management but continues to report to the CFO. The position has the responsibility of ensuring that the cost data, reports, and performance measures used in supply chain processes are consistent with the information in the financial management system. These individuals usually become the point of contact for costing information. The individuals serving in these positions report numerous challenges, including obtaining the nonfinancial data for developing effective cost drivers; the complexity associated with capturing and reporting cost information by product, division, supply chain, and customer; and developing effective approaches for assigning costs when a large portion of the costs are common to multiple products or customers. The analysts indicate that they experience little to no difficulty in working in a matrix assignment; however, they find the learning curve for understanding supply chain management and what it encompassed to be very daunting.

SUPPLY CHAIN COSTING INCREASES THE COMPLEXITY OF COST SYSTEMS

The pursuit of supply chain costing adds complexity to an organization's costing efforts. Internally, the firms find that they need to classify costs in multiple ways. Any exchange of cost information, to or from trading partners, increases complexity by adding more costs and drivers to the analysis.

Managers and those responsible for implementing supply chain costing need to recognize that cost information becomes progressively more complex as the firm moves through the supply chain costing steps described in this book. Some firms are still using only traditional cost systems and others, within the same supply chain, have detailed activity-based costing (ABC) systems based on multiple cost classifications. Firms just beginning the supply chain cost journey typically rely on traditional cost systems with a limited number of identified cost drivers and costs classified by function or natural accounts in the general ledger accounting system. Costing complexity increases as firms attempt to understand key cost drivers, both internal and external to the firm. The use of multiple drivers enables these firms to conduct more detailed analysis of their internal value chains.

The firms furthest along in supply chain costing employ cost techniques such as target costing, kaizen costing, cost-to-serve, or other process-based approaches to develop their costs. Many firms are making an effort to identify activities and trace costs. However, few firms have their supply chain employees assign their time (work) by activity. Instead they rely on industrial engineers and other process experts to determine the resources consumed by each activity and the resulting cost per activity and their activity cost drivers.

Understanding Supply Chain Costs

As firm management attempts to better understand supply chain costs, the need for multiple cost classifications increases. Costs may be classified by end-to-end processes (value streams) to better understand how different functions affect total process costs or the cost per output (outcome). The classification of costs by product or family group (product costing and profitability) provides greater insight regarding how product differences affect activity and process costs. Product classifications enable a firm to more accurately assign costs by strategic business unit (SBU) and better support each SBU.

Classification of costs by customer occurs where customer differences have a significant effect on cost. Those differences include product or packaging customization, order placement, cycle time, and delivery requirements. In some instances, firms extensively collaborate with selected customers to improve processes. In other cases, they identify how other process costs, such as research and development or manufacturing, are affected by customer demands. Depending on the size and uniqueness of the customer, the cost-to-serve (customer profitability) analysis sometimes breaks out costs separately for key or very large or key accounts and aggregates smaller, similar customers by class of trade. However, customer account profitability can be obtained even for very small accounts if warranted.

Cost classification by distribution channel, or supply chain, often is just beginning when firms commit to attempting to better understand how external drivers and business practices affect internal costs and the costs of other trading partners. Executives note that the most apparent need for this cost classification scheme occurs when the firm operates in distinct supply chains that use different business practices and thus generate large cost differences. If a manufacturer uses multiple channels and sells directly to the end user over the internet, through distributors, to large retailers through distribution centers, and does direct store delivery (DSD), the costs of each approach differ markedly. As an example, a supplier may want to recognize the need for capturing these cost differences to rationalize the use of multiple channels with the same retailer where the channel varied depending on the product, region, order size, retail store location, or end user.

Fluctuations in transportation and delivery costs has intensified interest in classifying costs by supply chain. Supply chain managers note that they sometimes acquire the same product from multiple suppliers or different locations. Rising transportation costs have caused these managers to more carefully consider and calculate the total landed cost (TLC) when sourcing, since higher transportation costs frequently surpass any savings obtained by always sourcing from the lowest-price supplier. Managers have a greater interest in comparing the costs of different supply chain strategies such as offshoring versus near-sourcing. Decisions in these areas commit the firm to future costs, and managers need to understand and explicitly evaluate the nature and size of this commitment.

 ## REASONS SUPPLY CHAIN COSTING MUST DIFFER FROM TRADITIONAL COSTING

There are constant examples and reminders that traditional general ledger accounting systems are of limited value in providing the types of cost information needed for modern supply chain costing. The focus of traditional costing systems is functional, using department cost centers designed to support external financial reporting, and strongly emphasizes product costing. These systems are based on transactions with customers and suppliers as well as internal transactions between segments of the firm. Traditional systems are internally focused. They are also historically focused and do not measure or report future prospective costs. Despite these shortcomings, most companies in the United States and abroad continue to rely on traditional systems as the primary source of cost information. In contrast, supply chain cost systems need to help the decision maker estimate and manage prospective costs because these costs can still be changed.

Technological limitations historically meant that cost data structured to support external statutory financial reporting for government regulators was by default the primary basis of internal cost reports. Cost accounting systems were developed within the confines of the functional internal cost structure to support mass production manufacturing. Their primary focus was on managing and controlling direct materials, direct labor, and inventory. There was limited emphasis on managing marketing, selling, customer service, and administrative costs or, often, even manufacturing overhead costs. Tools such as budgeting, capital budgeting, and standard costing were developed to help plan for future costs. Only recently, as new strategic cost management tools emerged, have more detailed costing systems gained traction in many firms and for specialty areas such as supply chain costing.

Supply Chain Costing Needs

Supply chain costing requires a different focus and emphasis. Cost information that spans the supply chain from inception to disposal is needed to effectively manage and control supply chain performance. Supply chain processes cross multiple functional and responsibility center lines. The most progressive managers stress that one of the primary points their firm emphasizes is to develop appropriate cost information for the overall process. Supply chain cost systems need to incorporate many of the characteristics of lean production methods with there being a particular emphasis on communication between functional areas and trading partners. Different types of cost information are needed to support strategic and operational decisions. Both are essential, but a major focus of the supply chain costing effort should be on future prospective costs. Chapter 11 discusses projecting costs, including budgeting and rolling financial forecasts.

Supply chain processes add value when they satisfy customers and still improve organizational profits. Both costs and revenues need to be managed. Internal and external customer requirements within the supply chain determine the products or services they provide. If a customer seeks to increase delivery frequency or modify their right of return, supply chain costing tools should help decision makers analyze how these changes impact profitability. Decision makers need to focus on more than simply reducing cost.

Many costs within supply chain processes are traditionally classified as part of distribution, marketing, selling, customer service, and administrative costs. Supply chain managers have long been aware that careful attention must be paid to these costs as well as traditional product costs. Some managers are having success in getting support for cost system modifications that elevate the level of attention paid to these types of costs. Some firms now link expenditure decisions within a supply chain process to projected changes in revenue and then monitor the actual results of the decision.

Recall that supply chain processes span firm units and functions and extend to customers and suppliers throughout the value chain. By design, supply chain costing systems should help in the analysis of what each process costs and how effectively the process functions. Decision makers must understand what occurs and why these activities are necessary.

EXHIBIT 5.1   Committed Costs versus Actual Supply Chain Costs

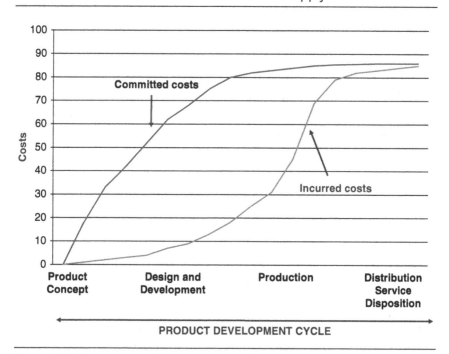

Source: Shahid Ansari, Jan Bell, and Thomas Klammer, "Target Costing," in the modular series *Management Accounting: A Strategic Focus* (Ansari, Bell, Klammer: Lulu.com).

Committed Costs

The majority of product or process costs become committed during conception and design. As shown in Exhibit 5.1, this commitment occurs much earlier than when the actual expenditures are made. Multiple studies demonstrate that 80% of total lifetime costs are committed before the first unit of a new product is produced. Even in the service areas, 60% or more of the lifetime costs are often committed prior to initial service delivery. The same is true for key supply chain decisions. A decision to use company-owned vehicles to make deliveries to customers commits the firm to a large portion of the delivery costs. A decision to set up a call center to handle customer orders and informational requests commits the firm to a large portion of the call center costs. It is essential to manage supply chain costs early in the process, thus there is an extensive focus on prospective or future costs throughout this book.

Supply chain costing needs to focus on costs incurred throughout the supply chain in order to manage these costs. It is essential to select the most appropriate tools for measuring and managing these costs. There must be a focus on understanding and improving supplier costs while managing the profitability of customers.

 ## DIFFERENCES BETWEEN TRADITIONAL AND SUPPLY CHAIN COSTING

Supply chain costing differs from traditional costing in several important aspects, summarized in Exhibit 5.2. These differences include objectives, focus, cost objectives, linkages, precision, scope, and visibility. The following discussion briefly compares and describes the differences and their importance.

Objective

Traditional costing focuses primarily on tracking expenses and supporting the development of financial reports. Although traditional costing provides important information, most of the reports generated offer little insight into how effectively the supply chain is operating or how managers' decisions are affecting value creation. *Supply chain costing focuses on providing the information needed to support cost-based decisions.* Managers gain greater visibility into how activities within supply chain processes consume costs and how their decisions affect the performance of these activities and drive costs differently.

EXHIBIT 5.2 Comparison of Traditional and Supply Chain Costing

	Traditional Costing	Supply Chain Costing
Objective	▪ To support reporting of financial data and results	▪ To support supply chain decision-making
Focus	▪ Allocation of costs to responsibility (budget) centers ▪ Cost control through budget management	▪ Determining the costs of boundary spanning processes ▪ Cost control by managing trade-offs across supply chain
Cost objects	▪ Functions ▪ Products ▪ Departments	▪ Activities and supply chain processes ▪ Customers ▪ Suppliers ▪ Distribution channels ▪ Supply chains ▪ Products
Cost drivers	▪ Simple volume measures	▪ Multiple drivers ▪ Recognize complexity ▪ Strategic decisions
Linkages	▪ Ignored ▪ Cost allocations used to reflect interdependencies	▪ Recognized and effect explicitly considered
Precision	▪ High apparent precision	▪ Low perceived precision ▪ Greater management insight
Scope	▪ Internal	▪ Internal and external value chain
Visibility	▪ Limited regarding factors driving costs	▪ Identifies key cost drivers in the supply chain and how process linkages affect cost and performance

Source: Exhibit adapted to include research results and previous comparison from Mike J. Partridge and Lew Perren, "Cost Analysis of the Value Chain: Another Role for Strategic Management Accounting," *Management Accounting* 72, no. 7 (1994): 22.

Focus

Traditional costing accumulates expenses by responsibility center. Budgets are used to compare planned versus actual expenses for variance analysis, and the responsible manager is held accountable for performance. Problems often arise because many factors beyond the manager's direct control determine the actual expense incurred. For example, a large downstream customer may arbitrarily elect to order more frequently, but in smaller quantities to reduce its average inventory levels. The total case volume moving through the manager's responsibility center does not change, but the increased number of orders may greatly increase order processing, resulting in actual expenses exceeding the budgeted expenses.

Supply chain costing addresses this problem by determining the costs associated with the processes spanning both firms. In this instance, order fulfillment costs may increase for the supplier but decrease for the customer. However, if collaboration occurs within the demand management process, the supplier may obtain decreased costs in the manufacturing flow process due to smoother demand patterns. Supply chain costing would reveal the cost trade-offs occurring at the supplier-customer trading partner interface and identify how managers' decisions affected costs in both firms. Traditional costing would only indicate that costs in one responsibility center (order processing) increased, and analysis would show that this was due to a customer altering a business practice.

Cost Objects

Traditional costing assigns costs by responsibility cost centers (functions or departments) or by products. However, the product alone generally does not create value for the customer. Instead, the services bundled around the product differentiate the supplier and create additional value for the customer. The customer may value the ability to customize the product, its availability, tracking, and tracing; the ability to order frequently; and the ability to depend on quick and reliable delivery. Tracking costs by product does not capture these costs or the costs incurred to serve specific customers.

Supply chain costing provides multiple views of how costs are consumed. In addition to assigning costs by products, costs can be viewed by customer or market segment, by supplier, by distribution channel, or by supply chain. The use of multiple cost drivers enables managers to view how differences between cost objects affect activity and process costs within and across firms.

Cost Drivers

The cost drivers used in traditional costing approaches involve a limited number of simple volume measures to allocate the costs that fail to capture the complexity occurring in most firms and supply chains. Some firms use the number of cases produced to allocate production costs and cases shipped to allocate distribution and marketing costs. This cost allocation factor violates costing's causality principle: the use of this production cost driver assumes manufacturing costs vary in direct proportion to the volume produced for all products. The use of a single cost driver fails to recognize differences in setup times, processes that may incur different costs, or packaging and handling differences within the production line. A similar situation exists in distribution and marketing. The cost driver assumes that marketing and logistics costs vary directly with the cases sold to customers. The use of a single driver ignores differences in lot sizes, transportation mode, distance traveled, order frequency, number of sales calls and effort, promotional spend, or customer service.

Supply chain costing uses multiple cost drivers to recognize the complexity found in most supply chains. Decision support hinges on the quality of information available for actual costs of key tasks and processes based on the resources consumed. Exhibit 5.3 illustrates how this data may be obtained. Supply chain decision makers need accurate and detailed information to analyze performance within a single firm or processes spanning multiple firms. This information cannot be obtained without the use of multiple cost drivers with the ability to trace both direct and indirect costs. Since many supply chain functions are aggregated under sales, general and administrative (SG&A), or other indirect categories, the use of cost drivers for assigning indirect costs is especially important. Without cost information and knowing what drives these costs at the activity level, supply chain managers will have no visibility regarding costs except at a very aggregate and unmanageable level.

Linkages, Precision, Scope, and Visibility

Supply chain management involves many complex linkages and relationships between sequential process steps, business units, and trading partners. These linkages involve the performance of several activities that affect cost and performance. Competitive advantages result from how well these activities are performed or how key interfaces are managed across the supply chain. Traditional costing ignores these linkages and does not provide cost information that indicates how well the supply chain is performing. Cost allocations are used to reflect any interdependencies. For example, customer service costs may be allocated based on sales volume to reflect the support provided to different customers. However, the allocation based on volume may not reflect the level of support actually provided or may mask problems occurring across the supplier–customer interface.

EXHIBIT 5.3 How Costs are Consumed Within the Supply Chain

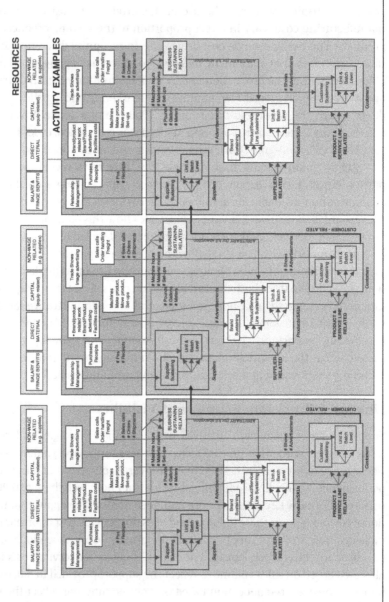

Supply chain costing explicitly recognizes the linkages occurring in the supply chain. Costs are traced to the processes or activities within these links so managers can identify how the business practices structured within the product service agreements (PSAs) between buyers and sellers are driving costs. If behavior changes, the resulting cost information will reflect this modified behavior.

Traditional costing provides a false sense of precision. For example, using cases shipped to allocate distribution costs suggests a high level of precision for case processing costs. Managers can determine, and frequently quote, the cost per case to several decimal points. However, they cannot explain how product or customer differences may affect case processing costs. Managers frequently perceive a lower level of precision with supply chain costing due to the use of multiple cost drivers that also involve some averaging. For example, the cost of the sales force making sales calls to customers may vary based on the travel distance, size of the order taken, or type of customer account. Multiple cost drivers will probably be derived based on an analysis of these factors. Despite the additional insight into what drives sales costs, managers perceive a lower level of precision due to the differences that cannot be fully captured even with the use of multiple activities and cost drivers. However, the analysis of supply chain costs highlights important information regarding what causes costs to differ and indications of expected cost changes in the future. The question for managers becomes whether it is better to be "precisely wrong" or "imprecisely correct" in their understanding of what drives costs.

A key difference between traditional and supply chain costing is the scope of cost information captured and made visible to management. Traditional costing only captures costs internal to the firm. In most instances, the information does not indicate how changes in the behavior of trading partners affects costs internal to the firm or externally in the supply chain. Supply chain costing extends the scope of cost information available to management. Supply chain costing determines not only the firm's internal costs but costs by firm and supply chain process.

Traditional costing provides limited cost visibility and insight for managers. The use of a limited set of cost drivers and objects provides only partial information regarding what factors are actually driving costs in the firm. Since the scope of information is constrained to the firm, management does not receive any information regarding how trading partners affect the costs incurred by the firm, and, equally important, how the firm affects costs elsewhere in the supply chain.

Supply chain costing provides significantly greater transparency of the relationship between management decisions and costs. The use of multiple cost drivers enables managers to recognize how their decisions affect costs, not only within their firm, but across the supply chain. The scope of cost information extends their line of sight beyond the boundaries of their firm so they can understand how their actions affect trading partners' costs and total supply chain costs. This visibility enables managers to make effective and intelligent cost trade-offs across multiple firms to lower overall supply chain costs. By creating more value for the end user, the trading partners will be rewarded with additional follow-on sales and larger market share.

CHAPTER 6

Overview of Cost Tools and Cost Classification

C OST SYSTEMS HAVE THE ability to portray costs in a variety of different ways and managers can select from a multitude of tools that can
be useful for measuring and reporting supply chain costs in ways that
support decision making. The supply chain cost measurement, estimation, and
reporting tools that firms use draw heavily from the management accounting
discipline. Supply chain professionals who have an understanding of costs,
cost classification, and the major tools that can be used for supply chain
costing will be able to work more effectively with management accountants
on costing issues and educate managers in and outside the firm on supply
chain costing improvement efforts.

The level of cost knowledge among supply chain professionals in firms
can range from very sophisticated to relying solely on general ledger accounts
for cost information. The differences in cost knowledge track closely with the
emphasis management places on cost control. Companies with more sophisticated cost systems have a management team that focuses on controlling
costs and understanding how their decisions and the behavior of their trading
partners drive costs within the firm. In some cases, executives indicate that a
"numbers culture" or a "strong cost-management culture" permeates their
company. In these firms there is a need to "run the numbers" whenever recom-
mending a decision, and there is a constant challenge to find ways to improve
customer service while simultaneously reducing costs.

In other cases, the focus on cost management and control is not nearly as evident. These types of firms compete strongly on aspects such as innovation, service, or quality, rather than primarily on cost issues. However, managers within these types of firms often indicate that they are seeking additional cost information to help them reduce costs. Observation suggests that smaller upstream suppliers are more likely to have limited cost management systems and less management insight regarding their supply chains.

WAYS TO THINK ABOUT SUPPLY CHAIN COSTING TOOLS

A fundamental purpose of managerial accounting information should be to support decision making and influence behavior at all levels—from CEOs to operational-level employees. Decisions can only impact the future; the past is already history. However, firms can learn much from historical information, such as by using trends and drawing inferences.

Exhibit 6.1 illustrates one approach to thinking about supply chain costs in the context of managerial accounting. Think of the exhibit as a taxonomy like that of biology with animal and plant kingdoms and their tree-branches-leaves structure downward into species. In this exhibit, the large domain of accounting is divided into four components in the taxonomy. The bookkeeping component deals with recording financial transactions, such as purchases and payroll. The financial accounting component deals with external statutory and regulatory reporting, such as for government agencies, banks, stockholders, and the investment community. External financial accounting follows compliance rules aimed at economic valuation and, as such, is typically insufficient for decision making. The tax accounting component is its own world of legislated rules. The internal management accounting component is most relevant for supply chain costing. Its purpose is to gain insights and support decision making. A way to think of the two center domains is that financial accounting is for *valuation* (e.g., inventories, costs of goods sold), and management accounting is for *creating financial value.*

This book restricts itself to only those aspects of managerial accounting involved with operational and cost measurement and supporting management decision making.

The Three Categories of Managerial Accounting

Exhibit 6.1 identifies three categories within managerial accounting that are of interest to supply chain managers: cost accounting, the cost autopsy, and

EXHIBIT 6.1   Accounting Domains

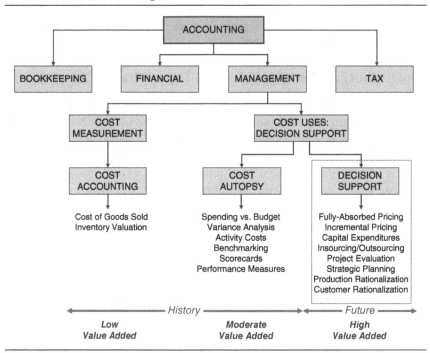

Source: Adapted from Gary Cokins, *Activity-Based Cost Management: An Executive's Guide* (New York: John Wiley & Sons, 2001), p. 33. Copyright Gary Cokins. Used with permission of the author.

decision support. Only a representative sample of the types of measures and tools that fall under each category are shown under each of these categories.

- **Cost accounting** historically focused on the calculation of cost of goods sold and the valuing of inventories in manufacturing firms. Only recently have service firms developed cost systems that emphasize a broader segment of a firm's total cost.
- **Cost autopsy**, some of which uses data derived from cost accounting, provides the historical view of past period costs—the rearview mirror. It represents the analysis of what has already taken place in the business to track performance.
- **Decision support** involves the future view of costs—through the windshield. It represents using cost autopsy information in combination with other economic information, including forecasts and planned changes (e.g., processes, products, services) to make those types of decisions that lead to a financially successful future.

Further review of Exhibit 6.1 shows a spectrum of the degree value-adding information for decision making increases as one moves from cost accounting to decision support—from low to high. Cost accounting data establishes a foundation, but it has low value for decision making.

The "What?," "So What?," and "Then What?" Questions

The cost autopsy information converts cost accounting data into a context for making decisions. The tools an organization chooses to use when performing cost autopsies can allow supply chain managers to clearly observe outcomes that they may never have seen before. Certain measures may demonstrate that costs are dramatically different from those derived from their firm's less mature costing method, such as allocating indirect expenses (i.e., overhead) thus violating costing's causality principle. Activity-based costing (ABC), discussed in Chapter 10, resolves this problem. A cost autopsy reports the reality of what has happened. This information provides answers to the "*What?*"—that-is, what did a product, a service line, an activity, a delivery, a sales call, and so forth cost last period?

An obvious follow-up question should be "*So what?*" A progressive management accounting system will create and make visible substantial information that had not been seen before. In fact, so much new information that it creates a question of "What is relevant from this new information?" Based on any questionable or bothersome observations, is there merit to making changes and interventions? How applicable to improving performance is the outcome we are seeing?

These types of questions lead to the more critical, and relatively higher value-added, need to propose actions and to make decisions. This is the "*Then what?*" What change can be made or what action taken? For example, should distribution routes be altered, and ultimately the impact of the change? Of course, changes lead to multiple effects on quality, service levels, and delivery times. Such changes also economically affect profits and costs. Decisions only impact the future, not the past that has become history.

However, there is a catch. When supply chain costing moves to the "decision support" box in the exhibit, analysis shifts to the realm of economic analysis. For example, a supply chain professional needs to understand the impact on future expenses resulting from any changes occurring in the supply chain. This shifts the focus to resources or processes and their capacities. The emphasis is on classifying cost behavior and understanding how costs and capacity can be adjusted. As is soon discussed, this means classifying the behavior of resources and their expenses as sunk, fixed, step-fixed, or variable.

COST CLASSIFICATION FOR MANY PURPOSES

Supply chain processes have different cost structures because firms are positioned differently in the supply chain, operate in diverse environments, select varied strategies, and employ different production and delivery processes. Identifying what types of costs and cost classifications are appropriate for evaluating multiple views of a firm's cost structure, including the type of and size impact of a decision, is a necessary precondition for effective supply chain costing.

Understanding that there are multiple views of costs and alternative ways to classify incurred and projected supply chain costs is critical for supply chain management. For many managers and employees, just the idea that there can be different costs, even for the same item, remains disconcerting. There is a strong desire to know the exact or precise cost. But a specific cost, which is always calculated based on incurred expenses and other factors, depends on the nature of the decision for which it will be used. Costs, like the pattern in a kaleidoscope, vary with how you look at them. Which cost views or classifications are useful for supply chain costing are primarily a function of the type of supply chain decision that is being made. The cost data a supply chain manager needs is a function of supply chain strategy, production or distribution method, supply chain structure, and the individual's level within the firm. Significant complexity is a characteristic of costing systems robust enough to provide managers with the information they need to do an appropriate analysis in this type of environment.

Costing systems extract data from transactions and their associated expenses. This data reflects what has already happened. Classifying and accumulating incurred costs in different ways helps us measure supply chain costs, assign responsibility for those costs, and use the information when evaluating supply chain managers. Accumulating actual cost information does not allow direct management of future supply chain costs, but the data is helpful for estimating prospective costs when properly measured and classified. Supply chain managers use actual and prospective cost data to help in their analyses. The objective is to make better strategic decisions and to effectively manage operational costs.

Information is measured and classified by the cost object of interest, be it a function, business segment, product, service line, distribution channel, customer, or supply chain process. The classification helps plan, maintain, and reduce costs while evaluating performance and managing strategic variables. Costing systems should provide information on whatever segment of the supply chain cost is of interest to decision makers. Ultimately, supply chain costs must be reconciled with the customers' willingness to pay the firm to design supply chain processes that maximize value.

The Need to Understand Costs to Answer Questions

To manage costs, supply chain professionals must understand their firm's cost structure. The cost accumulation system chosen should help answer questions such as what causes costs to vary, which costs are under the firm's control, which costs are driven by other trading partners' (supplier and customer) actions, and what the costs are of using various distribution channel options.

There are many ways to view or classify costs and to use or misuse this information. Functionally focused systems designed to support external statutory financial reporting for compliance with government regulators are of limited use for internal decision making. Supply chain costing requires multiple views of costs and the use of a variety of cost classifications. A managerial perspective of costing, focusing on both incurred and prospective costs, is needed to support supply chain strategy, process improvement, and better decision making. What cost view(s) are relevant depends on how the cost information will be used, and management's strategic decisions and choices of production methods. To illustrate, mass producers often have large inventories and use a variety of specialized labor. Cost systems logically focus on inventory and labor reporting. Lean producers frequently have little inventory and use flexible labor pools. Cost systems emphasize tracking and appropriately allocating indirect costs.

Historically, supply chain costs have been accumulated using functional classifications. The emphasis was on identifying who is responsible for costs. The economic theory of mass production is also the basis of several familiar cost classification schemes. Particularly important are the concepts of sunk, fixed, step-fixed, and variable costs. To clarify, step-fixed resources and their expenses are for resources that are acquired in discontinuous amounts. For example, one cannot purchase one-third of a machine or hire two-thirds of an employee; it is all or nothing.

Understanding how costs behave when production volume (or any other cost object of interest) changes is essential for supply chain costing. A variety of cost estimation tools are used to separate mixed costs into their sunk, fixed, step-fixed, and variable components.

Budgeting and standard costing are major responsibility-based costing tools that are integral parts of many supply chain cost estimation and measurement processes. Both tools put an emphasis on identifying which costs are controllable and by whom. Accounting systems capture the expenses of all transactions with suppliers and customers as well as internal transactions. Even with this transactional data, determining the amount of incurred cost to assign to a cost object, such as a supply chain process, involves significant estimates. How much cost is assigned to a cost object, such as a customer delivery, influences evaluations of managers and customers. These measures can also fundamentally influence managerial behavior and future decisions.

New costing concepts have emerged to support lean manufacturing methods and to reflect the growing importance of service firms and of extensive global competition. In these methods there is an emphasis on identifying cost drivers across cross-functional processes. The concept of a cost driver—something that causes costs to systematically change—is of particular interest for supply chain costing. Examples of cost drivers include deliveries, returns, material receipts, labor hours, calls received, and so forth. Costs can be analyzed and classified by cost driver type.

Value chain costing, lean accounting, customer profitability analysis, activity-based costing, and capacity analysis are newer costing concepts that are often particularly helpful in estimating or predicting costs. Which tools to use is a critical focus for supply chain professionals and is discussed in more detail in subsequent chapters that focus on both newer tools and the traditional costing tools that remain relevant parts of the supply chain costing toolbox.[1]

The Descriptive versus Predictive View of Costs

Exhibit 6.2 illustrates how a firm's view of its profit and expense structure changes as analysis shifts from the historical view to a predictive planning view. The latter is the context from which decisions are considered and evaluated. Remember, new decisions only impact the future.

The exhibit's left-hand side represents the historical time period, depicting the resource expenses the organization incurred. The resources *supplied* were either *used* to make products, deliver customer services, internally sustain the firm, or they went *unused*, and represent idle or protective capacity. One can describe the calculation of the output costs as the cost autopsy. Money was spent, and costing answers questions about where it went. This is the *descriptive* view of costs. Traditionally, firms have focused on tracing all expenses for a specific time period to outputs. The purpose is to measure what outputs consumed the resources and to determine the cost of each individual output. Some costs associated with outputs are directly tied to the output and are relatively easy to measure. Many other costs are indirect to the output and must be assigned to outputs using cost allocation techniques. Dealing with indirect costs is such an important part of supply chain costing that it represents a separate step in the supply chain costing journey.

The right-hand side of Exhibit 6.2 is the *predictive* view of costs. In the future, supply chain process capacity levels and types of resources can be adjusted as strategic decisions are made. Only resources can provide capacity. However, the classification of an expense as sunk, fixed, step-fixed, or variable depends on the planning horizon. The diagonal line reveals that in the very short term, most expenses are not easily changed and hence they are classified as fixed. As the time horizon extends into the future, capacity becomes adjustable. For example, assets can be leased instead of purchased. Future workers can be contracted from a temporary employment agency, rather than hired as full-time employees. Hence, these expenses become variable. The staircase line in the exhibit displays the step-fixed expenses that are incrementally added to provide increasing capacity of resources.

Changes in demand, such as the sales volume and mix of products and services ordered from customers, will drive the consumption of processes (and the work activities that belong to them). This in turn will determine what level of fixed, step-fixed, and variable resource expenses are needed to supply capacity for future use. In the case of purchased assets, such as expensive equipment, these costs are classified as sunk costs. Their full capacity and associated

EXHIBIT 6.2 Accounting Treatments and Behavior of Capacity (Expenses)

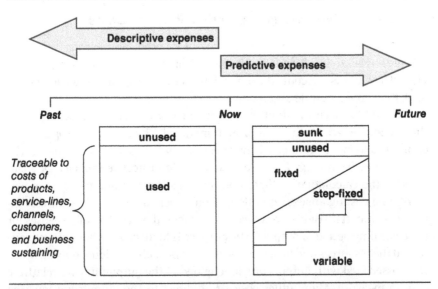

Source: Adapted from Gary Cokins, *Performance Management: Integrating Strategy Execution, Methodologies, Risk, and Analytics* (New York: John Wiley & Sons, 2001), p. 148. Copyright Gary Cokins. Used with permission of the author.

expense were acquired when an executive authorized the purchase order for the vendor. Some idle capacity is typically planned to meet temporary demand surges or as an insurance buffer for the uncertainty of the demand forecast. Since decisions only affect the future, the predictive view is the basis for analysis and evaluation.

The costing and classification processes used by a firm should provide information that helps supply chain professionals measure, plan, maintain, improve, and monitor supply chain process costs. There are a wide variety of costing tools and ways to look at cost that must be evaluated in the context of the supply chain and the firm's strategy, production processes, and cost structure. Selecting the appropriate costing tools and techniques for decisions and processes is an essential part of the supply chain costing journey.

SUPPLY CHAIN COSTING AS A COMBINATION OF COSTING TECHNIQUES

Supply chain costing incorporates a variety of techniques for developing and managing cost information. Several of the major techniques used by companies are shown in Exhibit 6.3. The tools' positioning within the simplified value chain is representative of where the listed techniques are likely to be useful, but the positioning fails to reflect the full scope of potential use for these tools. The primary purpose of the exhibit is to demonstrate that supply chain costing serves as an umbrella term for cost transparency and the costing techniques that develop or draw upon costs from multiple companies. In many ways, supply chain costing parallels the many management concepts and techniques encompassed within supply chain management.

The inclusion of many techniques under the umbrella of supply chain costing stems from management application. Managers select specific techniques, or combinations of techniques, to support targeted initiatives and to expand their knowledge of costs beyond the boundaries of their firms. These techniques are often complementary in that similar approaches are used for developing and analyzing cost information. Subsequent chapters demonstrate that the techniques used differ primarily in scope and the management decisions supported by each firm.

The costing techniques applied to support supply chain management span the extent of the supply chain as well as the processes that comprise it. As illustrated in Exhibit 6.3, most of the techniques currently focus within the firm (the four walls) or on the transaction costs between immediately aligned upstream

EXHIBIT 6.3 Supply Chain Costing Techniques

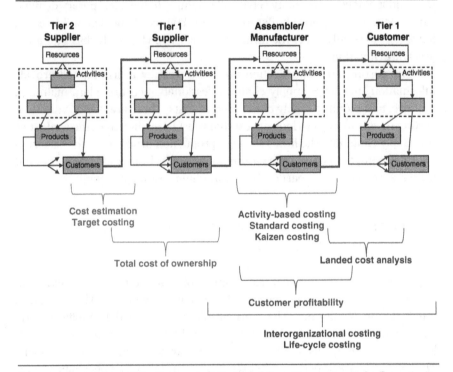

Source: Adapted from Gary Cokins, *Activity-Based Cost Management: An Executive's Guide* (New York: John Wiley & Sons, 2001), p. 169. Copyright Gary Cokins. Used with permission from the author.

or downstream trading partners. This is the "Assembler/Manufacturer" in the exhibit. As supply chain managers attempt to exert greater influence over the extended supply chain, depicted by the "Tier 1" and "Tier 2" trading partners upstream and downstream, they also attempt to expand their visibility over their trading partners' costs with their own trading partners. Depending on the function, process, trading partner, objective, and cost visibility, the techniques employed vary.

Major Supply Chain Costing Techniques

Exhibit 6.4 identifies several of the major supply chain costing techniques, briefly describes the technique, indicates where firms apply the technique within their supply chains, and lists the types of decisions where the technique and cost information can be applied. The exhibit does not include any discussion of general tools such as budgeting, capital budgeting, or capacity analysis that permeate supply chain cost planning. The next several chapters will elaborate on how these tools support supply chain costing.

EXHIBIT 6.4 Summary of Supply Chain Costing Tools

Technique	Description	Where Applied in the Supply Chain	Management Applications
Activity-based costing (ABC)	Assigns the direct and indirect costs to work activities and then reassigns those costs to products, services, channels, or supply chains that consume a firm's resources.	Typically applied to processes, comprised of activities, and managed within a firm in areas where indirect and shared costs represent a significant proportion of total costs.	Decision analysis and support that requires more accurate cost information and visibility of cost elements plus causal driver of costs. Primarily used in business process engineering, outsourcing, and customer profitability analysis.
Activity-based management (ABM)	Focuses on the management of activities as a means for continually improving the value delivered to the end user and to the firm through enhanced profitability.[2]	Process and activity management, primarily within a single firm. Can be extended to the processes and their activities comprising a supply chain.	Measuring and improving performance, reducing costs, and reengineering processes. Can be applied to activity and process management.
Balanced scorecard	Links and aligns performance measures across four perspectives: financial, customer, internal business process, and innovation and learning. Measures are linked through a cause-and-effect relationship.	Measure performance, primarily of a firm's internal processes. May be adapted to measure performance (e.g., service level, quality) by product line, customer, and distribution channel.	Measuring and improving performance, customer service, evaluating suppliers and third party providers, developing goals and objectives, determining the links between and aligning the four perspectives, and translating non-financial performance into financial performance.

(Continued)

Cost estimation	Models and techniques focus on determining the expected cost of a product. Estimates are derived from known factors or rates, estimating relationships, reverse engineering, and expert opinion.	Purchasing, product design and development, engineering, value engineering, and manufacturing.	Determine what a product should cost for negotiations with suppliers. Determine suppliers' and customers' process costs to expand cost visibility further across the supply chain.
Cost-to-serve	Assigns non-production costs by cause and by customer to determine the total cost to service a customer or market segment.	Downstream from production between a supplier and its immediate customer.	Determine customer profitability; identify means to improve profitability with customer accounts; reallocate resources between customers, optimize networks, segment markets, decide facility locations, schedule production, and control inventory levels.
Cost transparency	Customers and suppliers share detailed cost information about their in-house activities, pertinent to the supply of goods and services which links them. An extension of open-book negotiation, where the supplier, but not the customer, shares information.[3]	Purchasing, product design and development, and process reengineering of order-fulfillment process. Concept applicable to entire supply chain. Currently very limited, largely between immediate supplier and customer with information shared limited to the costs pertaining to a joint project.	Reduce costs through the joint development of good ideas by trading partners, thereby improving the mutual competitive position of both firms.

Customer profitability analysis (CPA)	Allocate revenues and costs to customers or market segments to determine their profitability.[4] The relationship between CPA and CTS can be explained as defining CPA as the manufacturing contribution of the products sold less the CTS of a customer or market segment.	Downstream between the firm and its immediate customers or market segments. Includes customer facing activities such as logistics, customer service, marketing, and sales.	More accurately determine customer profitability, identify means to improve profitability with customer accounts, reallocate resources between customers, optimize networks, segment markets based on customer profiles and profitability, determine dependence and risk associated with the proportion of profitable to non-profitable customers, reduce costs, decide facility locations, schedule production, and control inventory levels.
Direct Product Profitability (DPP)	Express the profit contribution of individual product lines by subtracting from gross profit all costs directly attributable to the product.	Applied principally in the grocery industry in the distribution of food products from firm's distribution center to retail store shelf.	Making merchandise decisions that increase the overall profitability of operations.
Economic Value Added (EVA)[5]	Attempts to capture the economic profit generated by a company by subtracting a charge for capital from net operating profit, EVA = NOPAT – (Capital employed × Cost of Capital)	Within a firm. Evaluate the value created through supplier and customer relationships.[6]	Evaluate the value created by a firm or the relationships created with suppliers or customers. Provides capability to translate non-financial performance into financial performance by linking performance measures, cost drivers, and value drivers into an integrated framework.[7]

(Continued)

Interfirm costing	A structured approach to cost management in supply chains. Transmits the cost reduction pressures faced by end firms to their supplier network.[8]	Primarily used in purchasing, engineering, and manufacturing.	Improve functionality, price, and quality of the products provided to the end user through improved design, value engineering, and cost reduction.
Kaizen costing	Focuses on reducing costs during the production stage of the total life cycle of a product.	Manufacturing and delivery processes for existing products.	Reduce product costs to achieve a target cost for a product currently being manufactured. Can be used internally or to transmit cost reduction targets to suppliers.
Landed costing	Captures the costs of freight and other activities performed to move product from origin to final destination. Costs in a landed cost analysis include freight, quality, receiving, material handling, administration, technology, and variable facility costs.	Determines the inbound logistics costs between a supplier and the company performing the analysis. May support cost-to-serve analysis by combining outbound and customer's inbound logistics costs.	Selecting carriers and third parties, optimize networks, study outsourcing, cost-to-serve, and process reengineering.
Life-cycle costing	Involves all of the costs associated with a system (e.g., aircraft, engine) or product	Research and development, production and construction, purchasing and acquisition, operations and maintenance, and system or product retirement. Since life cycle costing attempts to reduce costs by making design changes early in the life cycle, the technique may extend into suppliers.	Reduce total acquisition, manufacturing, operation, and retirement costs for a system or product. Provides an understanding of how decisions made early in the design of a product affect subsequent costs occurring later during the product life cycle.

Open-books costing	Supplier provides information regarding cost structure to the customer, and in return, the customer assists the supplier in identifying and pursuing cost reduction opportunities	Purchasing, manufacturing, product development and design, logistics	Sourcing decisions, price negotiation, cost reduction, product design, evaluation, and performance measurement of suppliers, carriers, and third party providers.
Standard costing	Develops standard costs for outputs or activities performed. Actual costs are compared to standard costs to determine whether variances exist. Variances are investigated to determine causes.	Widely used in manufacturing firms. Applications include manufacturing, logistics and customer facing functions with repetitive operations.	Standard costing widely applied due to its ability to support multiple purposes including: predicting future costs, setting cost targets, setting budgets, controlling costs and expenses, simplifying activities and processes, and tracing costs to products.[9]
Target costing	Management technique for new products (not existing ones) that determines customer requirements (price, quality, functionality, and time). Drives changes in the upstream supply chain component designs to achieve these requirements. Management effort focuses on three key processes:[10] determining the market [customer] driven price; product level costing—driving cost reductions within the firm; and component level target costing—extending pressure to upstream trading partners.	Within the research and development, marketing, and manufacturing processes of a firm. Sets cost reduction targets for suppliers to achieve for the components they provide.	Reduce costs of products currently in research and development. Extend cost reduction pressure backwards in the supply chain to suppliers.

(Continued)

Total cost of ownership	Determines the total cost of an acquisition, including the costs associated with sourcing, holding inventory, quality, and returns.	Sourcing, acquisition, purchasing.	Evaluate alternate sources of supply. Understand the effects of purchasing decisions on total costs incurred by the firm.
Value chain analysis	Analyzes the chain of activities extending from the ultimate source of supply to the end user in order to understand the activities and processes performed, the behavior of costs, and sources for potential competitive advantage.[11]	Within a firm's internal value chain or key processes. Can be extended to cover external activities and processes interfacing with the firm's value chain. Production, purchasing, logistics, marketing, and customer service.	Determine how suppliers and customers affect the firm's activities and costs, outsourcing, identify cost drivers at the activity level, develop cost/differentiation advantage, reconfigure the supply chain, assess supplier and buyer power, and exploit linkages with suppliers and buyers.[12]

NOTES

1. For a more detailed summary of various cost classifications see Shahid Ansari, Jan Bell, and Thomas Klammer, "The Kaleidoscopic Nature of Costs," in the modular series *Management Accounting: A Strategic Focus* (Ansai, Bell, Klammer: Lulu.com).

2. Peter B.B. Turney, *Common Cents* (Hillsboro, OR: Cost Technology, 1991).

3. Richard Lamming, Owen Jones, and David Nicol, "Transparency in the Value Stream From Open-Book Negotiation to Cost Transparency," in *Value Stream Management*, ed. Peter Hines, Richard Lamming, Dan Jones, Paul Cousins and Nick Rich, (Harlow, United Kingdom: Pearson Education Limited, 2000).

4. Erik M. van Raaij, "The Strategic Value of Customer Profitability Analysis," *Marketing Intelligence & Planning* 23, no. 4, (2005): 373.

5. EVA is a registered trademark of Stern Stewart & Company.

6. Douglas M. Lambert and Terrance L Pohlen, "Supply Chain Metrics," *The International Journal of Logistics Management* 12, no. 1 (2001): 1.

7. Terrance L. Pohlen and Thomas J. Goldsby, "VMI and SMI Programs: How Economic Value Added Can Help Sell the Change," *International Journal of Physical Distribution and Logistics Management* 33, no. 7 (2003): 565.

8. Robin Cooper and Regine Slagmulder, *Supply Chain Development for the Lean Enterprise Interorganizational Cost Management* (Portland, OR: Productivity, 1999) 16.

9. Colin Drury, "Standard Costing: A Technique at Variance with Modern Management?" *Management Accounting* 77, no. 10 (1999): 56.

10. Stefan Seuring, "Supply Chain Target Costing," in ed. Stefan Seuring and Maria Goldbach, *Cost Management in Supply Chains* (Heidelberg: Physica-Verlag, 2002).

11. John K. Shank and Vijay Govindarajan, "Strategic Cost Management: The Value Chain Perspective," *Journal of Management Accounting Research* 3, Fall (1992): 180.

12. Ibid, 196.

CHAPTER 7

Indirect Costs, the Influence of Cost Allocation, and the Need to Understand Activities

S UPPLY CHAIN PROCESSES ARE supported by many different activities and require a variety of resources. Cost structures for these processes vary because firms operate in diverse environments, emphasize different strategies, and use a variety of production methods. Identifying what costs are directly or indirectly associated with a supply chain process is an essential element of supply chain costing.

Only certain costs are directly associated with supply chain processes or process segments. Other costs are indirect, making cost allocations an inherent part of measuring supply chain costs. Improving supply chain costing means that firms must pay more attention to the indirect costs, which are a growing part of supply chain costs relative to the direct costs, because the increasing complexity of supply chains requires more indirect costs to manage the complexity. There is an increasing emphasis on carefully managing how costs are assigned or allocated. Executives strongly stress that cost allocation decisions drive people's behavior and influence the resulting performance measurements. Cost allocations send critical signals to management regarding how costs are assumed to be consumed in the performance of different activities in the firm or supply chain. This information directly affects how operations are managed and how individuals at various levels in the firm and supply chain behave. Activities drive most supply chain process costs and thus managing activities is essential for supply chain cost management.

Costing all or part of a supply chain process is the focus of this book. The cost objects of potential interest include a function, process, activity, product or customer, and, ultimately, the entire supply chain. The type of decision being made influences the cost object of interest and which types of supply chain costs need to be measured and analyzed. Historically, most cost measurement systems focused on cost objects that were relevant for external reporting but not for internal decision making. Now there is a growing emphasis on identifying activities as the cost objects of interest. This activity focus makes it easier to obtain the type of cost information that is more useful for managing supply chain processes.

INDIRECT COSTS AND ALLOCATION

Costs associated with a cost object of interest can be classified as direct or indirect. A direct cost is easily traced to the cost object. An indirect cost is common to more than one cost object and is not directly traceable to a single cost object. Whether a cost is direct or indirect depends on the cost object of interest. The fact that the same cost may be both direct and indirect in different circumstances is a frequent source of misunderstanding, particularly for individuals who are not accountants.

To illustrate why the cost object influences whether a cost is *direct* or *indirect*, consider some examples. The wages of individuals who work solely in the warehousing operation are direct costs of warehousing. However, for a particular shipment warehousing makes, these wages are indirect, and some portion of the wage cost needs to be allocated to the shipment to calculate its full cost. Likewise, the salary of a factory supervisor who spends time overseeing the warehousing operation is an indirect cost of warehousing. This salary is a direct cost if the factory itself is the cost object of interest. Finally, rent on a building that houses both warehousing and production is indirect to the warehousing operation. If warehousing were in a separate facility, the rent cost would be a direct cost.

Indirect costs exist for many reasons. Often it is physically impossible to trace the cost to the cost object. Insurance on a delivery truck that serves multiple customers cannot be directly tied to a single customer. In other situations, management decides to share resources among products or services. If any truck in the fleet may deliver to a major customer, rather than having a dedicated truck for this customer, then the transportation costs to that customer are indirect. There are times when it is not cost beneficial to directly trace a cost. The cost of replacing mud flaps on trucks may be treated as a part of general maintenance cost rather than traced to the individual truck, because the cost is immaterial.

Nature of Cost Allocations

Because some supply chain costs will always be indirect to a cost object, allocation is a critical part of every cost system. "Allocation is the assignment or sharing of indirect costs to cost objects. Basically, allocation involves dividing indirect costs by some measurable physical or financial quantity. The result of this division is a cost per 'something,' which is then used to assign costs to the cost object based on the object's use of the 'something.' Estimated or budgeted indirect costs are often used to predetermine an allocation rate."[1]

There are many ways to allocate costs, and the allocation process may be quite complex. For example, a firm may use physical quantity measures, such as labor hours, miles driven, calls received, or space used, as a basis for allocating costs. Alternatively, financial measures, such as labor dollars, could be the basis for making an allocation. Conceptually, any measure that can be operationalized could be chosen as an allocation base. In practice, allocation bases are ideally based on cause-and-effect relationships, the benefits received, fairness or equity, or the ability to bear cost.

Most firms devote considerable effort to determining the amount of indirect costs and the allocation base for assigning and tracing these costs to the cost object. How the firm plans to use the allocated cost information is typically a factor in the choice of allocation base. Cost information is substantially better and more accurate when the allocation scheme reflects how costs are caused or incurred. Allocations are improved when the allocation base is a primary factor that is driving the quantity of indirect cost. Activity-based costing (ABC), described in Chapter 10, is the commonly accepted costing method because it complies with costing's *causality principle*.

Cost allocations are useful for cost planning and cost management. They help supply chain professionals estimate the cost and profitability of providing services, such as in customer profitability analyses that will be discussed in Chapter 9. Allocations are a reminder that indirect costs need to be covered by selling prices. They make people aware that indirect costs are caused by what they do and focus them on the need to carefully consider these costs. Ideally this consideration results in actions that reduce indirect costs and/or convert these costs into direct costs. *How costs are allocated influences how people behave.*

There are three approaches to allocation that organizations may use. It is sometimes useful to allocate only controllable indirect costs to a supply chain subpart. Many costs are indirect but are attributable to an area because they benefit that area or service. A decision may be made to allocate all attributable costs to a supply chain or supply chain subpart. The third approach is to allocate all indirect costs to cost objects because ultimately full costs must be covered for the firm to earn a profit.

A good allocation method helps managers understand what *drives* or *causes* indirect costs to change. Allocations must tie work related decisions and actions to costs incurred within the organization. Understanding the link between what we do while we work and the kinds and amount of indirect cost incurred, enables indirect costs to be managed. One way to focus attention on what causes cost to change is to use an allocation scheme that reflects resource consumption patterns.[2]

INFLUENCE OF COST ALLOCATION

Historically, resources' capacity expenses have been classified as sunk, fixed, step-fixed, or variable. The classification depends on the planning time horizon because capacity may not be easily adjusted in the short term but more easily adjusted in future weeks or months (e.g., replacing full-time employees with temporary contactors). Many indirect costs are also fixed costs—costs that do not change in the short run (typically a year) when the volume of the assumed cost driver changes. When these costs are allocated, the average fixed cost declines as the volume of the allocation base increases. The cost chart shown in Exhibit 7.1 shows this decline for shipments and reflects the magic of economies of scale. The chart shows that spreading (allocating) fixed costs over more shipments drives down the average total cost until the volume reaches some level, even though the average variable cost for each shipment begins increasing much earlier.

Senior executives need a good understanding of this type of cost interaction as they plan the level of resources to commit to a supply chain process— such as manufacturing flows or order fulfillment—even though they may lack the capability to alter fixed costs in the short run. This knowledge also helps them avoid situations where managers were rewarded for artificially raising reported profits by spreading fixed costs over excess production that is then simply added to inventory and increases overall costs.

EXHIBIT 7.1   Effect of Volume on Average Fixed and Unit Costs

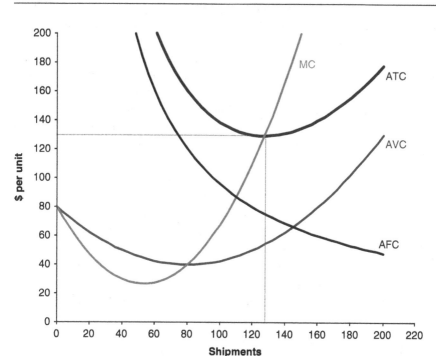

The Need for Sharing Indirect Cost Information

The presence of fixed, or step-fixed, costs can pose other problems for supply chain costing even when the managers incurring these costs recognize them as fixed and act accordingly when budgeting or planning for their operations. When these costs are included as part of the unit cost of an item or service, they become variable to the downstream customer. This situation creates tension within the supply chain as downstream customers seek unit cost reductions while upstream managers have little flexibility to reduce these fixed costs. Likewise, when fixed costs are reduced, the customer does not achieve a corresponding reduction in unit cost since any reductions in fixed costs are spread over the entire volume. This problem can only be overcome by sharing cost information so that downstream trading partners gain a greater understanding of their suppliers' cost structure.

Rather than continuing with often adversarial relationships among trading partners in a supply chain, the partners need to increase their collaboration.

This is because supply chains are competing against other supply chains for the share of wallet or purse of final customers at the end of the supply chain. The trading partners need to identify and pursue mutually beneficial cost and cycle-time reduction opportunities to improve their competitiveness.

Maintaining an awareness of the impact of indirect costs is an important element of supply chain costing. Supply chain managers often focus only limited attention on indirect costs internally and almost none when working with other internal and external members of the supply chain. Collaborative efforts and the exchange of cost information have primarily focused on direct costs. Since the flow of cost information is primarily one-way, the customer attempts to scrutinize the labor rates, capacity utilization, and process flows of its suppliers. Material costs are reviewed to determine where the customer may be able to leverage purchases across multiple suppliers, purchase in larger quantities, or possibly engineer out complex, expensive components and nonstandard parts. Only a limited number of suppliers share some cost information with customers, and that information is generally limited to costs directly associated with limited profit reengineering efforts. No indirect cost information is typically provided to prevent the customer from determining the suppliers' profit margins or gaining additional insight into their suppliers' operations.

There is no significant focus on understanding suppliers' indirect costs. Customers seldom challenge a supplier's overhead rates unless these rates are excessive or inconsistent with those of similar suppliers. Process improvements typically target direct labor or reduction of materials, scrap, or defects. Many indirect costs essentially go unmanaged.

There are a number of possible reasons this situation exists. There may be a lack of sophisticated cost management systems upstream of manufacturers, a relatively low proportion of indirect to direct costs with small upstream suppliers, or an inability to break out indirect costs and obtain any substantial savings in this area. It is likely that suppliers are unwilling to provide their customers with visibility beyond the manufacturing line, since they may be "burying" additional margin in their overhead rates. Suppliers typically do not provide information on their indirect costs when working on collaborative actions with their customers. They consider the information proprietary and only provide the direct costs of those activities within the scope of the project. Indirect costs could provide insight into their strategies and associated cost trade-offs being employed.

The Process View of Costing

Managing with a process view creates a growing need for better management accounting information. Managing end-to-end processes and the work activities that "belong" to and comprise processes go together. By defining a *business process* as comprising two or more logically related work activities intended to serve end customers, the need for integrating processes, outputs, and measured costs becomes even more apparent as an important requirement for managers and teams. Money is the language of business.

Traditional general ledger accounting systems usually deny managers visibility of many of the costs that belong to the end-to-end business processes. This is because multiple cost centers may be doing similar work. Each cost center is a silo, with barriers to viewing the end-to-end processes across all the cost centers. This is particularly apparent in the stocking, distribution, marketing, and selling expenses that traditional accounting reports as "expenses to the month's period" using expense account codes. With traditional cost allocations, these sales, general, and administrative expenses (SG&A) are not proportionately traced to the costs of the unique products, containers, services, distribution channels, or customers that cause those costs to occur.

ABC, discussed in Chapter 10, resolves this deficiency. What follows is a description of how activity-based management (ABM) leverages the ABC principles.

The Two Views of Costs: The Assignment View versus the Process View

There are two ways to organize and analyze ABC work activity cost data: the cost assignment view (ABM) and the process view (ABC). Since there is substantial confusion between their two views, even among accountants, they are described and clarified in Exhibit 7.2.

The *horizontal* process view, which is the ABM view of costs, sequences and additively builds up costs, whereas the *vertical* cost assignment view, which is the ABC view of costs, transforms resource expenses into output costs by continuously reassigning costs based on cause-and-effect tracing (i.e., cost allocations). The ABC cost assignment and the ABM process costing are two different views of the same resource expenses and the work activity costs that consume the resources. They are equivalent in amount, but the display of the information is radically different in each view.

EXHIBIT 7.2 The CAM-I ABC Cross: What Questions Are Answered?

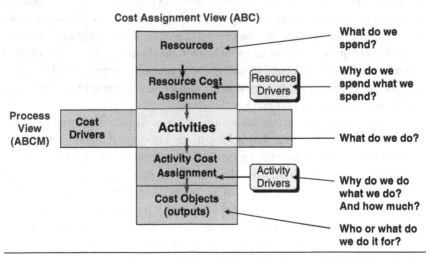

Cost Assignment View (ABC)

What do we spend?

Why do we spend what we spend?

What do we do?

Why do we do what we do? And how much?

Who or what do we do it for?

Source: The Consortium of Advanced Manufacturing International (CAM-I). Used with permission.

The *horizontal* process cost view is governed by the time sequence of activity costs that belong to the various processes. The *vertical* cost reassignment scheme is governed by the variation and diversity of the unique products, service lines, types of orders, distribution channels, and customers. Think of the vertical ABC cost assignment view as being *time-blind*. It does not care if a work activity comes before or after another work activity. In contrast, the ABM process costing view, at the activity stage, is output *mix-blind*. It does reflect how the diversity and variation of products and service lines uniquely consume the activity costs.

Vertical Cost Assignment View

As illustrated in Exhibit 7.3, the vertical axis reflects costs as being sensitive to demands from all forms of product, service line, distribution channel, and customer diversity and variety. The work activities consume the resources, and the products and customer services consume the work activities. The ABC cost assignment view is a cost-consumption network chain. When each cost is traced based on its unique quantity or proportion of its driver, *all* the resource expenses are eventually reaggregated into the final cost objects. There is a 100% expenses-to-costs reconciliation. This method provides much more accurate measures of product, service line, distribution channel, and customer costs than the traditional and arbitrary "butter spreading across bread" cost allocation method.

EXHIBIT 7.3 The Vertical View of Assigning Costs

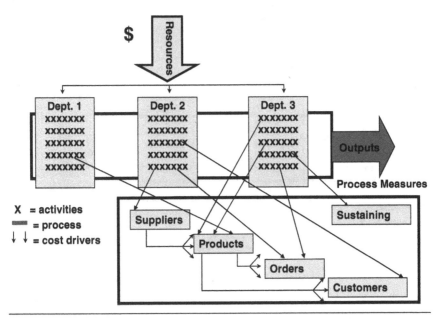

Source: Adapted from Gary Cokins, *Activity-Based Cost Management: An Executive's Guide* (New York: John Wiley & Sons, 2001), p. 63. Copyright Gary Cokins. Used with permission of the author.

Horizontal Cost Assignment View

The ABM horizontal view of activity costs, as illustrated in Exhibit 7.4, represents the business process view. This is often referred to as the lean accounting view. A business process can be defined as two or more activities or a network of activities with a common purpose. Activity costs belong to the costs of business processes. Across each process, the activity costs are sequential and additive. ABM strings, like pearls in a necklace, the activity costs in an ABC system.

In this orientation, activity costs satisfy the requirements for popular flow-charting, process mapping, and process modeling techniques. Business process–based thinking can be visualized as tipping the organization chart 90 degrees horizontally, and not the often self-serving silos of departments in the organization chart. ABC provides the activity costs for the ABM process view costing that are not available from the general ledger, which is restricted by the barriers of cost centers.

EXHIBIT 7.4   The Horizontal View of Sequencing Costs

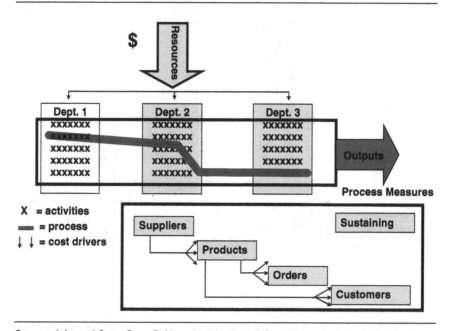

Source: Adapted from Gary Cokins, *Activity-Based Cost Management: An Executive's Guide* (New York: John Wiley & Sons, 2001), p. 64. Copyright Gary Cokins. Used with permission of the author.

In summary, the ABC vertical cost assignment view explains *what specific things cost* and *why things have a cost*. This provides insight into *what causes costs*. The ABM horizontal process view displays *how costs additively build up over time*.

The Process View—Value Stream Mapping

Exhibit 7.5 illustrates a three-dimensional view of Exhibit 7.4. It is referred to as a value stream map. The stacks are the activity costs, and the height of each stack measures the amount of the activity cost. Each activity can be segmented, with a third dimension of costs referred to as cost attributes. A popular cost attribute is one that classifies activities as being value added (VA) or non – value added (NVA).

EXHIBIT 7.5   Processes: Six Sigma, Lean Management, and Value Stream Mapping

Processes include activities that have high to low *value-adding* content.

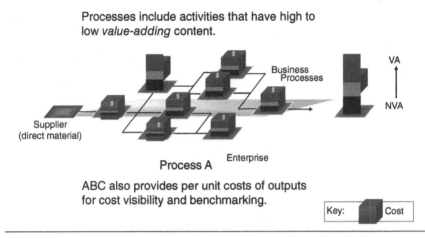

ABC also provides per unit costs of outputs for cost visibility and benchmarking.

Source: Adapted from Gary Cokins, *Activity-Based Cost Management: An Executive's Guide* (New York: John Wiley & Sons, 2001), p. 68. Copyright Gary Cokins. Used with permission of the author.

ACTIVITY-BASED MANAGEMENT FUNDAMENTALS

Activities are what a company does, and activities consume the resources' expenses. Materials, supplies, capital equipment, technology, and people are used to do work, and all these resources have a cost. Knowing what activities cost is useful in eliminating unnecessary activities and reducing cost. It can help lower the cost of performing the activities by facilitating a redesign of how these activities are done.

Executives in leading firms are working to improve their understanding of work activities; how activities are performed; the resources they use; how they are coordinated across the organization; and how these activities affect the cost, quality, and timeliness of service to customers. There is a growing realization that such an understanding is essential to managing activities. The understanding, managing, and costing of activities is very different than implementing a full-blown activity-based costing system.

Activity-based management (ABM) is used to identify the activities that occur, learn why they take place, and document how they are accomplished. The purpose of analyzing and costing activities is to improve work processes. ABM uses a process view to understand what causes costs and focuses on how to redirect and improve the use of resources to increase the value created for customers and other stakeholders. The tool is useful for making process improvements, doing operational and profitability/pricing analysis, and is an inherent part of strategic decision making.[3]

"ABM is a cost management tool that improves organizational decisions by focusing attention on the organizations' *work, how* they do it, *why* they do it, and at what *cost* they do it. ABM employs activity analysis. *Activity analysis* is used to *analyze the outputs, cost, and performance of organizational activities*. It involves understanding the tasks that are done and searching for better ways of doing those tasks. It also identifies the resources that activities consume and what causes this resource consumption or cost to be incurred. The result is improved and more cost-efficient work processes."[4]

The focal cost object in ABM is the activity. Knowing the cost of activities is one part of managing these activities, and this knowledge is helpful in developing improved cost information for distribution channels, customers, and specific services. Supply chain costing is increasingly focused on managing supply chain processes, and ABM is an essential part of supply chain process management.

ABM analysis may be thought of as starting with small tasks that combine into activities that make up the process of interest. Exhibit 7.6 illustrates a way of visually thinking about this progression.

EXHIBIT 7.6　Relationship of Tasks, Activities, and Process

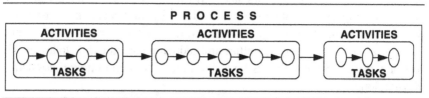

Source: Shahid Ansari, Jan Bell, and Thomas Klammer, "Activity Based Management," in the modular series *Management Accounting: A Strategic Focus* (Ansari, Bell, Klammer; Lulu.com).

Performing an ABM Analysis

When performing an ABM analysis, a common approach is to start with a single department or area and then expand the analysis into other departments that are an inherent part of the process or a segment of the process of interest. Another approach is to divide the effort into a series of steps. An example of these steps when the object of analysis is a single department as shown in Exhibit 7.7.

While activity analysis is common, few firms have formalized their approach to activity-based management to this extent.

The analysis done for ABM requires obtaining enough detail to understand what is being done and to identify possible inefficiencies. It is important to avoid capturing so much detail that information analysis becomes burdensome. Information is typically gathered using a combination of observation, interviews, and storyboarding or affinity diagramming. In all cases, the cost of an activity is still an estimate because cost assignment inevitably involves at least some allocation.

There are many levels that decision makers may select to analyze and measure supply costs using ABM information and alternative cost classifications. Each analysis level requires the decision maker to look at costs differently. In all cases, some activity costs are direct and others are indirect. Which costs are controllable varies with the time frame of the decision being considered. Cost analysis may be cross-functional within the firm or extend to firms throughout the supply chain. Analysis may be done within a department, function, internal process, or for a full supply chain process.

EXHIBIT 7.7   ABM Analysis Steps

Obtain the *existing cost* information and reports on the focal department.

Determine the major *processes* that occur within the department.

Identify the *inputs* (actions or events) that start each process and the *outputs* or results that the process produces.

Determine the *activities* involved in the various processes. Document the current activity flow in detail and list all *tasks* that are part of each activity.

Identify all *resources* used (people, machinery, supplies, space, etc.) by each activity.

For each major activity, define an *output measure.* This measure may be financial or nonfinancial.

For each major activity, define a *performance measure.* These measures may be financial or nonfinancial.

Record the *actual performance,* on the selected performance measures. The measures may be quality, cost, or time.

Use the performance to *determine how well you are performing* the activity.

Brainstorm *improvement* ideas.

Source: Shahid Ansari, Jan Bell, and Thomas Klammer, "Activity Based Management," in the modular series *Management Accounting: A Strategic Focus* (Ansari, Bell, Klammer; Lulu.com).

There are seldom measurement problems when the analysis shows that a cost is direct to an activity. For example, many firms have a dedicated team of employees who unload all incoming shipments from the company's suppliers. The salaries of these individuals are direct to the activity—unloading incoming shipments.

When costs related to an activity are indirect, it becomes necessary to allocate some portion of this cost to the activity. The allocation involves making decisions about which costs are indirect and about the appropriate allocation base to use for each cost or group of costs. If a janitor cleans the receiving dock as well as other parts of the warehouse, a portion of the janitor's salary is a cost of the "unloading incoming shipments" activity. Hours worked would probably be a reasonable allocation base. The receiving dock is part of the larger warehouse. Some portion of the total warehouse cost is logically allocated to the activity—unloading incoming shipments. The allocation base of choice may be square feet or some other physical measure.

How much cost is controllable is often directly linked to the time frame of the decision. If an economic downturn reduces the number of shipments being received, the firm may have only a limited ability to adjust the costs of the activity—unloading incoming shipments. Union contracts may limit the ability to decrease worker headcount. Most of the facility cost related to the loading dock is probably fixed. Alternatively, assume a firm makes a strategic decision to restructure its operations and have third-party suppliers ship directly to customers rather than to the firm's warehouse. Over time the majority of the costs associated with the activity—unloading incoming shipments—can be eliminated. These costs become controllable, but, of course, they are being replaced by other costs.

Why Use ABM and ABC?

Progressive companies use both ABC and ABM.

Adopting ABM principles helps supply chain managers develop a better understanding of work processes. The analysis requires individuals to identify the activities that occur, learn how they are performed, and document the ways they link within and across organizations. ABM is useful for decision making because better information is available for product design and process improvement, as well as for planning and control.

Adopting ABC principles facilitates strategic decisions more than operational ones. ABC provides visible and layered profit margin information that reports which products, service lines, and customers are more or less profitable, as well as the varying level of costs from suppliers other than the price of materials purchased from a supplier.

ABM is helpful for understanding what work is being done and how much that work costs. Complex supply processes are broken down into work activities rather than by function. This breakdown allows decision makers to see how activities contribute to goal achievement. Understandable activity cost data can be communicated through the organization. It allows employees to focus on completing activities more efficiently. Activity cost data help individuals see how their actions influence their organization and even other organizations. Because there is an operational focus to the cost data, it is easier for operating personnel and managers to understand and communicate information about activities. By highlighting interdependencies, ABM helps people understand why activities occur and which activities are redundant or unnecessary. This analysis lowers cost, reduces process time, and improves quality.

ABM refocuses attention onto the activities that cause costs. It is operationally focused and emphasizes the importance of understanding and measuring how and why activities occur. Continuous improvement is encouraged because activity cost data helps users compare costs for similar activities and encourages continual questioning of how and why these activities occurs. ABM encourages employees to participate in improvement efforts but does require a culture of empowerment to exist.

ABC supports strategic rationalization decisions involving pricing, adding or dropping products and services, and answering questions like which types of customers are more attractive to retain, grow, win back, or acquire—and how much to spend pursuing those actions.

NOTES

1. Shahid Ansari, Jan Bell, and Thomas Klammer, "Measuring and Managing Indirect Costs," in the modular series *Management Accounting: A Strategic Focus* (Ansar, Bell, Klammer; Lulu.com).
2. Ibid.
3. A useful discussion of ABM is found in the IMA Statement of Management Accounting, *Implementing Activity Based Management: Avoiding the Pitfall* (IMA, 1998).
4. Shahid Ansari, Jan Bell, and Thomas Klammer, "Activity Based Management" in the modular series *Management Accounting: A Strategic Focus* (Ansari, Bell, Klammer; Lulu.com).

CHAPTER 8

The Need for Value Chain Analysis

MODERN SUPPLY CHAIN COSTING requires a reevaluation of the traditional view of costing and a broadening of the scope of the actual and projected cost data collected by the firm. Supply chain costing emphasizes a process view and spans multiple internal functions. A broader perspective assists managers in evaluating how process changes will affect changes in costs and revenues over time, as well as in capturing the effect other members in the supply chain have on internal costs and overall supply chain profitability.

Value chain analysis (VCA) is a uniquely important tool for supply chain costing. The following section outlines the essential elements of VCA and describes why this technique is useful for evaluating the total cost of key supply chain processes. Leading firms in executing supply chain costing have a good understanding of their internal value chains and are engaging in costing efforts that extend beyond their firm into the external supply chains.

 ## VALUE CHAIN ANALYSIS

Two schools of thought have emerged regarding how to visualize and analyze the value chain. The original view, suggested by Michael Porter, depicts an internal value chain comprised of the activities and processes that a firm completes "to design, produce, market, deliver, and support its product or service."[1]

A broader and more relevant view for the supply chain cost journey is the one described by John Shank and V. Govindarajan: They suggest that the "value (supply) chain for any firm is the value-creating activities all the way from basic raw material sources from component suppliers through to the ultimate end-use product delivered into final consumers' hands."[2] This is consistent with this book's definition of the supply chain. The external value chain and external supply chain are, in essence, identical. The term *value chain analysis* (VCA) is used when referencing this technique since previous studies, much of the accounting literature, and many executives also use this terminology.

An Example

To illustrate, consider the supply chain for gasoline. It starts with exploring and finding crude oil, developing the field, producing (pumping) oil, and transporting (via a pipeline or a tanker) to a refining facility, where it is converted into gasoline (and other products). The gasoline is then transported to a storage terminal from where it is transported again to retail gas stations or other outlets and sold as branded or unbranded product. Exhibit 8.1 depicts the value chain for gasoline. Firms may be positioned in one, two, or even all the steps within a value chain.

EXHIBIT 8.1 A Simplified Value Chain for Gasoline

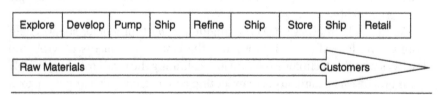

Source: Shahid Ansari, Jan Bell, and Thomas Klammer, "Value Chain and Strategic Cost Management," in the modular series *Management Accounting: A Strategic Focus* (Ansari, Bell, Klammer; Lulu.com).

Dealing with Rising Costs

Rising costs across their supply chains, as well as increasing pressure to find ways to reduce these costs, confront supply chain managers. Typically, they have focused inward when attempting to reduce costs. Reducing headcount, streamlining internal processes, and seeking lower-cost suppliers are common approaches when seeking cost reductions. Having said this, many managers recognize that this traditional perspective misses opportunities for cost reduction elsewhere in the supply chain. Executives must consider how their firm can work with other trading partners to reduce supply chain costs. The approach that has proven most successful combines supply chain costing and VCA within the context of individual supply chain processes.

VCA is a cost management process that analyzes costs, such as supply chain costs, across linked enterprises. This analysis helps identify where the majority of costs are in a supply chain process and thus where to focus cost management efforts, document why actions of upstream supply chain organizations influence downstream supply chain costs (and vice versa), and evaluate where the more or less profitable segments of the supply chain processes are, thus facilitating appropriate cost management strategies.

The growth of lean production processes within the supply chain represents one of the major reasons VCA has become a more important cost planning tool. In a lean environment it is essential that firms work closely and exchange planning and operational data with suppliers and customers. Incorporating cost planning as part of this process within the value chain helps avoid decisions that commit the firm to the wrong cost structure. Exchanging cost and operational data with trading partners and evaluating key relationships within each of the supply chain processes is beneficial for cost reduction and increased efficiency and effectiveness.

Another reason to complete a value chain analysis and attempt to identify costs within the value chain is to better understand how the linkages and interrelationships between trading partners affect the costs and profits of other entities. Executives acknowledge that many of their costs are driven by their trading partners' performance. A VCA can be used to demonstrate to a firm's trading partners how to improve coordination, reduce waste, speed up delivery, avoid delays, and reduce errors.

Performing a VCA and identifying value chain costs for a supply chain process represents a significant challenge for most firms. Obtaining cost information internally often requires managers to fundamentally rethink how costs are classified and used. This challenge is one of the reasons this book emphasizes that a variety of tools and approaches may be an inherent part of supply chain costing. Activity analysis is one essential element of this effort. There is also a need to alter the behavioral and cultural environments that are in place within the organization to gain acceptance of restructured cost measurements.

An even bigger challenge is obtaining cost information related to the external elements of the supply chain processes. Two-way sharing of actual cost information is extremely rare, even for organizations that focus extensively on building strong ties to suppliers and customers as part of their effort to drive costs out of the entire supply chain. Communication in the supply chain occurs primarily between trading partners during transactions. The information exchanged depends on the firms' respective location in the supply chain and the products or commodities exchanged. Processes that involve manufacturing or assembling tend to exchange a wider range of information that includes product design, specifications, and demand information. Consumer product supply chains tend to communicate a narrower range of information such as forecasts, shipping, demand, and inventory information. Most firms report that the information communicated is relationship-dependent. Information exchange generally occurs between management teams attempting to use the supply chain to obtain a marketplace advantage or in relationships with trading partners with growth strategies. Even among firms recognized as being at the forefront in supply chain management, these relationships represent a relatively small proportion of their trading partners.

 ## BASICS OF VALUE CHAIN COST ANALYSIS

A supply chain costing model enables managers to simulate how changes within the supply chain are likely to impact the firm and its trading partners. Having a better understanding of how different market segments, distribution channels, and product/service offerings affect costs and performance can yield a competitive advantage. A firm and its trading partners can concentrate on those activities where the greatest opportunities exist to differentiate the supply chain when they have this understanding.

Ansari, Bell, and Klammer recommend a four-step value chain analysis model: documenting supply chain activities and relationships within the supply chain, estimating the cost and profit margins at each step of the chain, mapping the firm's internal supply chain activities, and analyzing the internal cost structure to understand what factors drive costs and how these costs compare to the trading partners' costs across the supply chain.[3]

The analysis begins by documenting the activities within the value chain. Key relationships and the contribution of each trading partner are identified. Exhibit 8.1 illustrates a gasoline supply chain. Some firms, such as Exxon or British Petroleum, span the entire supply chain, whereas many others participate in just a few segments. Exhibit 8.2 shows where several individual firms participate, or "fit," in the gasoline supply chain.

EXHIBIT 8.2   Some Corporations in the Gasoline Supply Chain

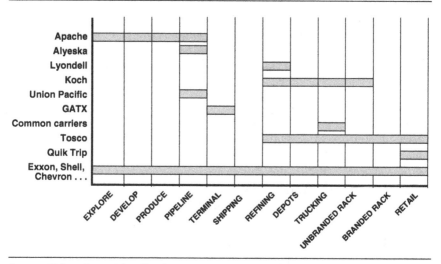

Source: Taken from John Shank, Eric Spiegel, and Alfred Escher, "Strategic Value Analysis for Competitive Advantage," *Strategy, Management and Competition,* vol. 10 (March 1998).

Steps in Using VCA to Analyze Supply Chain Costs

A VCA should be performed for each of the supply chain processes in which a firm participates. The analysis involves mapping the supply chain process and the activities each firm in the supply chain performs within the process. The level of detail depends on the complexity of the different activities and where opportunities appear to exist. However, the analysis must extend across the entire supply chain. The analysis concentrates on identifying those activities where trading partners interact with one another.

The next step involves developing an understanding of the cost and profit margins at each stage of the supply chain process. As noted earlier, most of the firms find directly obtaining this type of information extremely difficult, if not impossible. Not only is there an unwillingness to share this type of sensitive data, but supply chain process cost data is often not readily available because of how the cost systems used internally or by other trading partners aggregate cost information.

Despite these challenges, reasonable estimates can often be obtained by making use of the wide variety of available public information. A certain amount of cost and margin information related to supply chain costs is available from the financial reports of public companies that operate in specific sectors of the supply chain. Securities and Exchange Commission (SEC) filings and numerous financial databases provide easy access to data. Information on private firms may be more difficult to obtain, but company websites and rating agencies such as Dun & Bradstreet can provide some additional insights. Executives at several leading firms indicate that they often have a better understanding of many of their supplier's costs than the supplier.

Industry studies, trade association reports, and benchmarking data for many of the functions within individual supply chains are available from a variety of sources. Professional societies such as the Council of Supply Chain Management (CSCMP) and the Association for Supply Chain Managers (name rebranded from APICS—the American Production and Inventory Control Society) make a wide variety of data on supply chain processes available to their members. Conference presentations provide many cross-organizational, information-sharing opportunities. These events can deepen a manager's knowledge of the supply chain and its members. This knowledge helps fill in informational gaps and allows for reasonable cost and profit estimates when performing a value chain analysis.

The third step in VCA refocuses attention internally. Here lies the mapping of the internal value chain and the links to the previously documented external value chain. A diagram of the internal value chain—such as that shown in Exhibit 8.3 for a paperboard printing company—is created for each major supply chain process. Both support areas and the primary manufacturing activities are included in this mapping.

After documenting the internal supply chain and its components for a supply chain process, an analysis of the cost of each internal step is made. An activity analysis within the supply chain facilitates the identification of those cost factors causing costs to occur. Activity-based costing (ABC) information (discussed in Chapter 10) often proves useful for restructuring and reallocating traditional functional cost information into data that is specific to internal supply chain processes. Links between internal processes are made explicit, as are the links of processes with external value chain members. A key objective of this analysis is to determine how internal costs compare with the trading partners' costs of performing similar activities within the supply chain. The analysis results may suggest shifting functions elsewhere in the supply chain where they can be performed at a lower total cost.

The final documentation resulting from a VCA shows managers where the firm incurs costs, what drives them, and which steps in the supply chain are most costly or provide the greatest opportunity for cost reduction. Each activity is carefully scrutinized to determine whether the cost is controlled internally or being driven by external sources. An analysis of these activities is largely based on knowledge and experience rather than a structured set of decision rules.

EXHIBIT 8.3   Midway Containers Internal Value Chain

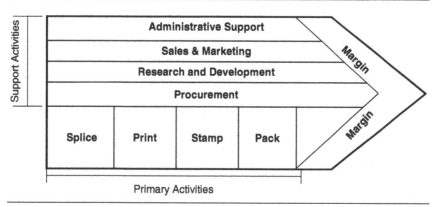

Source: Shahid Ansari, Jan Bell, and Thomas Klammer, "Value Chain and Strategic Cost Management," in the modular series *Management Accounting: A Strategic Focus* (Ansari, Bell, Klammer; Lulu.com).

VCA represents collaborative, team effort in most firms. Accountants, production, distribution, engineering, and many other functions come together to identify supply chain process improvement opportunities. VCA provides an excellent platform for firms to identify the activities and value-creating processes where the firm and its trading partners have a strategic advantage.

A Statement of Management Accounting (SMA) issued by the Institute of Management Accountants (IMA) provides a useful description of how a VCA can be used for assessing where in the supply chain trading partners can turn to obtain a competitive advantage. The statement authors break down the analysis used into several parts. Internal cost analysis is used to determine the sources of profitability and the relative cost positions of internal value-creating processes. Internal differentiation analysis helps managers understand the sources of differentiation (including the cost) within internal value-creating processes. Vertical linkage analysis focuses on understanding the relationships and associated costs among external suppliers and customers to maximize the value delivered to customers and to minimize cost.[4]

 ## USING VALUE CHAIN ANALYSIS RESULTS

A VCA of a supply chain process reveals how a firm's activities fit into the overall supply chain, documents competitor's positions, and shows how each step influences costs and profits. A firm's supply chain managers can use this information to improve performance in several ways:

- Avoid entering or continuing to operate in "no profit" segments of the supply chain or a process whenever possible. A key objective of many supply chain costing efforts is the development of customer, channel, or supply chain profitability analyses. Knowing the costs and returns in different segments of the supply chain helps management decide where and what resources to commit or pull back.
- The VCA provides information about whether the firm should consider opportunities for additional integration of its operations or whether less integration makes more sense.
- Management can improve performance by deploying resources into those areas that create or increase value. If a firm has a cost advantage or employs unique technology that provides a competitive edge, it makes sense to deploy additional resources to maintain these advantages. For example, some firms invest heavily in specific logistics functions because of their expertise in extracting additional cost savings for the supply chain.
- Many opportunities to reconfigure the supply chain to further reduce costs will be identified, particularly over time. For example, some firms outsource noncore or high-cost activities to their trading partners, require their suppliers to co-locate near them, or have their supply chain fundamentally redesigned by changing how goods are shipped or how orders are processed and filled.
- Growing opportunities exist to work directly with other value chain members to improve overall performance. Some firms are developing alliances with customers and suppliers that are yielding substantial cost savings while providing quicker and higher-quality service.
- Performance improvement increasingly requires sharing operational and eventually cost information, both across internal functions and

with external members of the value chain. This sharing remains a formidable challenge for most firms, but the firm has a greater chance for success when it is already moving toward lean processes and thus increasingly working with both customers and suppliers. As firms become more dependent on one another, the amount of shared operational and cost information increases.

▪ Mapping the value chain helps managers increase their understanding of supply chain processes and their dependence on those trading partners that have the greatest influence on driving costs. This knowledge should make it easier to identify and implement win-win alliances within the supply chain. Behaviorally, managers must learn to look beyond their immediate, transactional relationships. In key relationships, an attitude shift toward working more closely with those trading partners to achieve cost reductions rather than acting as adversaries during price negotiations is essential. An understanding of how the firm and its trading partners drive both internal and supply chain costs is fundamental for informational sharing and improved long-run decision making. However, learning to share cost information and detailed activity data, even internally, often requires a major culture shift for most managers.

THE VALUE OF COOPERATIVE COSTING ACROSS THE VALUE CHAIN

An example illustrates how one firm began to consider the supply chain as a single entity for costing purposes. Management reported that a large customer with multiple retail locations sought higher delivery frequency to lower average retail inventory, maintain fresher products, and increase on-the-shelf availability. In response to this request, the supplier employed a combination of VCA and an activity-based approach to determine how more frequent store deliveries would affect total supply chain costs.

The VCA of the order fulfillment process produced an activity map similar to that shown in Exhibit 8.4.[5] The customer participated in the value chain analysis and provided information on the direct costs for the activities affected by a change in delivery frequency. The supplier provided similar information but did not share indirect costs for any of the activities. The supplier's management team indicated that their cost system already had assigned indirect costs to their activities, and they could assess how a process change would affect direct as well as indirect costs.

EXHIBIT 8.4 Supply Chain Map of the Order Fulfillment Process across a Single Dyad in the Supply Chain

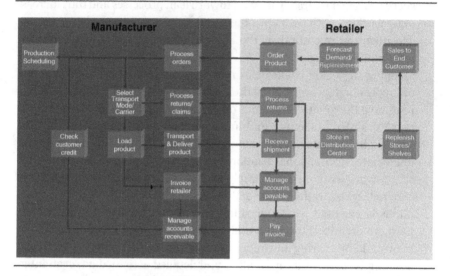

The analysis used an activity-based approach to determine the cost for each activity performed across both firms during the process. For each activity, the firms jointly identified a corresponding cost driver—the factor that causes a change in activity performance—and the amount of resources, such as labor or material, consumed by the activity. Exhibits 8.5 and 8.6 provide a summary of the activity-based analysis performed for the order fulfillment process from both the supplier's and customer's perspectives.

The exhibits provide alternative cost drivers for each activity. These alternative drivers enable the use of additional activities to capture differences in how the activity may be performed and the cost associated with those differences. For example, most shipments were accomplished via direct store delivery; however, truckload (TL), less-than-truckload (LTL), and parcel shipments were used by the supplier for different stores or customers. These differences became more important as the analysis progressed, because more frequent deliveries resulted in smaller shipments and shifted some of them to alternative modes with higher transportation rates.

Based on the cost analysis across both firms, the supplier recommended several changes to lower total process costs. These changes included using direct store delivery (DSD) drivers to stock the shelves to bypass the customer's receiving and check-in processes. The retailer would provide point-of-sale information daily to improve the supplier's scheduling of deliveries, amount shipped, and forecasting used in production and setting inventory levels. In addition to these changes, the retailer and supplier jointly determined how these process changes would affect sales, on-the-shelf availability, and inventory levels for the retailer. The joint analysis determined how the process change would affect the retailer's profitability across all stores. The supplier independently assessed the effect on their profitability by simulating how changes in activity levels would likely affect sales, inventory levels, forecasting accuracy, and production costs. Although several costs were exchanged between the firms, neither firm had total cost transparency of the other trading partner's costs.

EXHIBIT 8.5 Supplier's Activity Costs

Activity	Potential Cost Drivers	Activity Cost
Process orders	# of EDI, phone, fax or salesperson orders	$ per order
	# of SKUs	
Pick and load product	# of lines, cases, tiers, or pallets	$ per order pick
Transport and deliver product	# of LTL, TL, or parcel shipments	$ per delivery
	# of miles, drops, pallets	
	# CWT	
Manage returns	# of lines, SKUs, returns, or cases	$ per return
Perform accessorials	# of cartons or pallets	$ per accessorial
Invoice customer	# of invoices, lines, or SKUs	$ per invoice
Evaluate backhauls	# of orders, shipments, or pallets	$ per backhaul
Perform credit check	# of orders or customers	$ per credit check
Manage accounts receivable	# of orders	$ per receivable

The analysis results indicated that total supply chain costs would be reduced by implementing the process change with the supplier's recommendations. The retailer obtained lower ordering, receiving, returns, and inventory carrying costs. The supplier's delivery costs increased, but offsetting cost reductions were obtained in returns, order processing, invoicing, production (not shown), and inventory that carried costs through improved demand visibility.

In addition, both firms obtained increased sales due to higher on-shelf product availability and fresher product. Without cost visibility across both firms, the process adoption would have been highly unlikely because of the perception of costs simply being shifted from one firm to another. Other changes needed to occur within the process to gain acceptance from both firms and to reduce total cost. The analysis identified opportunities to make cost trade-offs to lower total costs and showed the effect these changes would have on the supply chain and on each trading partner.

EXHIBIT 8.6 Customer's Activity Costs

Activity	Potential Cost Drivers	Activity Cost
Order product	# of EDI, fax, phone, internet, or salesperson orders	$ per order
Process customer demand	# of customer demands, SKUs, or lines	$ per customer demand
Process returns	# of SKUs, cases, lines	$ per return
Receive shipments	# of LTL, TL, parcel, backhaul, or DSD deliveries	$ per shipment received
Incheck shipment	# of cases, pallets, lines, SKUs, or shipments	$ per SKU received
Replenish shelves	#SKUs or cases	$ per replenishment
Manage accounts payable	# of orders or lines	$ per order
Pay invoice	# of invoices or lines	$ per invoice

USING COST ESTIMATION CAPABILITY ACROSS THE VALUE CHAIN

Cost sharing among value chain members is rare, but some firms attempt to estimate their trading partner's costs. These firms employ sophisticated and highly proprietary cost estimation models to determine a supplier's manufacturing costs. Estimates of supplier costs can be developed independently and do not necessarily require collaborative relationships to obtain reasonably accurate costs. The cost information incorporated into these cost estimation models come from the firm's knowledge of their trading partner's processes, business strategies, technology, and other information obtained during the acquisition process. Analysts supplement this data by obtaining publicly available information from government databases such as Bureau of Labor statistics. In addition, the models include information that could be obtained without the suppliers' cooperation, such as facility size, location, capabilities, and date constructed.

These models are generally used during price negotiations. However, some firms have expanded their capabilities to estimate all their trading partners' costs. Using this information and their cost estimation models, the firms are able to closely approximate their suppliers' costs. In many instances, the individuals using these models find they have better estimates of process costs than the supplier's management team. However, these models require considerable effort and sustained maintenance to remain of value to supply chain decision makers.

The experience gained in developing costs for immediate upstream or downstream trading partners enables the most advanced applications of these cost estimation tools to estimate costs from the ultimate source of supply through to the final end user. Certain firms use their cost estimation models to determine process and activity costs for second- and third-tier suppliers to obtain a complete understanding of their inbound supply chain costs and the total delivered costs to the end user. These models provide the capability to quickly determine how network changes, such as relocating a facility from one country to another, will drive costs throughout the supply chain.

Supply chain flowcharts are another approach used to estimate supply chain costs (see Exhibit 8.7). The flowchart helps identify the supply chain structure and is used to determine the cost and value added by each trading partner. The information required for this analysis is usually obtained from industry or trade reports and analyses, consultants, benchmarking reports, or a "make-versus-buy" analysis if the company were to perform the same function as the trading partner. By assigning costs within the supply chain flowchart, management can examine all the steps—and the associated costs— of each trading partner within the supply chain. To determine their leverage in working with upstream suppliers, a chart illustrating their buys as a proportion of the supplier's business is sometimes included. Large proportions indicate that the customer will be more likely to negotiate or collaborate with upstream suppliers than in supply chains, where their spending represents a small proportion of upstream suppliers' business. Although the estimates used in these flowcharts may not be detailed, the cost information highlights where the greatest payback exists in the supply chain for improvement efforts.

The combination of cost estimation and flowcharts provides a powerful tool for analyzing cost drivers within the supply chain and assessing how process

EXHIBIT 8.7   Supply Chain Flowchart

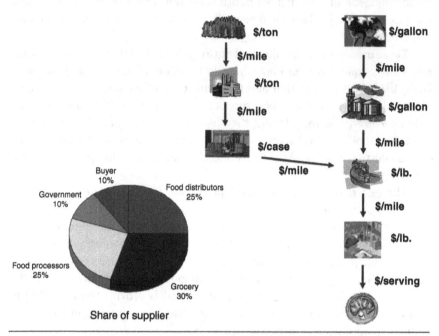

Source: Case study example disguised to protect firm identity. Exhibit includes additional information obtained from Peter Kajüter and Harri I. Kulmala, "Open-Book Accounting in Networks Potential Achievements and Reasons for Failures," *Management Accounting Research* 16 (2005), pp. 179–204.

changes will affect costs throughout the supply chain. These tools highlight opportunities to leverage the value-adding efforts of each trading partner. By analyzing process flows, management can identify where eliminating unnecessary steps and waste from the value chain can lead to cost reductions and shorter lead times. Management can develop more effective strategies based on all the trading partners' costs and capabilities.

This understanding of the value chain and the ability to estimate trading partner costs is frequently used in the development of alternative sourcing strategies. Large, well-established suppliers generally have little incentive to collaborate on cost reduction initiatives. In many instances, the customer may represent only a small proportion of their total revenue, and any cost savings would be relatively small. The suppliers perceive that disclosing any cost information will lead to reduced margins. To overcome this obstacle, the downstream customer can use cost estimation techniques to demonstrate the cost and revenue implications of a proposed process change to alternative suppliers. The analysis identifies the process steps, required capability, and associated costs. Potential suppliers could then more easily assess whether their current processes can accommodate this new product. The customer can provide additional information such as price, volume, and forecasts to assist the supplier in making the decision whether to produce this product.

Cost estimation is often used to simulate the causal effect between end-user demand and trading partners' costs and performance across the entire supply chain. The ability to simulate process changes is one of the most significant capabilities offered by supply chain costing and cost estimation. Managers can simulate whether changes in flexibility, cost, quality, and time produce a competitive advantage at the end-user level. The simulation enables an assessment of the contribution of each trading partner and how they affect value creation in the supply chain. Based on the analysis, specific trading partners can be targeted for collaborative efforts or alternative providers. This approach is a different and important use of supply chain costing and cost estimation. Instead of focusing on internal improvement, managers are using cost and performance information to influence external behavior. A key for management is to determine how best alter the behavior of their trading partners in harmony with their firm's cost structure. However, management of both firms must already possess a thorough understanding of their cost structure and how it will vary with any proposed changes.

NOTES

1. Michael E. Porter, *Competitive Advantage* (New York: Free Press, 1993).
2. John K. Shank and V. Govindarajan, *Strategic Cost Management* (New York: Free Press, 1993).
3. Shahid Ansari, Jan Bell, and Thomas Klammer, "Value Chain and Strategic Cost Management," in the modular series *Management Accounting: A Strategic Focus* (Ansari, Bell, Klammer: Lulu.com).
4. IMA Statement of Management Accounting, *Value Chain Analysis for Assessing Competitive Advantage*, IMA, 1996. While this is an older document, there is a detailed explanation of each of these analysis segments along with good exhibits and multiple examples that are helpful for anyone interested in learning more about this tool.
5. Process and cost information disguised at the request of the firm.

CHAPTER 9

Customer and Distribution Channel Profitability Analysis

T HE ONLY VALUE A company will ever create for its shareholders and owners is the value that comes from its customers—current ones and the new ones the company acquires in the future. To remain competitive, companies must determine how to keep customers longer, grow them into bigger customers, make them more profitable, serve them more efficiently, and acquire more profitable customers.

But there is a problem with pursuing these ideals. Customers increasingly view suppliers' products and standard service lines as commodities. This means that suppliers must shift their actions toward differentiating their services, offers, discounts, and deals to different types of existing customers to retain and grow them. Further, they should concentrate their marketing and sales efforts on acquiring new customers who have traits comparable to those of their relatively more profitable customers.

As companies shift from a product-centric and service line–centric focus to a customer-centric focus, the myth that almost all current customers are profitable needs to be replaced with the truth. Some highly demanding customers may indeed be unprofitable! Unfortunately, many companies' management accounting systems aren't able to report the customer profitability information needed to support analysis for how to rationalize which types of customers are more attractive to retain, grow, or win back, as well as which types of new customers to acquire—and which types of customers are not attractive.

This shift in attention from products to customers means managers are increasingly seeking granular non-product-associated *costs to serve* customer-related information as well as information about intangibles, such as customer loyalty and social media messaging about their company and its competitors. Today in many companies there is a wide gap between the CFO's function and the supply chain management, marketing, and sales functions. That gap needs to be closed.

 ## THE PROBLEM WITH TRADITIONAL ACCOUNTING

Here is the basic problem. With accounting's traditional product gross profit margin reporting, managers can't see the more important and relevant "bottom half" of the total income statement picture—all the profit margin layers that exist and should be reported from customer-related expenses such as distribution channel, selling, customer service, credit, and marketing expenses.

The supply chain, marketing, and sales functions already intuitively suspect that there are highly profitable and highly unprofitable customers, but management accountants have been slow to reform their measurement practices and systems to support the supply chain, marketing, and sales functions by providing the evidence. To complicate matters, the compensation incentives for a sales force (e.g., commissions) typically are based exclusively on revenues. Companies need to focus on growing profitable sales, not just increasing market share and growing sales. Compensation incentives for the sales force should be a blend of both customer sales volume and profits.

Who are the troublesome customers, and how much do they drag down profit margins? More important, once this question is answered, what corrective actions should managers and employees take to increase the profit from a customer? Measurements and a progressive management accounting system are the key.

Modern supply chain costing requires cost systems that have been restructured to provide a broader scope of actual and projected cost data so that managers can analyze the profitability of a variety of cost objects, such as products, service lines, projects, distribution channels, and customers. Customer profitability analysis is an obviously important tool within the umbrella of supply chain costing. This chapter describes this tool in more detail.

GOOD (LOW MAINTENANCE) VERSUS BAD (HIGH MAINTENANCE) CUSTOMERS

Every supplier has good and bad customers. Low-maintenance "good" customers place standard orders with no fuss, whereas high-maintenance "bad" customers demand nonstandard offers and services, such as special delivery requirements. For example, the latter constantly changes delivery schedules, returns goods, demands special rather than standard services, or frequently contacts the supplier's help desk. In contrast, the former just purchases a company's products or service lines and is rarely bothersome to the supplier. The extra expenses for high-maintenance customers add up. What can be done? After the level of profitability for all customers is measured, they all can be migrated toward higher profits using "profit margin management" techniques.

SUPPLY CHAIN MANAGEMENT'S NEED FOR CUSTOMER PROFITABILITY INFORMATION

In customer profitability analysis, the cost and revenue object of interest becomes the customer or the distribution channels to customers. More precisely, customer profitability analysis involves the process of tracing and assigning revenues and costs to customers or market segments based on costing's causality principle to determine their profitability.

Customer profitability analysis, including cost-to-serve expenses, represents a major step toward implementing supply chain costing. In many firms, analyzing how external customers drive costs represents their first initiative to capture costs and activities across multiple trading partners. Activity-based costing (ABC) principles and a system to support ABC are essential for assigning costs to customers. ABC is described in detail in Chapter 10.

Customer profitability analysis is a tool that helps measure both the revenues generated and the resources used to serve specific customers, groups of customers, or distribution channels. This analysis helps managers identify and focus on the relatively more profitable customers and place less effort on the less profitable or unprofitable customers. Because of the product and service variety that permeates today's business environment, not all customers are equally profitable. A customer profitability analysis often shows that a small percentage of customers generate a large proportion of a firm's profits, and that many customers are actually unprofitable. Cost-to-serve focuses on the assignment of costs by customer to determine the total cost to service a customer or market segment. Customer profitability analysis—the technique more widely emphasized in management accounting—is the focus of the discussion throughout the remainder of this chapter.

Like value chain analysis, customer profitability analysis requires a modification in the way costs are viewed and managed. Supply chain costing is complicated by the variety of choices made available by the advent of lean processes. For example, what does it cost to sell identical products under different names or brand numbers in big-box stores, in mom-and-pop outlets, and over the internet? How are choices to deliver products directly to retail stores, to distribution facilities, by mail or UPS to individual customers, and by other means justified? Which customers or distribution channels are relatively more or less profitable? These are increasingly important questions in a world where a firm must compete with many other suppliers for customers with new and complex expectations.

Understanding customer profitability is critical to making decisions about what and how to sell and deliver different products and services. Management must determine which of the many market niches and different types of customers they wish to serve. Considerable management interest exists in determining which customer groups are most loyal, which require extra levels of support or service, how customer actions affect costs, and whether there are customers the firm needs to let go—to terminate the relationship and let competitors take on those customers and lose profits from them.

EXHIBIT 9.1 Information Managers Need in Today's Environment

Who are the firm's "best" (most profitable) customers?

Who are the "problem" customers? How can they be made more profitable?

What is the value of keeping or increasing customer loyalty?

What customer actions result in increasing selling, service, or support costs? How can the firm work with these customers to avoid such cost increases?

Which customers should get price discounts and receive special promotions?

What customer support activities are costly and how can these activities be done at less cost?

Are there more profitable means of distributing products or service, such as over the internet?

Source: Adapted from Shahid Ansari, Jan Bell, and Thomas Klammer, "Customer Profitability Analysis," in the modular series *Management Accounting: A Strategic Focus* (Ansari, Bell, Klammer: Lulu.com).

Exhibit 9.1 lists some of the customer information supply chain managers need in today's environment. The information systems that managers need to answer these and similar questions are significantly more complex than the traditional systems many firms continue to use.

AN APPROACH TO CUSTOMER PROFITABILITY ANALYSIS

When performing customer profitability analysis, information about the revenue generated by a customer and the direct costs of the product or service the customer buys is usually readily available. However, the gross margin information that typically results is not a good estimate of customer profitability in a world where customer demands on support services vary widely.

Completing a customer profitability analysis requires an understanding of how and why there are differences in the support costs associated with serving a customer, group of customers, or a particular distribution channel. Information on who the customers are as well as what, when, how, how often, and even why they buy is essential. There is a need to accumulate data on what it costs to sell, deliver, provide customer support, and meet other customer-generated costs. This type of data often resides in different functional systems such as logistics, sales, marketing, and finance. The data usually needs to be reclassified by type or activity to be useful. The importance of cross-functional information sharing is critical. Exhibit 9.2 shows customer support activities classified into four major types of subprocesses and lists several examples of the types of activities that support each process.

Some of these activity costs may be readily traceable to individual customers or channels if the firm has properly structured information. The salary of a salesperson dedicated to a single customer is easily traced to that customer. Other costs may be shared among several customers or market segments and will require significant additional analysis and the use of reasonable cost allocations. The cost of the customer support personnel who respond to inquiries from a group of 10 large customers might be allocated based on the percentage of time spent with each customer. Still other costs, such as designing and maintaining a website, may be general to all customers and it may be inappropriate to allocate this type of costs to customers when doing a customer profitability analysis.

EXHIBIT 9.2   Customer-Related Subprocesses and Activities

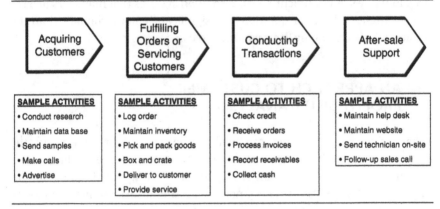

Acquiring Customers	Fulfilling Orders or Servicing Customers	Conducting Transactions	After-sale Support
SAMPLE ACTIVITIES	**SAMPLE ACTIVITIES**	**SAMPLE ACTIVITIES**	**SAMPLE ACTIVITIES**
• Conduct research	• Log order	• Check credit	• Maintain help desk
• Maintain data base	• Maintain inventory	• Receive orders	• Maintain website
• Send samples	• Pick and pack goods	• Process invoices	• Send technician on-site
• Make calls	• Box and crate	• Record receivables	• Follow-up sales call
• Advertise	• Deliver to customer	• Collect cash	
	• Provide service		

Source: Adapted from Shahid Ansari, Jan Bell, and Thomas Klammer, "Customer Profitability Analysis," in the modular series *Management Accounting: A Strategic Focus* (Ansari, Bell, Klammer: Lulu.com).

Several basic steps are part of customer profitability analysis:[1] create customer profiles, compute the revenue generated from each customer, compute the cost of activities consumed in servicing customers, compute customer profitability by combining the revenue and cost data, and use the analysis to design the right customer mix and strategy.

Much of the Data Already Exists

This information often resides in marketing, since most organizations already have a fairly detailed profile of their customers. Information on what goods and services customers purchase and how often they purchase them (such as preferring morning deliveries) is readily available. Firms use this information to make special offers or to inform customers of new products or services.

Computing the revenue generated by a customer from all sources is relatively straightforward. Payment records are an obvious source of this information. Part of the analysis may become a bit less certain where there are indirect revenues, such as what a bank can earn from cash kept in a customer checking account. When a supply chain process, such as manufacturing flow or order fulfillment, is part of the product cost, estimating how much of the revenue to assign to the process requires informed judgment.

Revenue generation costs money. A transportation company must buy fuel, pay drivers, buy insurance, rent or buy facilities, repair equipment, and so forth to generate a stream of delivery revenue. Determining how much cost to assign to an individual customer or class of customer requires a careful analysis of what drives the costs so a reasonable allocation of these costs to the customer can be made. There are also significant other costs that need to be considered to estimate customer profitability. For example, what does it cost to acquire and keep a customer? How often does a customer return goods, require special deliveries, make service inquiries, or demand unique services? What is the cost of each of these extra activities? The analysis must attempt to consider all the costs associated with a customer or class of customer.

Customer profitability analysis is often done for several timeframes, ranging from a year to a lifetime. Managers can use this profitability information to structure or restructure the customer mix or to modify customer strategy. Assume the delivery costs for a customer or a group of similar customers are too high. The shipping firm may work with customers to restructure how it makes deliveries and thus convert unprofitable customers into profitable customers.

When the analysis is complete, it is common to classify customers into groups based on their relative profitability. A high-revenue, low-cost customer is more valuable than one that generates high revenues but also has high costs. The least desirable customer is one that generates low revenues and high costs. It would make sense to eliminate this customer from the mix unless it can be made more profitable.

Reasons to Rationalize Which Customers to Focus On

Recall from Exhibit 9.2 that managers want to know the value of maintaining customer loyalty. Typically, loyal customers buy more and may be somewhat less price-sensitive. This customer provides an ongoing stream of profits without the firm's having to incur the costs of acquiring a new customer. In fact, the loyal customer may even help the firm generate new customers. Actions taken to encourage customer loyalty may also help move other customers into a higher level of customer profitability.

A firm may choose to keep a low-profit customer. Demographics might suggest that this customer will become more profitable over time, perhaps because of anticipated growth or higher income levels. Cultivation of this customer for the generation of higher lifetime profits is more important than avoiding short-term losses or low profitability. A firm may also choose to keep low-profit customers in the short term because a significant percentage of costs are committed in the near term, and there are not opportunities to acquire higher-profit customers immediately. It is essential to find ways to lower costs or modify unprofitable customers' behavior so it makes sense to retain them.

VALUE OF CUSTOMER PROFITABILITY ANALYSIS

Customer profitability analysis forces decision makers to identify and understand the activities required to serve customers, evaluate how customers behave, and associate costs with these activities and behaviors. Customer relationships are understood and valued, as there is a focus on ensuring customer satisfaction rather than just minimizing costs. However, customer profitability analysis also shows why it is unwise to simply provide whatever the customer wants. It imposes discipline on management decisions by making the cost to serve visible throughout the firm. More focus is put on what is best for the organization than on what is best for a functional area such as marketing or production.

There is an increasing emphasis on developing customer costing techniques. This emphasis stems from the tremendous diversity in the services being performed for downstream trading partners and the recognition that this diversity results in major differences in workload, resources, and costs to the firm. Managers believe that in some instances these differences make customers unprofitable to the firm, but their existing costing systems do not possess the capability to isolate costs by customer.

The traditional general ledger cost systems employed by most firms focus on product costing and do not have the capability to accurately determine the costs of serving different customers. A product costing approach relies on a limited number of cost drivers such as labor or materials to assign costs. Traditional information systems typically do not give much attention to customer-related costs, such as order filling, sales support, billing and collection, credit checking, or warehousing. Customer-related costs are aggregated under sales, general, and administrative (SG&A) expenses and, as an indirect cost, are arbitrarily allocated to products based on a proportion of direct labor, sales volume, number of units produced, square feet/meters, or some other basis. Such measures do not represent good measures of what it costs to serve customers who make diverse demands on supply chain activities. To be more specific, they violate costing's causality principle.

Activity-Based Costing (ABC) Resolves Deficiencies with Traditional Costing

Customer-driven costs, while often large, are often invisible to decision makers and thus do not receive sufficient management attention. The use of arbitrary cost allocation methods provides managers with little visibility and insight into what drives these costs or how diversity in customer requirements or behavior drives differences in customer costs and profitability. Customers often have a greater effect than products on how many costs are incurred. This situation is especially true in customer-facing processes or functions such as sales, marketing, logistics, and customer service. Most managers do not have accurate information regarding customer profitability because of the problems associated with traditional costing.[2]

Customer profitability analysis overcomes the limitations of traditional costing through the use of activity-based costing (ABC). Firms that employ or develop customer profitability analysis rely on an activity-based approach for assigning costs to distribution channels and customers. ABC determines the cost of work activities performed to service customers and uses cost drivers to assign the cost of those resources consumed by these activities. An activity-based approach permits the assignment of indirect costs (e.g., SG&A), commonly referred to as "overhead," to customers through the use of activity drivers to calculate unit-level cost consumption rates such as cost per customer order, cost per delivery, cost per sales call, and cost per customer return. These activities can be expanded to reflect the diversity of customer requirements. Exhibit 9.3 shows how the order-picking activity could be further disaggregated to reflect differences by customer orders.

EXHIBIT 9.3 Developing Activities to Capture Differences in Customer Requirements or Behavior

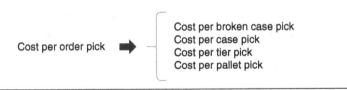

Activity-based costing (ABC) is a management accounting method that reasonably accurately traces the consumption of an organization's resource expenses (e.g., salaries, supplies) into its products, SKUs, service lines, and to

the types and kinds of distribution channels and customer segments that place varying degrees of workload demand on the company. It should no longer be acceptable not to have a rational system of assigning so-called nontraceable costs to their sources of origin—the resource expenses. ABC is that system. Yet, sadly, many companies still do not use ABC. The consequence is that managers are receiving flawed and misleading cost information, which means misleading profit margin information.

The use of an activity-based costing (ABC) approach substantially increases the accuracy of cost and profitability information provided to management. It replaces the broadly averaged cost allocations by tracing and assigning how resource expenses are consumed by outputs using cause-and-effect relationships with cost drivers. Exhibit 9.4 compares the costs and profitability obtained from a traditional approach versus an activity-based approach. The traditional approach assigns SG&A expenses to each customer based on their proportion of sales revenue. The ABC approach assigns the components within SG&A based on actual consumption. These results send very different signals to management. The traditional approach implies that indirect costs vary in direct proportion with sales. Consequently, any additional sales volume would appear to be equally effective in increasing the firm's profitability. However, not all customers are created the same, and their behavior will drive a different mix of activities being performed within the firm. The activity-based analysis traces costs to customers based on how they consume these different activities. The results of an activity-based analysis may produce dramatic shifts from the profitability reported by traditional cost systems. These differences are driven by the extent of the firm's indirect, customer service costs, and the service demands placed on the firm by its different customers.

Customer profitability analysis provides powerful information that supports management decision making. At the individual firm level, managers can manage costs and revenues to improve the profitability of individual firms. At the aggregate level, customer profitability can assist managers in two areas. Customer profitability analysis provides insights regarding the firm's risk and its dependence on specific customers or market segments. Management can use the analysis to develop market segments based on profitability and develop corresponding strategies.

Management can also use the results to determine how best to manage revenues and costs to improve overall profitability. Without a customer profitability analysis, managers do not have a true picture of how individual customers affect the firm's costs. As a result, the greatest benefit of the analysis is accurate information regarding which customers are profitable and

EXHIBIT 9.4 Comparison of Customer Profitability Computed Using Traditional versus Activity-Based Approaches

Customer Profitability (Traditional Costing)	Company	Cust A	Cust B	Cust C
Sales ($M)	20,000	4,500	5,500	10,000
Less returns & allowances	2,000	0,250	0,500	1,250
Net Sales	**18,000**	**4,250**	**5,000**	**8,750**
Cost of Goods Sold	9,500	2,200	2,600	4,700
Manufacturing Contribution	**8,500**	**2,050**	**2,400**	**4,050**
Sales, General & Administrative	5,700	1,283	1,568	2,850
Controllable Margin	**2,800**	**0,768**	**0,833**	**1,200**
Customer Profitability (Activity Based)	Company	Cust A	Cust B	Cust C
Sales ($M)	20,000	5,000	6,000	9,000
Less returns & allowances	2,000	250	500	1,250
Net Sales	**18,000**	**4,250**	**5,500**	**8,750**
Cost of Goods Sold	9,500	2,200	2,600	4,700
Manufacturing Contribution	**8,500**	**2,050**	**2,900**	**4,050**
Variable selling and logistics costs:				
Sales & advertising	1,200	0,310	0,290	0,600
Transportation	2,000	0,200	0,250	1,550
Warehousing	0,500	0,050	0,075	0,375
Order processing	0,300	0,020	0,060	0,220
Customer relationship	0,700	0,100	0,200	0,400
Inventory carrying costs	1,000	0,100	0,200	0,700
Segment contribution margin:	**2,800**	**1,270**	**1,825**	**0,205**

which are not. Managers can use this information to adapt or develop strategies to make underperforming customers more profitable. Customer profitability analysis might reveal that many of a company's smaller customers are unprofitable. By "breaking even" on these customers, the firm could substantially improve overall profitability. Managers could then respond by using a lower-cost delivery process and by offering customers incentives to use a less expensive order placement process. These changes would enable the firm to improve the profitability of these customers without degrading customer service or losing sales.

EXHIBIT 9.5   Cumulative Plot of Customer Profitability

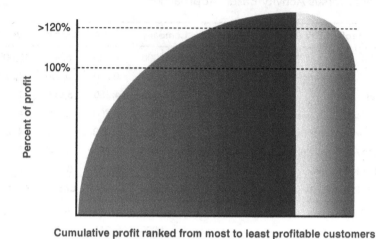

Cumulative profit ranked from most to least profitable customers

Source: Adapted from Gary Cokins, *Activity-Based Cost Management: An Executive's Guide* (New York: John Wiley & Sons, 2001), p. 103. Used with permission of the author.

Cumulative Profit Graphs: The "Whale Curve"

Customer profitability analyses can be used to determine the risks and dependence existing in a firm's customer base. A cumulative plot of customer profitability from most profitable to least profitable is used to demonstrate the level of risk and dependence (Exhibit 9.5). These graphs are often referred to as "whale curves" because they have the shape of a whale.

For example, a review may show that a relatively small proportion of customers accounts for all the firm's profits. These firms subsidize the costs incurred in supporting the remaining firms. In this situation, the firm is highly dependent on a small number of firms for its profitability. Managers need to mitigate their risk by focusing on these customers. These firms will be targeted for higher service levels and sales and marketing retention efforts. In addition, managers should attempt to reduce their dependence on these firms by increasing the profitability of the remaining customers. They can do this by increasing the revenues from these customers, changing their behavior to lower costs, or developing stronger customer relationships. A different plot of customer profitability may reveal an opportunity to improve profitability by focusing only on a small number of very unprofitable. By focusing on just these firms, managers can significantly improve profitability by determining what is causing the cost-to-serve to exceed revenues and then taking appropriate action.

Customer profitability analysis can be used to segment the firm's market based on profitability. Managers can review customers in different categories to determine whether the customers with similar profitability share a set of attributes. Based on this analysis, managers can use the profile to target customers with similar attributes. They understand what makes these customers profitable and the requirements to serve them. In addition, managers can recognize which customers to avoid if they match the profile of unprofitable customers. This recognition gives managers an edge in targeting potential customers—an edge that their competitors are unlikely to replicate, given the extent of customer profitability analysis used in most supply chains.

Expanding the CFO's Service to Managers

Much has been written about the increasing role of CFOs as strategic advisors and their shift from bean counter to bean grower. Now is the time for the CFO's accounting and finance function to expand beyond financial accounting, reporting, governance responsibilities, and cost control. They can support the supply chain management, sales, and marketing functions by helping them target the more attractive customers to retain, grow, and win back and to acquire the relatively more profitable ones.

NOTES

1. The steps listed are taken from Shahid Ansari, Jan Bell, and Thomas Klammer, "Customer Profitability Analysis," in the modular series *Management Accounting: A Strategic Focus* (Ansari, Bell, Klammer: Lulu.com). This module includes a detailed number example of the customer profitability analysis process.

2. Douglas M. Lambert, "Which Customers Are the Most Profitable?" *CSCMP's Supply Chain Quarterly* 2, no. 4 (2008); Reinaldo Guerreiro, Sérgio Rodriqus Bio, and Elvira Vazquez Villamor Merschman, "Cost-to-Serve Measurement and Customer Profitability Analysis," *The International Journal of Logistics Management* 19, no. 2 (2008): 389.

CHAPTER 10

Tools for Reducing Supply Chain Costs

S UPPLY CHAIN COSTING ENCOMPASSES a variety of tools and software technologies. The appropriate method often varies with the question being asked, the position of the firm across the supply chain, and different circumstances that exist in the firm or supply chain. Some cost tools are particularly useful for improving the supply chain cost structure, while others are more valuable for cost planning, understanding profit margins, or as part of a strategic analysis of supply chain costs. Certain tools work well in mass production environments, while others better support lean or manufacture-to-order production methods.

Considerable overlap exists among several different costing tools, and most decision-making teams are likely to find that they will extensively use only a few of the many possible costing methodologies. How cost information influences employee behavior and their decisions may cause different management teams to prefer alternative tools.

A key part of supply chain costing is measuring the amount of costs incurred in the "as is" state. Managers at all levels and across trading partners need to understand what and why things currently cost what they do. Executives and managers seek to answer questions such as:

- "Where does the firm make or lose money?"
- "What is the landed cost of the product at the customer's receiving dock?"

- ■ "How well do actual costs align with standard costs?"
- ■ "Where is there the greatest opportunity for cost reduction?"
- ■ "Which customers are relatively more attractive to retain, grow, win back, or acquire?"

With significant data restructuring, historical and descriptive supply chain costing can partially answer these questions. The need for information in a different form explains, in part, the growing popularity of applying activity-based costing (ABC) principles to supplement traditional direct costing. Likewise, the growth in diversity and variation in areas such as products, service lines, distribution channels, customers, and so on has caused a relative increase in the indirect and shared expenses compared to the direct expenses that an organization incurs to manage the resulting complexity. These cost increases have led to greater management emphasis on understanding indirect and shared costs and a growing reliance on information technology.

For example, a manager wanting to know what variations in products or services cost needs good information on the direct and indirect costs of the product or service. The cost is "what" the manager wants to know, but management also needs to know what to do with the cost information—this is the "so what" question. Without good information on current costs, conclusions are being made on intuition, flawed and misleading information, or office politics.

The following segments provide an overview of several cost reduction tools, with a focus on standard costing and activity-based costing (ABC). These tools expand management's cost visibility outside the firm and over broader segments of the supply chain. They accelerate or focus on particular types of costs, help stimulate questions that lead to discovery of better ways to measure costs, and encourage discussion and debate about potential changes that can reduce costs. The information these tools provide can often indicate an obvious need for change, even without deeper analysis. A major problem with these tools (beyond those specifically linked to individual tools) is that they may provide insufficient information to validate the impact of suggested changes on overall supply chain costs, particularly because of the lack of a specific focus on future costs. This requires budgeting and what-if analysis so there is a predictive view of costs. These tools are discussed in Chapter 11.

STANDARD COSTING

Standards are pervasive in organizations. Companies such as UPS have standards for a wide variety of delivery functions. Others, such as pharmaceutical companies, conform to strict quality standards in drug development and production. Firms have many cost-related standards, particularly for purchased goods and services. Standard costing is a well-established management accounting tool. It has traditionally been applied primarily in manufacturing for the financial balance sheet valuation of inventories and income statement cost of goods sold (COGS). It is also used to analyze and control costs, primarily the direct costs.

Firms demonstrating the greatest cost knowledge have expanded standard costing to incorporate nonmanufacturing processes. Their standard cost systems include major supply chain processes such as order fulfillment, demand management, customer service, research and development, and returns management. These cost systems are able to distinguish how these activities are performed when conducting transactions with different suppliers, customers, or distribution channels. Obtaining this capability requires the development of several thousand standard costs to reflect the many ways an activity could be performed. The ability to capture these cost differences facilitates cost-to-serve and customer profitability analyses. The application of standard costing to a wider range of processes has positioned these firms to better develop, analyze, and control supply chain costs.

EXHIBIT 10.1 Essentials of Standard Costing

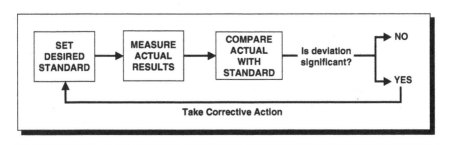

Source: Adapted from Shahid Ansari, Jan Bell, and Thomas Klammer, "Customer Profitability Analysis," in the modular series *Management Accounting: A Strategic Focus* (Ansari, Bell, Klammer: Lulu.com).

A standard cost is a predetermined cost. It is an estimate of the cost of resources an organization expects to consume to produce one unit of a product or service. In a standard cost system, costs actually incurred are compared with a predetermined estimate of what cost should be required. The difference is a cost variance from what management expected. Variances are reviewed, the reason for significant variance is identified, and corrective action is taken when appropriate. Exhibit 10.1 is a depiction of a standard cost system.

Standard costing is particularly effective when the production or service process is understood, stable, and optimized, such as in an automobile manufacturing line. Standard cost systems were originally created for use in mass production environments where there are repeated purchases of the same materials, many repetitive labor tasks, and dedicated equipment that is used for a single product. Traditional standard costing is less useful in make-to-order and lean production environments where constant change in the products or services make establishing standards for labor or material purchases more difficult. Likewise, standard cost systems historically were not widely used in service industries, such as banking and insurance companies, due to the difficulty in capturing the performance and cost data needed to develop standards and actual costs.

Firms on the leading edge of supply chain costing have recognized that there are many repetitive elements in their supply chain processes and therefore support the use of standard costing. Even as supply chain processes have grown increasingly lean, management recognizes that many of the same activities meet the requirements for standard costing. In many firms and processes, the development of standard costs for these activities makes sense. Typically, the approach taken in developing standard costs parallels the methodology employed in activity-based costing. ABC applies activity driver quantities primarily for the indirect expenses that provide the cost rates.

A team might begin by mapping the key processes and supporting activities performed by the firm. Then identify the resources consumed in performing each of these activities to determine total activity and process costs. Based on normal capacity and output levels, the team can calculate a standard cost for each activity. These activities would be at a sufficiently aggregate level so that individuals are not required to track or report their work hours by activity, although such a refinement may be an integral part of the process as supply chain costing efforts move forward.

Controlling and Reducing Costs

Managers can use standards to control costs and to drive cost reductions. Actual costs can be routinely compared to standard costs to ensure performance is meeting expectations. Major variances would be investigated to determine their cause and decide whether any management action is warranted to improve performance. The process of mapping work flows and determining the resources consumed can be beneficial. Additional benefits come from using the standards to control costs and to drive cost reductions. This information can challenge the need to perform some activities and suggest eliminating activities by changing procedures or business practices. Examples in a manufacturer are changing the warehouse layout, modifying the handling of material and information, improving quality, and reducing the number of times a part or document is handled. Management can target high-cost activities for reengineering studies or outsourcing. They can continually review the activities to ensure that their performance is consistent with the overall process strategy, and to determine how to further streamline the processes by reducing additional costs or time. Budgets for the upcoming year can be developed based on forecasted activity level multiplied by the standard cost to perform that activity.

The development and maintenance of standard costs creates a unique costing competency within firms on the leading edge of supply chain costing. Management not only knows the cost to perform activities and processes, they also recognize how their trading partners' behavior affects activity performance and costs. Managers can have a much better idea of their trading partners' costs than their management counterparts in those firms. They can attribute this knowledge to the work done in developing their standard costs and in working to further reduce the time and cost required in performing these activities. They can then work with their customers or suppliers to reduce costs across both firms. Although managers do not necessarily need to exchange cost information with their trading partners, they can use their knowledge of their costs and their trading partners' costs to make more effective decisions. This knowledge enables supply chain managers to gain a competitive advantage over competitors who lack this information.

Managers at all levels in firms can know the key cost measures for their area of responsibility. They can make decisions based on process and activity costs as well as customer profitability analyses. The standard cost system promotes a cost-conscious culture within firms. Although cost is important, management should not base their decisions solely on costs. They should consider cost to be a tool to assist them in making better decisions as to how to improve profitability and evaluate different strategies.

Standard costing is not particularly useful for managing committed costs, such as rent or depreciation, or discretionary costs, such as advertising. Managers should carefully evaluate where in their supply chain processes standard costing makes sense.

ACTIVITY-BASED COSTING (ABC)

Activity-based costing (ABC) is a technique used to assign the direct and indirect expenses of a firm first to the work activities that employees and assets, such as equipment, perform. It then assigns activity costs to the products, service lines, customers, or supply chains consuming those activities. Costs that can be directly associated with a service or process are not a problem. But currently, manufacturing and distribution deal with broadly diverse products and SKUs. Managing this diversity is complex, and the indirect and shared expenses often represent substantial portions of a firm's total costs.

The primary value of ABC stems from its capability to more directly assign indirect expenses. ABC links costs to what causes those costs. Activities are identified, and the resources' expenses used by these activities are measured. ABC then assigns the activity costs to cost objects, such as a service, product, distribution channel, or customer, based on the activities used by that cost object.

A complete implementation of an ABC system is often perceived as being extremely complex. But it does not need to be. Effective ABC systems can be right-sized to a level that is good enough, with reasonable visibility and accuracy, to support good decisions. Implementing ABC can be accomplished in a few weeks, not in months, using a rapid prototyping method discussed later in the chapter. ABC is a management accounting method and does not require the precision and accuracy required for external compliance statutory financial reporting. A right-sized ABC system results when we recognize that one quickly gets to diminishing returns on extra cost accuracy for the incremental additional administrative effort to collect, validate, and calculate the data, and we stop when the additional accuracy is not worth the effort. Effectively ABC uses the Pareto 80/20 rule, asking "Is the higher climb worth the better view?"

The results from an effective ABC system can be used to continually review for process improvement opportunities. Costs across all business processes are assigned to products, service lines, distribution channels, and customers. An ABC analysis can then be used to develop the standard costs for each activity. A firm can share and exchange some of its cost information with select customers and suppliers to achieve cost savings.

Some confuse the term *activity-based management* (ABM) with the term *activity-based costing* (ABC). To clarify, ABC is the math of calculating costs. ABM is the actions and decisions after the ABC data is made available.

ABC principles can provide data for managers to do special studies of what activities cost in specified cost object areas such as a department, internal process, or throughout the supply chain. Activity analysis is essential for improving supply chain costing.

Implementing ABC with Rapid Prototyping

ABC rapid prototyping followed by iterative remodeling of each of ABC's prior model's results has been proven to be a superior approach to successfully implementing and sustaining ABC systems. It is a way to overcome the temptation (and habit by accountants or consultants) to construct an ABC system that is too large, too complex, and too detailed prior to the organization's ability to absorb what ABC is all about and how it can work for the organization. ABC rapid prototyping is accomplished in just a few days at a workshop facilitated by a skilled ABC practitioner. It is also an effective way to drive out the natural fear and resistance to ABC through training and participation.

EXHIBIT 10.2   Rapid Prototyping with Iterative Remodeling (crawl, walk, run, fly)

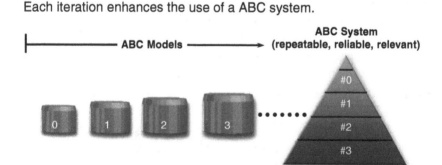

Make your mistakes early and often, not later
when the system is too hard to change.

Source: Adapted from Gary Cokins, *Performance Management: Integrating Strategy Execution, Methodologies, Risk, and Analytics* (New York: John Wiley & Sons, 2001), p. 73. Copyright Gary Cokins. Used with permission of the author.

ABC rapid prototyping is effective because the organization is modeling their own organization's expenses and calculated costs, and not a fictitious one's. Employees, managers, and executives relate to it because they recognize the people, processes, work, and outputs (e.g., services). People learn better through doing.

ABC rapid prototyping is an implementation approach where the initial ABC model 0 is immediately followed with iterative remodeling of the same expenses and calculated costs included in the prior model, but deeper and with more resolution and visibility. Any issues related to source input data can be quickly flushed out. Exhibit 10.2 gives a sense of the process for a succession of models plus some key benefits. Iterative ABC prototyping with expanding granularity and more detail (but same scope) accelerates learning about model design and cost behavior. The exhibit illustrates how the ABC models can eventually become a permanent and reliable production ABC system within a few weeks, not months as is often perceived.

 ## ABC FUNDAMENTALS

ABC differs from traditional cost accounting because it focuses first on work activities and then on products and service lines and ultimately on distribution channels and customers. Multiple activity cost drivers are used to more accurately calculate product or service costs. Exhibit 10.3 illustrates a subset of an enterprise-wide ABC system focusing on how indirect expenses, such as those for supervision, are first flowed to activities such as put-away or setup and then reassigned to the cost object, in this illustration to products handled in a distribution center for different divisions.

EXHIBIT 10.3 Activity-Based Costing Assignment Process

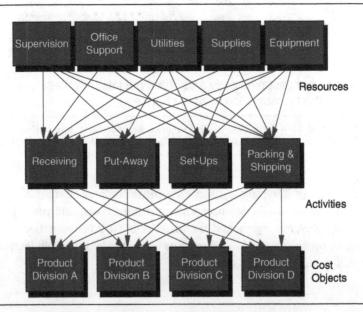

Traditional methods of allocating indirect expenses use broad averages such as sales volume, number of units produced, or number of labor hours. This is like spreading peanut butter across bread. None of those types of cost allocation factors reflect the cause-and-effect relationship between the cost objects and the work activities they consume. When ABC costs are compared to the traditional and simplistic costing that violates costing's *causality principle*, one discovers that some products or SKUs are substantially overcosted (relative to correctly tracing the resource expense consumption) and the others must be undercosted. This is because it is a zero-sum error calculation. The total expenses must reconcile exactly with costs of the cost objects. Hence, traditional costing results in flawed and misleading costs and profit margins. Sadly, managers use that information to support their decisions.

The ABC method models cost reality by understanding that the outputs, such as products and SKUs, first place demands on work activities belonging to processes (e.g., moving parts, inspecting SKUs), and then the workloads draw on the various resource capacities and their expenses spending. With ABC the resource expenses are first assigned to work activities, and then the activity costs are reassigned to the outputs, called *final cost objects*. ABC traces the outputs to the work activities based on activity cost drivers, such as "the number of SKUs inspected." In this way, ABC adheres to the accounting *causality principle*—the resource and work activity consumption are proportionate to a cause-and-effect relationship with the outputs they supply expenses to.

In complex, support-intensive organizations, there can be a substantial chain of indirect activities prior to the work activities that eventually trace into the final cost objects. These chains result in activity-to-activity cost assignments, and they rely on *intermediate* activity drivers in the same way that final cost objects rely on activity drivers to reassign costs into them based on their diversity and variation.

The *direct costing* of indirect expenses is no longer an insurmountable problem, given the existence of integrated commercial ABC software. ABC allows intermediate direct costing to a local process, to an internal customer, or to a required component that is causing the demand for work. That is, ABC cost flow networks no longer have to "hit the wall" from limited spreadsheet software that is restricted by columns-to-rows math and the lack of visibility to see how the costs flow. Commercial ABC software is arterial in design. Via this expense assignment and tracing network, ABC reassigns 100% of the resources' expenses into the final products, service lines, channels, customers, and business-sustaining costs. In short, ABC connects customers to the unique resources they consume—and in proportion to their consumption.

ABC Multiple-Stage Cost Assignment Network

Exhibit 10.4 is a snapshot view of the business conducted during a specific time period. It depicts an ABC cost assignment network that consists of the three modules connected by cost assignment paths calculating the cost of cost objects (e.g., outputs, product lines, service lines, customers).

Resources are at the top of the cost assignment network. They provide the capacity to perform work and represent all the available means that work activities can draw on. Resources supply capacity to be used or unused. Unused and excess capacity may be needed for surges in sales volume. Resource expenses can be thought of as the organization's checkbook to pay employees or for purchases from suppliers: money exits the treasury. Examples of resource expenses are salaries, operating supplies, or electrical power. These are the period's cash outlays and amortized cash outlays, such as for depreciation, from a prior period. It is during this step that the applicable resource drivers are developed as the mechanism to convey resource costs to the work activities that consume the resources.

"Expenses" must be distinguished from "costs." They are not the same thing. All costs are *calculated* costs. It is important to recognize that assumptions are always involved in the conversion and translation of expenses into costs. The assumptions stipulate the basis for the calculation. Expenses occur at the point of acquisition with third parties, including employee wages. This is when money (or its obligation) exits the company's treasury. In that special moment, "value" does not fluctuate—it is permanently recorded as part of a legal exchange. From the expenses, all costs are calculated representations of how those expenses flow through and are consumed by work activities and into outputs of work. In sum, resources are traced to work activities. It is during this step that the applicable resource drivers are developed as the mechanism to convey resource expenses into the activity costs.

A popular basis for tracing or assigning resource expenses is the time (e.g., number of minutes) that people or equipment spend performing activities. Note that the terms *tracing* or *assigning* are preferable to the term *allocation*. This is because many people associate allocation with a redistribution of costs that have little to no correlation between source and destinations—the "spreading of peanut butter across bread." Hence, to some organizations, overhead cost allocations are arbitrary and are viewed cynically when they violate accounting's *causality* principle.

The activity module is where work is performed. It is where resources are converted into some type of output. The activity cost assignment step contains

EXHIBIT 10.4 ABC/M Cost Assignment Network

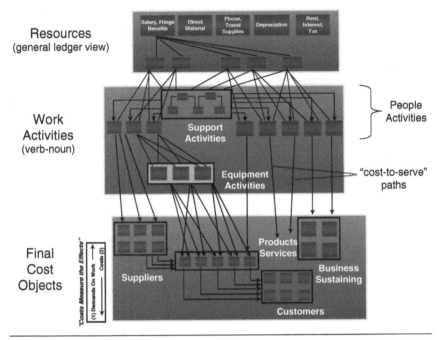

Source: Adapted from Gary Cokins, *Activity-Based Cost Management: An Executive's Guide* (New York: John Wiley & Sons, 2001), p. 53. Used with permission of the author.

the structure to assign activity costs to cost objects (or to other activities), utilizing activity drivers as the mechanism to accomplish this assignment.

Cost objects are at the bottom of the cost assignment network and represent the broad variety of outputs and services where costs accumulate. The customers are *the final-final cost objects*; their existence ultimately creates the need for a cost structure. For some supply chain cost models, the customer may be a retail store or branch outlet. Cost objects are the persons or things that benefit from incurring work activities. Examples of cost objects are products, service lines, distribution channels, customers, and outputs of internal processes. Cost objects can be thought of as the "for what" or "for whom" work is done. Once established, the cost assignment network is useful in determining how the diversity and variation of things, such as different products or various types of customers, can be detected and translated into how they uniquely consume activity costs.

A major advantage of ABC is that it displays the work activity costs that are buried in traditional costing's lump-sum (hidden) and inaccurately calculated costs of indirect and shared expenses. It also shifts attention to reducing the frequency or quantity of the activity driver as the lever to reduce the costs.

A disadvantage to ABC is that it requires the collection of additional data, specifically the estimation or tracking of resource time to work activities and the activity cost driver quantities to the outputs. However, this extra administrative effort is not as onerous as sometimes perceived if these estimates focus on the transactional data for the relevant "vital few."

EXHIBIT 10.5 Activity-Based Costing Captures Cost Differences Driven by Products, Customers, or Supply Chains

Activity	Activity Cost	Activity Volume	Cost/Activity
Process Returns	$386,418.86	2,700	$143.12
Hold Inventory	$7,837,909.66	10,500	$746.47
Perform Consolidation Moves	$241,446.08	48,000	$5.03
Pull/Putaway Inventory	$583,079.04	70,000	$8.33
Pick/Build Pallets	$235,229.17	20,000	$11.76
Pick Case	$726,338.24	11,000,000	$0.07
Pick Tier	$173,723.04	81,292	$2.14
Pick Pallet	$182,084.56	14,000	$13.01
Process Shipments	$632,682.25	1,000,000	$0.63
Process Promotions	$186,084.56	68	$2,736.54
Receive Production	$1,196,708.51	65,432	$18.29
Accept/Dispatch	$216,081.06	18,509	$11.67
Load Trucks	$912,728.03	14,950	$61.05
Ship Interplant Transfers	$2,709,324.23	2,582	$1,049.31
Receive Interplant Transfers	$164,976.10	1,750	$94.27
Ship UPS	$410,074.93	38,436	$10.67
Ship by Cust Pickup	$172,144.61	62,790	$2.74
Ship Direct TL	$1,919,303.22	1,650	$1,163.21
Ship Direct LTL	$1,098,932.95	8,427	$130.41
Ship Pool/TL	$4,095,749.30	4,100	$998.96
Process EDI Order	$110,536.15	652,446	$0.17
Process Telephone/Fax Order	$649,934.44	347,554	$1.87
Perform Billing	$151,511.03	1,000,000	$0.15

Despite the effort required to implement ABC, the technique appears well suited for supporting supply chain costing. ABC provides the capability to isolate costs at the activity and process levels. The use of attributes attached to costs enables managers to distinguish between the direct and indirect cost components to determine how volume or other variables actually drive costs. Much of the complexity existing in supply chains is driven by the differences and variations in products (e.g., colors, sizes, and ranges), volumes, customer requirements, and supplier capabilities. The ability to discern how differences affect costs will require the use of multiple activities. For example, the order fulfillment process may involve deliveries by truckload, less than truckload, or parcel. Some orders may be full pallet, mixed pallet, tiers, or cases (Exhibit 10.5). To accurately determine these differences in costs, multiple activities must be used to capture the cost differences.

LANDED COSTING

Landed costing captures the costs of freight and other activities performed to move product from its origin to its final destination. A landed cost analysis would include freight, quality, receiving, material handling, administration, technology, and facility costs. *Landed costing* is a term for determining the cost of the final cost object, such as an SKU at a retail outlet's receiving dock or store shelf. This is a well-known cost approach within the broader scope of supply chain costing. As commonly used, landed costs appear to focus primarily on direct or readily traceable costs such as purchase price, freight, custom duties and tariffs, commissions, insurance, and material handling.[1]

Firms sourcing from international origins or those using multiple distribution channels have interest in landed cost models. Rising energy prices and global sourcing focus management attention on the importance of this costing technique.

Management uses the information from landed cost analysis when making decisions in many areas. These include choices related to port of entry; the use of transportation intermediaries; and selections of modal, intermodal, carrier, and dray services. Landed cost data is useful in choosing when to distribute via direct store delivery, distribution center, and/or cross-dock facilities. It is also a factor in shipment size decisions, such as individual shipment versus consolidated shipment, less-than-truckload versus truckload, and less-than-container-load versus container load.

The analysis performed by a large retailer demonstrates the information required to perform a landed cost analysis. The activities captured will vary depending on the processes used by a firm, the cost trade-offs exercised by management, and the level of cost and nonfinancial information available in the firm's information management EDI systems. The retailer's management used a landed cost analysis to determine the most effective network for replenishing retail stores. The analysis considered alternative networks, including direct store delivery, shipments through company-run distribution centers, and the use of company-run cross-dock facilities. Since many fixed costs would not change under these scenarios, the analysis encompassed only direct costs. Exhibits 10.6, 10.7, and 10.8 illustrate the type of data this firm used in its landed cost analysis.

EXHIBIT 10.6   Cross-Dock Facility Activities, Cost Drivers, and Activity Costs

Cross-Dock Facility*	Activity	Cost Driver	Cost per Activity Driver in $
	Pallet handling	Per pallet	
	Pallet breakbulk	Per SKU	
	Pallet consolidation	Per SKU	
	Planning and scheduling	Per shipment	
	Transloading	Per shipment	
		Per pallet	
		Per carton/unit	

* inbound and outbound activities similar to DC operation but with different activity costs assigned

The cost information required to support this analysis was not readily available within the retailer's cost management system. The team used an activity-based approach to develop standard costs for each activity driver. In several instances, the team found that the activity volumes needed for the analysis were not captured by their cost system or their transportation or warehouse management systems. As a result, they had to manually comb through documents to obtain the required information. Based on their analysis, management decided to employ cross-docks in their network. However, they required their suppliers to use EDI to make scheduling of carriers and shipments through the cross-dock facility work effectively.

EXHIBIT 10.7 Distribution Center Activities, Cost Drivers, and Activity Costs

Costs Incurred by Distribution Center	Activity	Cost Driver	Cost per Activity Driver in $
Inbound freight	Direct charge	Per CL	
		Per LCL	
		Per pallet	
		Per carton	
Receiving			
	EDI by PO	Per PO	
	EDI by PO line	Per PO line	
	Scheduling and matching to PO	Per PO line	
	Claims	Per claim	
	ASN by shipment	Per shipment	
	Documentation processing	Per shipment	
	Pallet unload/count/processing	Per pallet	
	Mixed pallet unload & processing	Per line	
	Carton unload & processing	Per carton	
	Piece/unit unload & processing	Per piece/unit	
	Adjustments	Per adjustment	
Putaway and storage (DC)			
	Pallet putaway	Per pallet	
	Case putaway	Per case	
	Piece/unit putaway	Per unit	
Inventory	Pallet count	Per pallet	
	Case count	Per case	
	Piece count	Per line	
	Adjustments	Per adjustment	
Storage			
	Pallet storage	Per pallet	
	Case storage	Per sq ft/ location	
Order picking			
	Pallet pick	Per pallet	
	Case pick	Per case	

(Continued)

Costs Incurred by Distribution Center	Activity	Cost Driver	Cost per Activity Driver in $
	Broken case pick	Per unit/line	
	Re-packaging	Per carton	
	Mixed pallet build	Per pallet	
Inventory			
	Inventory carrying cost	Avg inventory per SKU	
Outbound transportation			
	PO scheduling	Per PO	
	ASN transmission	Per shipment	
	Dispatch	Per shipment	
	Documentation processing	Per shipment	
	Outbound freight	Direct charge	
	Pallet count/load	Per pallet	
	Mixed pallet count/load	Per mixed pallet	
	Case count/load	Per case	
	Piece count/load	Per piece/unit	
	Packaging/shrinkwrap	Per line	

A landed cost analysis can be used to gain a competitive advantage. A trading company combined its knowledge of international sourcing and of transportation to develop a landed cost tool for its customers. The tool, an Excel-based spreadsheet, enables customers to select the mix of SKUs and quantities, based on weight and cube, that maximizes container utilization and produces an acceptable container load (CL) or less-than-container-load (LCL) rate. The customer can select the port of entry and mode choice to the final destination. The algorithms behind the screen calculate the total landed cost for the customer. The trading company has already determined the freight, handling, and container-stuffing costs by product, from its suppliers to their third-party consolidator that stuffs the containers, prepares customs documentation and notification, and drays the container to the origin port. Contracts with the shipping

EXHIBIT 10.8 Retail Activities, Cost Drivers, and Activity Costs

Costs Incurred by Retail Stores	Activity	Cost Driver	Cost per Activity Driver in $
Ordering and payment costs			
	Replenishment order	Per line	
	PO preparation	Per PO	
	EDI transmission by PO	Per PO	
	EDI transmission by PO line	Per PO line	
	Matching receipt to PO	Per PO line	
	claims	Per claim	
	Invoice processing and payment	Per invoice	
Receiving			
	Documentation	Per shipment	
	Pallet unload and inchecking	Per pallet	
	Mixed pallet unload and inchecking	Per line	
	Case unload and inchecking	Per case	
	Piece/unit unload and inchecking	Per piece/unit	
	Adjustments	Per adjustment	
Putaway			
	Pallet putaway	Per pallet	
	Case putaway	Per case	
Stocking			
	Replenishment	Per SKU	
	Displays	Per SKU	
Inventory			
	Inventory carrying cost	Avg inventory per SKU	

lines, intermodal marketing companies, and drayage companies generate the international and domestic freight costs. This capability has produced a unique competitive advantage by enabling customers to maximize container utilization to lower their costs, to compare the total landed cost of importing through different ports, and to know what their total landed cost will be at the time they place the order. Due to the unique capabilities within this spreadsheet, the trading company has patented the spreadsheet design.

 ## KAIZEN COSTING

Kaizen costing supports continual improvement and cost reduction for items in current production and processes. Kaizen costing is simply a systematic approach that makes use of information from multiple costing tools.

The kaizen costing process begins by targeting a product or process for continuous improvement. Targeting may result from quality, time, cost, or flexibility issues associated with the process or product. If a significant effort is anticipated, a kaizen event may be designated and a specialized, cross-functional team may be established. The team typically begins with a cost reduction target based on feedback from marketing or customer service regarding the value proposition that needs to be afforded to the customer or end user. The team examines opportunities with the product or process to reduce costs without detracting from the value proposition. In many instances, the improvement effort improves quality while obtaining a lower cost. Exhibit 10.9 illustrates some sources for originating cost reduction opportunities.

The results of the kaizen event are documented in a standardized format for review by the controller or CFO. The documentation ensures that any cost savings are recognized in the standard cost system, or that the recommended actions will indeed produce a cost savings to the firm. An activity-based analysis may be used to identify changes in resource consumption or to identify any released indirect or direct resources. In many instances, the projected cost savings are "soft," in that the firm will benefit from the recommendation, but cost savings may not necessarily occur (i.e., there is no effect on the bottom line).

EXHIBIT 10.9 Cost Reduction Opportunities

Labor reduction or elimination due to fewer handlings or a simplified process requiring less processing time

Commonality of parts with other items—eliminates specialized items from being produced or purchased

Material or parts price reductions by ordering from a different supplier, negotiating a lower price, or working with the supplier to reduce their costs

Specifications exceeding actual requirements and increasing costs

Freight, packaging, material handling, and inventory—do opportunities exist within logistics to reduce costs or eliminate cycle and safety stocks?

Alternate materials—can lighter or less expensive materials be used without compromising form, fit, and function?

Waste—can scrap or rework be eliminated through a process change or specification?

Complexity—can fewer parts, drawings, varieties, SKUs, etc. be eliminated to generate fewer transactions and inventory?

Warranty and returns—what factors have driven warranty and other returns and how can these be eliminated?

Facility—by changing the process, handling, or storage, can space be released for other functions?

Quality—can the process be made more consistent with lower variance to make scheduling and throughput time more predictable?

NOTE

1. When focused on activities, landed cost analysis may be considered a subset or specific application of activity-based costing. The term *landed cost* is preferable to some because it does not carry some of the complexity connotations many associate with ABC.

CHAPTER 11

Supply Chain Cost Planning Tools

A S CUSTOMERS ORDER MORE or less volume of products, change the mix of a firm's products they use, or alter demands for services, several questions become critical for supply chain managers. What is the financial impact of these changes for the firm? What will future profit-and-loss statements look like? How will profit margins change? If a change is made, what will be the impact on resources and future expenses?

When questions like these are asked, one needs more than a crystal ball to answer them. This is when the focus turns to the *predictive view* of supply chain costing. A variety of costing tools exist that are valuable for supply chain cost planning. This chapter examines several of these tools.

The best time to manage costs is before they are incurred. By carefully evaluating actions in advance, supply chain managers can avoid decisions that commit them to higher than necessary future costs. Modeling cost behavior, listening to customers, carefully evaluating value chain relationships, estimating future costs, analyzing the acquisition of capital assets, and focusing on core competencies are all important elements of cost planning.

Cost estimation is an inherent part of every supply chain costing tool. Measures of incurred costs are useful for predicting future costs. Budgeting, capital budgeting, target costing, and even simple cost volume profit models are each built on multiple types of cost estimation.

Cost volume profit (CVP) models are among the most widely understood and used cost planning tools. Managers use CVP models to help improve cost structures and to provide quick "go no-go" answers on projects. Powerful "what-if" models based on CVP allow managers to study the effects of changing prices and production quantities on costs and profits.

BUDGETING—USING WORK ACTIVITIES

The annual budget is the most widely used management accounting planning and control tool in most organizations. Budgeting is the primary tool that businesses use to help plan resource inflows and outflows and to maintain costs and profits at an acceptable level. A budget is a quantitative financial plan that requires both physical and financial estimates. For example, an estimate of the number of miles trucks will drive is converted into a financial estimate of fuel costs.

Ideally the budgeting process should require individuals to focus on what they do (their work activities) and on what resources (money, time, goods) they need to complete these activities. The budget is a tool that can be used to reach agreements on and commitments to pursue common objectives and then direct spending to items essential for meeting these objectives. The budget is where supply chain managers make their case for the resources they need. At their core, these budgets are about resource capacity planning—the ability to convert and reflect physical operational events into the language of money: expenses and costs.

The annual budget is often perceived as a fiscal exercise done by the accountants that: (1) is disconnected from the executive team's strategy, and (2) does not adequately reflect future volume drivers. The budget exercise is often scorned by managers as taking months to prepare and then being obsolete soon after it is produced; requiring two or more executive "tweak" adjustments to the numbers they want; shortchanging the departments that have valid increased needs in the coming year; retaining and incorporating process inefficiencies from the current year; and being biased to politically muscled managers who know how to sandbag their budget request. There is a collective organizational groan at budget time.

Enlightened managers are increasingly demanding budgets that can be readily adjusted to reflect changes in their circumstances. There is growing use of short-term rolling financial forecasts where future period assumptions, especially sales volume and product mix forecasts, become more certain.

Knowledge of the activities that occur, what people do, what resources they use, and what these resources cost are essential elements of supply chain costing. Building budget requests based on this type of activity knowledge, activity-based budgeting, is almost certain to result in more realistic supply chain resource requests and more effective cost management.

The budgeting process represents an important part of the supply chain cost management toolkit. Given the importance firms attach to better understanding their activities (such as setting standards), the development of supply chain budgets based on work activities is likely to be particularly valuable. It is a natural evolution from the current budget process to a more effective tool for planning cost information.

Activity-Based Budgeting: An Improved Cost Planning Tool

An *activity-based budget* focuses on the work required to complete a process or activity (such as loading a truck). This information helps managers improve planning, identify opportunities for cost improvement, and make the budget adjustments that are inevitable in a dynamic environment. It helps managers determine that adequate capacity exists to complete planned activities and to identify areas where capacity is significantly underutilized. Large portions of the supply chain processes fall into the categories of manufacturing overhead, distribution, selling, and administrative costs—areas that in traditional budgeting are often given the least attention, even though the relative level of costs in these areas are rapidly increasing. Preparing a budget based on the work activities in these areas will focus more attention on measuring and managing supply chain costs.

Advances in activity-based costing (ABC) principles, which were discussed in Chapter 10, aid in calculating projected outcomes. Simply stated, if a historical ABC model is constructed and its results are calculated for the *descriptive* view of past period costs, the ABC model can be calculated backward for the *predictive* view of costs. In contrast to historical ABC, where the resource and expense is known but the costs of processes with their work activities and outputs are not (they are calculated), reverse estimates are used for budgeting. Estimates are based on forecasts of the future period sales volume and product mix of outputs, including services, and the resulting resource expenses to supply capacity are derived. In this scenario, the outputs are known (estimated), and the manager solves for the unknown resources.

Activity-based budgeting (ABB) is still a relatively new cost planning tool and budgeting tool that many supply chain managers are likely to be unfamiliar with. To understand it, go back and review Exhibit 10.4 and imagine that all the line arrows, which are the cost drivers, are now going in reverse from bottom to top. That is what is happening every minute, day, week, and month. The demands on work flow upward and the costs measure the effect downward. But there is a bonus byproduct from ABC. It is also calculating the unit-level cost consumption rates. These rates are important. Here is why.

ABB draws on Industrial Engineering 101 principles. It is a form of capacity requirements planning. By forecasting not only the sales volume and product mix but also the quantity of all the other activity cost drivers (e.g., the number of truck deliveries, the number of customer sales calls) from the final cost objects to the work activities and multiplying these drivers by the unit-level cost consumption rates, the result is the projected costs of the work activities. These then calculate the required resource expenses to match the demand load with the needed supply of capacity—the number and types of employees and the spending amount with suppliers and contactors. To accomplish this, accountants need to think like engineers!

Exhibit 11.1 lists seven steps that should be part of the supply chain budgeting process when this approach is used. Documenting exactly what activities occur and what causes the volume of the activity to change is essential for understanding the supply chain process. The individuals who do the work activities understand it best. They are in the best position to recommend changes when resources are tight, because these employees better understand how the budget relates to what they do. In addition, budgets based on activities are generally easier for operating individuals to understand, and there is more likelihood that there will be buy-in to meeting budget targets.

EXHIBIT 11.1 Steps in Preparing a Support Budget

---

1) Document the major activities in each part of the supply chain process.

2) Identify what causes the volume of an activity to occur for each major activity—the activity drivers.

3) Estimate the amount of each activity driver that will be needed.

4) Identify the resources (people, space, equipment) needed to perform the activities.

5) Estimate the cost of providing the necessary resources.

6) Develop a spending request that documents the basis for the request.

7) Consolidate requests into the master budget for the department, function, division, or firm.

Source: Shahid Ansari, Jan Bell, and Thomas Klammer, "Activity Based Budgeting," in the modular series *Management Accounting: A Strategic Focus* (Ansari, Bell, Klammer; Lulu.com).

To be useful for planning, budget estimates must be realistic. Historically, budgets, particularly support budgets, were built primarily on incremental percentage changes, up or down, from each cost center's prior-year spending. In a stable environment this may be acceptable, but in a dynamic environment budgets must be easily adjustable to changed circumstances. The use of rolling financial forecasts, based on recent transactions and events, as well as the use of activity cost information to build and adjust budget, gives more validity to change estimates and makes the budgets better planning tools.

In many organizations, the budget has become primarily a control tool—in most cases ineffective—rather than a planning tool. Managers are held to spending targets based on annual budgets that are widely viewed as unreliable before the budget period even begins. A "use it or lose it" mentality exists. Game playing with the budget estimates becomes common. Short-run behavior detrimental to the organization, but helpful in meeting the budget, becomes the norm. *Activity-based budgeting has the potential to revitalize the budget as an important supply chain planning tool.*

 ## TARGET COSTING

Supply chain professionals are under constant pressure to take costs out of supply chain processes. Because most costs are committed even before production begins, it is more effective to manage costs early. Target costing and its variations are tools that firms increasingly use to estimate and manage the cost of a new product or service during their design and development and before they are introduced.

The ability to design and implement these cost reduction opportunities prior to "first piece" production enables firms to achieve considerable cost savings. They then have the greatest opportunity to meet the customers' requirements at the lowest cost during the concept and design phases. The decisions made during this phase commit the firm to costs that would not be incurred until into production and deployment (see Exhibit 5.1). Changes made later, such as through kaizen costing, would be unable to achieve the same level of potential cost reduction.

Target Costing Process

Target costing is market driven. A *target cost* is an estimate of the amount of cost that can be incurred while still permitting the firm to earn a required profit. A market price that will maximize revenues is established first and the required profit margin is subtracted to calculate the target cost. It is an equation. Price minus profit equals the target cost. A cost-plus-a-profit markup pricing mentality is traditional, but it ignores the arguably more important variable—the optimal price to maximize revenues.

The cardinal rule with target costing is that the target cost becomes the maximum allowable cost. So, as the product concept, design, specifications, and components are planned, if the initial sum total of the purchased or manufactured components and the labor costs to make the individual product exceeds the maximum allowable cost, it fails the cardinal rule. This creates pressure on the product designers to alter the prototype design of the product so it can be more efficiently manufactured, reducing labor costs and using fewer or lower-priced purchased components from suppliers. Before first-piece production can be approved, the product's cost must be at or below the target maximum allowable cost from the equation.

Unlike traditional costing, target costing includes all types of costs—production, selling, and administrative. It also considers all life-cycle costs. Product and process design occur concurrently to maximize cost reduction opportunities. Information from activity-based costing can be useful by viewing ABC cost rates to make and assemble similar existing products and apply them to the new product's design.

Exhibit 11.2 illustrates the inputs that determine the target selling price and the target profit margin that net to the maximum allowable cost. From the bottom upward in the exhibit, as the estimated product sums to the "expected cost," it is continuously tested until the expected cost equals (or is lower than) the maximum allowable target cost. Until it does, pressure is transmitted with cost reduction actions until the matching is satisfied.

The use of cross-functional teams (that include outside entities within the value chain) is essential. Typically, achieving a target cost is not feasible unless a firm creates collaborative relationships with all members of the supply chain.

Comprehensive target costing is a complex process. Many steps and activities must occur to achieve the target cost. Exhibit 11.3 identifies seven major activities that occur just to establish the target cost for a potential product or service. These activities are representative of the uncertainties that firms face as they consider introducing a new product or service. Another eight major activities (see Exhibit 11.4) occur as the firm works to alter the product design, including its components, to attain the target cost. Target costing is a reiterative process that involves constant refinement of efforts. Every iteration brings the firm closer to meeting the target cost or reaching a decision to abandon the product or service.

EXHIBIT 11.2   New Product Target Costing

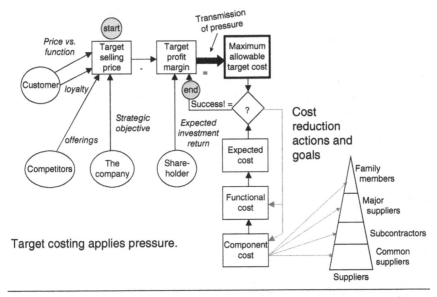

Source: Adapted from Gary Cokins, "Integrating Target Costing and ABC," *Journal of Cost Management* (July/August 2002), p. 14. Copyright Gary Cokins. Used with permission of the author.

EXHIBIT 11.3   Activities to Establish Target Costs

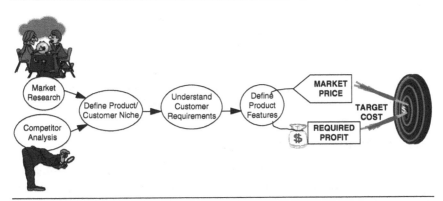

Source: Shahid Ansari, Jan Bell, and Thomas Klammer, "Target Costing," in the modular series *Management Accounting: A Strategic Focus* (Ansari, Bell, Klammer; Lulu.com).

A major benefit participating firms gain from their target costing efforts is enhanced process understanding and information that is relevant for many ongoing organizational decisions. Learning to be a team player and becoming more tolerant of cost ambiguity are essential for target costing. Neither of these behavioral changes is easy.

Target costing is a management technique for determining customer requirements (price, quality, functionality, and time) and using this information to drive product design changes and changes in the upstream supply chain to achieve these requirements. Management effort focuses on three key processes: determining the market (customer) driven price; product-level costing (driving cost reductions within the firm); and component-level target costing (extending pressure to meet market requirements to upstream supplier trading partners). Supply chain costing provides the cost information needed to support target costing. As activity and process costs are established across trading partners, management can identify where the greatest opportunities exist to achieve customer requirements.

EXHIBIT 11.4 Activities for Attaining Target Costs

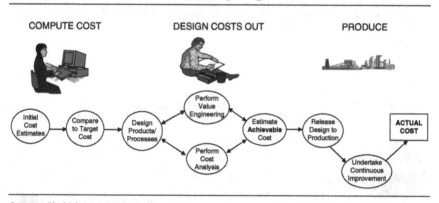

Source: Shahid Ansari, Jan Bell, and Thomas Klammer, "Target Costing," in the modular series *Management Accounting: A Strategic Focus* (Ansari, Bell, Klammer; Lulu.com).

Target Costing Variations

Target costing requires a long-term commitment from the organization, significant cost estimation skill, and typically major behavioral and cultural changes within the organization and the supply chain. Many firms are performing pieces of the target costing process but few have implemented a comprehensive target costing process. Other organizations are applying techniques that parallel target costing. Managers establish a target unit cost and use the target to drive cost reductions within their firms and suppliers. The key differences between their approaches and a formalized target costing approach are found in their analysis; not formally establishing a target costing program and not strictly adhering to a cardinal rule of target costing that the target's maximum allowable cost can never be exceeded. Target costing also requires a supportive cost management system. Most Western companies do not have a cost system integrated with product design and supportive of target costing.[1]

Exhibit 11.5 shows that these firms initiate their efforts in a manner similar to formal target costing programs (see Exhibit 11.3). Senior management establish a target cost by identifying what they believe is the price a new product needs to achieve. Much of this information originates from the marketing staff or represents direct input from key customers. The firm's retailers, distributors, and dealers provide information about actions being taken by competitors and identify where sales have been lost due to not meeting customer requirements in different market segments. Customer requirements and the research and design staff play a critical role in determining what future marketplace requirements would be for new products or models. Sustainability, labor constraints/higher productivity, capability to incorporate new technology, and fuel prices are among the factors driving market requirements. Similar to target costing, managers develop the target cost by subtracting their profit objective (often stated as a contribution margin toward profit and fixed costs) from the target price.

EXHIBIT 11.5 Approach Used for Determining Target Cost

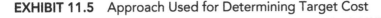

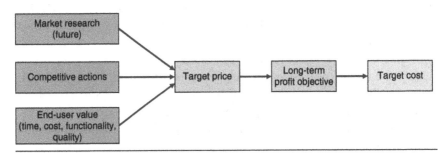

Firms in the aviation industry have incorporated techniques similar to target costing within performance-based logistics (PBL). The Department of Defense initiated PBL in an effort to increase performance levels while decreasing costs. PBL incorporates several techniques embedded in target costing. The end user (military services) defines their requirements, which reflect stretch targets in the performance levels and lower total operating costs. There are two key differences in this approach. First, a target cost is attached to a performance outcome and not necessarily to a product, and second, suppliers are selected by the customer based on their capability to meet the requirements and achieve the target cost. However, achieving the target cost is a must.

The steps taken within the firms using a target costing variation generally match those included in the product-level costing process (see Exhibit 11.6). Multi-functional teams examine the modules or assemblies comprising the end product. Target costs are established based on previous manufacturing or sourcing experience with the items. The component target cost reflects their best estimate of what cost reductions could be obtained while comparing existing product features with customer requirements. Gaps frequently occur between the overall product target cost and the sum of the component target costs. The team has the responsibility of determining how best to close the gap. In many instances, they use a value engineering approach to achieve cost reductions by improving productivity through fewer process steps, eliminating waste, reducing complexity (fewer components), using less material or less expensive alternatives, employing new technology or equipment, shifting production to an upstream supplier capable of producing at a lower cost, or outsourcing functions to a third-party provider. Trade-offs frequently occur between assemblies. Costs sometimes need to increase in some assemblies to meet customer requirements or to achieve a cost reduction in another module within the end product. The approach and documentation used to support this process is identical to that used for kaizen costing, the major difference being that they are attempting to achieve the target cost for a new product rather than an existing product.

Firms frequently turn to their upstream supplier trading partners to achieve the target costs established by senior management. The cost targets are generally aggressive and many of the opportunities to reduce cost have already been achieved through previous cost reduction efforts. The process used to work with their trading partners closely follows the component-level target cost process.

EXHIBIT 11.6 Product-Level Costing Approach

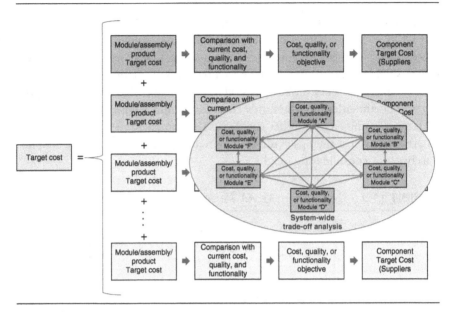

During the costing effort, firms work with their suppliers in a similar fashion; however, they typically do not perform a two-way exchange of cost information. They identify targets to be achieved and work with their suppliers to obtain the target costs, usually through a reduction in the component or service price. Suppliers are asked to provide their cost information with varying degrees of success and information utility. Large, dominant suppliers generally refuse to provide cost information or collaborate. Smaller suppliers can be leveraged to participate; however, their cost systems generally cannot provide the cost "intelligence" required to support target costing. New suppliers are generally more willing to provide cost information as a means to increase market share.

During the component-level target costing process (see Exhibit 11.7), buyers play a lead role in identifying suppliers where a cost or functional improvement can be obtained. Where suppliers are considered too costly and uncooperative, the buying team attempts to develop alternative sources capable of meeting the end user's requirements with their components. In some instances, the buying team works with functional counterparts to develop the source by providing technology, drawings, or engineering support.

If cost justified, the firm may purchase and supply equipment to the supplier. In other instances, a cross-functional team may work with existing suppliers to examine the suppliers' processes and identify cost reduction opportunities as well as a means to meet or exceed customer requirements. Depending on the supplier's sophistication and cost systems, the team uses this information to focus value engineering efforts. Based on the information, either the supplier or customer team initiates several actions, again similar to kaizen costing and documentation. The firm's cross-functional team compares findings with those obtained from other suppliers. The comparisons sometimes reveal where further cost savings could be obtained, such as by combining supplier purchases or consolidating freight.

EXHIBIT 11.7   Component-Level Target Costing

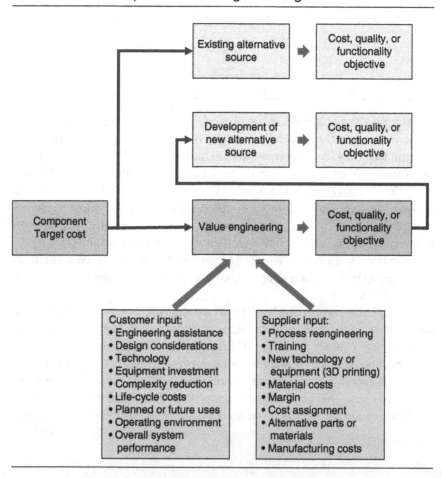

The overall target costing process is usually tracked at the division level responsible for the end product. Cost reductions are documented and forwarded to the controller for verification. Senior management is periodically updated on the progress and actions necessary to achieve the target cost.

Life-Cycle Costing

The importance of managing the cost of a service or process over its life is rapidly gaining acceptance as firms deal with a rapidly changing environment. The "low-bid supplier wins" mentality of the mass-production era—and in government contracts—is widely recognized as no longer being appropriate. Leading decision makers, especially in firms with a "cost" mentality, recognize that considering all costs and revenues, a concept known as *life-cycle costing*, is essential when making investment or purchase decisions that will influence future costs. Life-cycle costs include acquisition, operating, and abandonment costs.

For the customer, life-cycle costs include all outlays related to a product or service from its inception to its abandonment. When a firm buys a truck, the acquisition costs include the purchase price, taxes, and title fees. Operating costs include fuel, insurance, maintenance, and repairs. Abandonment costs include resale inflows less costs of disposal such as title transfer. Considering these costs in advance provides a far different picture of the overall cost of owning a truck than just focusing on the acquisition cost. A life-cycle cost analysis can help the customer compare alternatives when making purchase decisions. While these benefits are obvious, the life-cycle approach is often not used when making purchase decisions.

As a producer or service provider, life-cycle costs include the cash inflows and outflows associated with all activities that occur from the product or service's inception to its abandonment. Lifetime sales must exceed lifetime cost or it is certainly not worthwhile to provide the product or service. Assume a new service is going to be provided. There are one-time costs to design and promote the service and buy equipment. Then there are recurring costs associated with selling and supporting the service, as well as recurring revenues generated by service sales. Finally, there are abandonment costs related to disposal of equipment, termination of contracts, and so forth. Typically, the cost of operating and maintaining a resource or process far exceeds all other costs. The cost of operating equipment may reach 2 to 20 times its initial cost. More importantly, a large percentage of lifetime costs are committed prior to the decision to provide the product or service. There is a clear linkage to the earlier target costing discussion.

Life-cycle costing is commonly associated with engineering and developing cost estimates for large projects such as buildings, defense programs, highways, and so forth. Public agencies increasingly use this analysis tool to assist in making construction, rehabilitation, and maintenance decisions. Several states have documents that detail how to do life-cycle costing. Completing a life-cycle cost analysis is a combination of art and science. Developing and using a systematic analysis process throughout an organization helps assure that appropriate elements are properly and consistently considered. Exhibit 11.8 provides one example of the types of steps that can be useful in doing a life-cycle cost analysis.

The cost segment on capital investment analysis that follows also includes a list of steps associated with the capital budgeting process. When reviewing the steps for capital budgeting in Exhibit 11.9, consider how similar many of the suggested steps are to those for life-cycle costing listed in Exhibit 11.8. Essentially, life-cycle costing and capital investment analysis are similar approaches for evaluating strategic supply chain costs—particularly when cash flows are discounted.

EXHIBIT 11.8 Key Steps in a Life-Cycle Costing Analysis

Define problem and state objective

Identify feasible alternatives

Establish common assumptions and parameters

Estimate costs and times of occurrence for each alternative

Discount future costs to present value

Compute and compare LCC for each alternative

Compute supplementary measures if required for project prioritization

Assess uncertainty of input data

Take into account effects for which dollar costs or benefits cannot be estimated

Advise on the decision

Source: Sieglinde Fuller and Stephen Peterson, NIST Handbook 135, *Life-Cycle Costing Manual for the Federal Energy Management Program* (U.S. Government Printing Office, 1996).

Managers note that their firms have made investments to support supply chain processes without information related to either their capital investment decision processes or any life-cycle costing information. Supply chain managers certainly understand the importance of these concepts; however, they persistently emphasize the operational and short-term cost analysis of supply chain information. Researchers of capital investment practices have consistently encountered considerable reluctance on the part of firms to share information on the specifics of these practices, and many firms have even found it difficult to find benchmarking partners.[2]

 CAPITAL INVESTMENT ANALYSIS

Capital investment analysis, or capital budgeting, is the process organizations use to evaluate and select long-term investments in tangible or intangible assets. It helps answer questions about whether the return on investment (ROI) from a proposed purchase of an asset, such as equipment or a system, is justified. A good capital investment analysis process helps supply chain managers analyze and plan when and how to add long-term capacity costs in a manner consistent with the firm's long-term strategy. Most organizations remain reluctant to discuss the details of their capital decision models, but managers are very much aware that it is easier to manage capital costs before making the investment. Managers understand the importance of capital investment decisions and that these decisions influence supply chain costs for a substantial period.

The Steps

Exhibit 11.9 shows eight major steps that are part of a common approach to the capital investment analysis process. Research results show it is not uncommon for firms to make long-term investments without linking these investments to the firm's strategy—the first step in the process. While the need for such a linkage should seem obvious, an analysis of the literature and discussions with many business executives demonstrate that the link is often assumed rather than systematically documented.

Capital budgeting analysis typically involves comparing a baseline with an alternative scenario that includes investing in an asset for which the expected benefits will continue well beyond a year's duration. Some refer to the associated investment justification analysis as "same as, except for" or comparing the *as-is* state with the *to-be* state. Care should be taken to do an adequate search for feasible alternatives. Too often, managers select the first proposal with an acceptable return and overlook better alternatives because they were not identified.

EXHIBIT 11.9 Steps in the Capital Budgeting Process

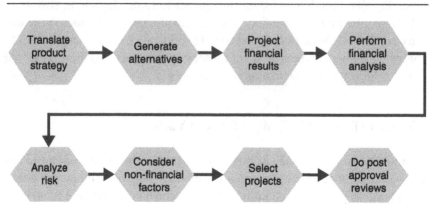

Source: Adapted from Shahid Ansari, Jan Bell, and Thomas Klammer, "Customer Profitability Analysis," in the modular series *Management Accounting: A Strategic Focus* (Ansari, Bell, Klammer; Lulu.com).

The "project financial results" step is where acquisition, operating, and terminal (or abandonment) costs over the life of the project are estimated. In developing these estimates, firms rely on forecast projections, such as demand volume units, and the associated incremental impact on revenues and resource expenses. Experience shows that it is easy to overlook certain types of cash inflows and outflows. It is useful to assign project champions to develop illustrative lists of cash flows that might occur.

Performing financial analysis encompasses the use of discounting techniques such as net present value and internal rate of return. These tools make it feasible to compare the value of estimated cash inflows and outflows that occur at different times. These discounted cash flow equations rely on the forecasts of demand and on unit-level consumption rates of the workload. There are also other analysis tools ranging from simple payback models to exotic estimation tools, such as those based on chaos theory, that are used in different situations. Historically, the tendency has been to focus too extensively on the third and fourth steps of the capital budgeting process. This narrow focus can lead to extensive analysis of projects that are "easy" to make cash flow estimates for, such as buying trucks or forklifts. Critical one-time strategic decisions, such as outsourcing part of a supply chain or decisions with hard to estimate benefits, such as investing in "green" technology, are too often made with limited analysis.

Note that a review of risk factors and consideration of nonfinancial factors, such as the impact of quality and time, are essential before making project investment decisions. It is easy to get caught up in the financial analysis and overlook these critical elements of the capital process while making investment decisions. The final step in the capital budgeting cycle is to review prior decisions and learn why estimation mistakes occurred in order to help improve future analysis efforts. Feedback is essential for better future supply chain decision making.

Capital investment decisions are important because they commit the organization to certain types of cost structures and specific supply chain processes. Almost every large firm has detailed procedures in place for making capital investment decisions. Yet research and interviews reveal that few firms believe that their capital investment decision process is world class. Many important strategic decisions are still made based on top management's "gut feeling." Most firms are reluctant to benchmark in the capital investment analysis area. This unwillingness to share information impedes process improvement. This is a major problem that needs to be addressed in many parts of the supply chain costing journey.

Make versus Buy—General Outsourcing Decisions

The outsourcing decision is a strategic, long-term capital investment decision. Before outsourcing there needs to be a careful business case developed to justify which services are going to be performed by third parties. This type of decision should only be made using the logic and math of capital budgeting. Cost and revenue differences that measure "same-as, except for" incremental changes need to be identified. Activity-based costing techniques should be applied because the primary variable is the work activities that the third-party contractor performs to replace the current in-house work activities. Since cost is not the only variable that shifts, a service-level agreement with the contactor should be a standard practice.

Unfortunately, the make-or-buy decision is often still treated as a short-term relevant cost decision, where the focus of attention is on how variable costs change. The traditional cost accounting treatment for make or buy involved a comparison of the buying price for the product or service with the cost savings that resulted from making this purchase—the variable costs that went away. The long-term impact on costs is not given much attention. The need to consider other factors such as quality or timeliness is noted, but typically given little attention in the quantitative case used for the decision.

There are many reasons a firm may consider outsourcing or insourcing. One reason often cited is, of course, cost savings. The decision may also allow the firm to restructure where it focuses its spending or even its fundamental strategic focus. It may provide quality improvements for customers, take advantage of the knowledge and expertise of the service provider, or make better use of capacity or management skills. An outsourcing decision can place a focus on the core competencies of the organization versus the third party, such as cafeteria services or uniform cleaning, where the third-party contractor is more skilled and/or may enjoy economies of scale due to serving multiple customers, thus providing greater efficiency and effectiveness.

A decision to fundamentally change an organization by outsourcing major functions or processes entails considerable risk. It is politically charged, particularly when work is sent overseas or to organizations that pay lower wages or provide fewer benefits. Promised benefits often fail to materialize, perhaps because the decision did not properly consider all costs. An organization can lose control of quality and productivity. There is a loss of knowledge and expertise within the organization that may make it difficult to rectify a poor outsourcing choice. The firm may be also subject to more security and fraud risks. *Outsourcing decisions are strategic long-term decisions that should consider life time costs and be analyzed using appropriate capital investment tools.*

 ## CAPACITY ANALYSIS

Capacity is a measure of the resources available as a supply to match the sales demand quantity of goods or services that a firm expects to sell. Knowing whether adequate or excess capacity already exists or will exist after selecting alternatives (based on life-cycle or capital investment analysis) is an important part of supply chain costing. There are many potential uses for capacity analysis at the operating, tactical, and strategic level.

Capacity is often thought of primarily in the context of the existing operating structure of the organization. While every firm has multiple measures of capacity, these measures are seldom integrated. The type of general capacity analysis model described shortly does not yet appear to be familiar to most supply chain professionals, even though its use has been instrumental in improving how firms use existing capacity and reducing the need for investments in additional capacity.

The capacity model introduced below (the CAM-I model)[3] is probably the most comprehensive of the general models related to capacity described by

McNair[4] in her comprehensive review of capacity models. The CAM-I model helps communicate the overall state of capacity. Traditional capacity measures typically focus on only planned or actual capacity and make it easy to overlook the extensive amount of idle and nonproductive capacity that is present.

Capacity represents a physical measure of product or service capability that is based on a combination of rate and time ($C = R \times T$). It is a measure of what *can* be done, not how much *is* done. Time is the constant in this measure.

Total or *rated capacity* is the maximum an asset or process can produce with no constraints. Assume an order call center can handle 1,000 calls per hour. Its total capacity is 24,000 calls a day ($24 \times 1,000$), 168,000 calls a week ($24,000 \times 7$), and so forth. Total capacity can then be separated into the portions that are productive, nonproductive, and idle. A brief description of each follows.

Productive capacity is the use of capacity to make good (i.e., error-free and meeting specifications) products or deliver good services. A forklift loading trucks for 1,500 hours in a year would be a measure of the productive use of the forklift.

Nonproductive capacity is capacity that is used but does not result in making a good product or delivering a good service for the customer. Doing setups, performing maintenance, incurring waste, and having resources on standby are elements of nonproductive capacity. These activities may be essential, but they are still unproductive in terms of the customer. If a forklift is unable to load trucks because there is no driver or materials are unavailable, it is unproductive. If a load is dropped or the forklift requires an oil change, it is unproductive.

Idle capacity is capacity that is available but unused because of policy decisions or the market. Some capacity is idle because it is off-limits, some may be unusable in the existing market, and other amounts may be useable but are not being used for various business reasons. Some idle capacity is referred to as "buffer capacity" to anticipate surges in demand that can be met without cycle time delivery delays. If management decides to operate only two shifts, the forklift will be idle part of each day. If a competitor reduces demand for a firm's product, the forklift may be idle because of fewer shipments.

Exhibit 11.10 displays these three capacity portions in the second column, titled "Summary Model." The third column decomposes the second column, and the fourth column further decomposes the model.

EXHIBIT 11.10 CAM-I Capacity Model

Rated Capacity	Summary Model	Industry Specific Model	Strategic Specific Model	Traditional Model
Rated Capacity	Idle	Not Marketable	Excess Not Usable	Theoretical
		Off Limits	Management Policy	
			Contractual	
			Legal	
		Marketable	Idle but Usable	Practical
	Non-Productive	Standby	Process Balance	Scheduled
			Variability	
		Waste	Scrap	
			Rework	
			Yield Loss	
		Maintenance	Scheduled	
			Unscheduled	
		Setups	Time	
			Volume	
			Changeover	
		Process Development		
		Product Development		
	Productive	Make Good Products		

Source: Thomas Klammer and the CAM-I Capacity Interest Group, *A Manager's Guide to Evaluating and Optimizing Capacity Productivity* (Irwin Professional Publishing, @CAM-I,1966), p. 17.

Capacity is an expense. It only resides within a firm's resources (e.g., employees and assets); it does not reside in the work activities. Activities are capabilities. Using capacity more efficiently can reduce expenses and help firms avoid investing in unneeded capacity. Common adages are "more with the same" and "the same with less." One of the alternatives that should be considered when making strategic supply chain decisions is redesigning the supply chain processes by working with suppliers and customers to reduce nonproductive and idle capacity.

A careful analysis of the states of capacity that exist for processes and products provides a wealth of information to decision makers and can have major implications for the cost of supply chain processes. A major firm in the semiconductor industry carefully analyzed their nonproductive costs and worked to minimize those costs. As a result, they were able to improve their ability to produce productively enough to avoid investing in additional plants that would have cost the firm over six billion dollars.

Research shows that traditional capacity measures often focus on only a portion of available capacity. As a result, idle and nonproductive capacity are often taken as givens and are not carefully managed. Becoming aware of this blind spot has resulted in operating changes in organizations. For example, many firms now do preventive maintenance on assets, such as delivery vehicles, outside normal working hours. This frees up additional capacity, reducing the need for extra equipment, such as trucks, or allows the firm to accept a larger volume of delivery orders.

Capacity analysis is essential for making visible the state of existing capacity, particularly idle and nonproductive capacity. This information is useful in helping avoid making unneeded investments. An analysis of prospective capacity is also useful for evaluating the scope of potential capital projects.

NOTES

1. R. Cooper and R. Slagmulder, *Target Costing and Value Engineering* (Portland, OR: Productivity Press, 1997).
2. Based on insight from Thomas Klammer, one of this book's authors, who has a stream of research related to the capital budgeting practices industry uses and has worked extensively with other researchers and many individuals in industry involved with the capital decision process.
3. The model discussed in this section is based on work done by CAM-I and originally published in Thomas Klammer, *Capacity Measurement and Improvement, A Manager's Guide to Evaluating and Optimizing Capacity Productivity* (Chicago, IL: Irwin Professional Publishing, 1996). A comprehensive summary of part of the model itself is found in Shahid Ansari, Jan Bell, and Thomas Klammer, "Measuring and Managing Capacity," in the modular series *Management Accounting: A Strategic Focus* (Ansari, Bell, Klammer; Lulu.com).
4. C.J. McNair, *Implementing Capacity Cost Management Systems* (Montvale, NJ: Institute of Management Accountants, 2000).

CHAPTER 12

Align Performance Measures with the Strategy

ERFORMANCE MEASUREMENT POSES SEVERAL unique challenges for supply chain management. Executives and managers need to understand how the supply chain affects performance within their firm. In most instances, external trading partners have a major effect on how and why a firm performs certain activities. Executives and managers must understand how their internal performance affects the performance of their trading partners and the different activities that are performed by upstream suppliers or downstream customers. All trading partners should realize that their supply chain is competing against other supply chains for the share of wallet or purse of the customer at the end of the supply chain, and the purchase price will matter to that customer.

An understanding of these interactions requires a significant exchange of information—the right information between firms. The information must be specific to the relationship and clearly demonstrate how interactions between the supply chain and the firm affect performance in both directions. In addition, executives need the ability to translate nonfinancial performance into financial value creation for the firm, its stockholders and owners, and for the firm's trading partners in the supply chain.

The ability to translate improved process performance into value makes a compelling argument when attempting to persuade trading partners to align their business practices with supply chain objectives. Executives and managers across the supply chain need to understand how changing business practices will affect nonfinancial performance, such as cycle time, product availability, quality, on-time delivery, customer satisfaction, or obsolescence. They also need to understand whether aligning their performance will create additional value for their firm. A key part of this alignment process requires that managers reexamine the nature of their supply chain costs and select or modify the tools used to capture cost information in ways useful to supporting decision making. As different costing tools are incorporated into the supply chain cost management process, performance measures need to evolve. Likewise, as trading partners collaborate and align performance, additional insight will be required regarding how changes in the supply chain are affecting performance, costs, and value.

LINKING COST AND PERFORMANCE

Supply chain costing can provide management with better capability to translate supply chain performance into financial performance. Effective supply chain management does more than reduce cost. It creates value for the end user and other stakeholders. Although cost reduction is a highly desirable result, supply chain management can create value by increasing sales, gaining additional market share, reducing inventory, or improving asset productivity. The cost drivers embedded in supply chain costing can be used to demonstrate how supply chain process changes will impact the four components of the value equation: revenues, cost of goods sold (COGS), expenses, and assets. This is illustrated in the section linking costs, performance, and value found later in this chapter.

Supply chain costing must be linked to the performance measurement system. The linkage is necessary to ensure that supply chain costing is not implemented in isolation from other factors such as quality and throughput cycle time. Linking supply chain costing to performance measures means managers will focus more on understanding their costs and what drives cost in their organization. The combination of cost and performance information represents a major step forward in cultivating a cost-conscious culture within the firm.

Sharing nonfinancial information is and will remain a critical part of supply chain processes. The capability to translate nonfinancial information into financial information is essential because the language of senior executives is finance. Key decision makers will require that the value created through supply chain management be measured and sold in financial terms. The translation will also help gain acceptance from trading partners. Firms affected by a proposed change in a supply chain process will need to be convinced of the financial merits of the change. Demonstration of improved financial performance will be especially important when additional costs or investments are required by the trading partner. The use of tools such as the balanced scorecard (BSC) can facilitate this process.

Measuring the financial benefits and burdens resulting from supply chain initiatives will help determine if they are being equitably allocated across trading partners. An equitable allocation does not necessarily mean equal and should be based on the level of investment, risk, and performance. Measurement can help ensure that the supply chain is producing financial performance consistent with the strategic objectives of the firm and other trading partners.

Selecting good supply chain performance metrics, doing appropriate measurement, and acting on the measurements is an essential part of the supply chain costing journey. The measures should increasingly focus on process and give managers clues about what may happen, that is, be leading indicators. Activities throughout the organization (and ideally across the supply chain) that relate to a particular outcome are the focus of these measures. The performance measurement system should emphasize problem solving through the use of root cause analysis and attempting to eliminate the cause of the problem. Value is created by having multiple groups across functions and organizations actively collaborating on measures and performance analysis.

Issues with Many Existing Performance Measures

There is still a strong emphasis on short-term performance measures and many examples of how this emphasis conflicts with efforts to improve supply chain management. However, managers understand the importance of having a broad variety of real-time measures in place to support efforts to improve modern supply chain processes. Financial and nonfinancial measures that broaden management focus beyond monthly or quarterly results and support strategic supply chain decisions are essential, and will require changes in existing performance measurement systems. However, even when strong incentives to change exist, implementation is a major challenge. Change is even more problematic if top management is not viewed as "walking the talk."

When performance measures do not align with an entity's objectives and strategies, they often drive the wrong type of behavior. The result is higher supply chain costs and at least a partial failure in supply chain management. Exhibit 12.1 includes several examples of what can happen when there is misalignment between internal performance measures and supply chain objectives. Operating managers often react to performance measures that are not linked to the organization's strategic plan. As the examples show, failure to link measures with objectives will produce situations where managers respond inappropriately or drive the wrong behaviors in the organization. Often the performance measures are not forward looking and thus are of little help in improving processes. Even worse, top management is often unaware of the extent of this disconnect or misalignment.

EXHIBIT 12.1 Disconnect between Performance Measures and Supply Chain Management Objectives

---

Inferior quality goods are shipped at period end to meet an area's quarterly revenue or tonnage targets. Additional costs are then incurred in the next quarter to have the goods returned, ship the right quality of goods, and interact with the customers who received the inferior goods.

Customer support is charged with responding to customer questions and inquiries. Staffing levels are cut to meet wage budget targets. Calls and electronic inquires are then not responded to on a timely basis, problems escalate from minor to major, and existing and potential customers are lost or order less.

To meet raw material purchase price standards purchasing managers severely pressure a critical supplier to accept unreasonably low selling prices in a weak economy. As demand rises the supplier is unwilling or unable to provide the additional materials the firm needs. The firm becomes that supplier's customer of last choice.

Critical shipments to customers are delayed so the shipping manager can meet percentage targets for full truckload deliveries. The customer must shut down production because of missing goods and classifies the shipping firm as an unreliable supplier. The customer significantly lowers future orders.

Critical company infrastructure expenditures are delayed to avoid increasing depreciation costs that would keep the company from making this year's target profit. The company is then forced to pay a premium for the space and equipment needed to support next year's demand for services because of the construction delay.

Production is outsourced based on a promise of lower labor costs. Control over quality and production timing is lost, delivery costs soar, and the time spent managing the production process increases dramatically. Overall costs increase.

R&D personnel receive a bonus for developing a cheaper product component. The production department must incur higher costs to handle the fragile component and control the toxic waste it releases during production.

One common characteristic of these examples is that an action is taken that makes an employee or functional area look good in the short run, but has negative long-term consequences to the firm because there is a misalignment in performance measures and supply chain objectives and strategies. Such results occur when senior managers focus too extensively on short-term financial results. Responding to questions about variances and budget shortfalls seldom results in systematically changing future performance. These efforts are not linked to strategy and systemic cost improvement. Instead, managers modify what they do to avoid having to deal with questions about variances and budget differences. The result is little or no process improvement.

Another characteristic of these examples is that the performance measures are narrowly focused on a function or small part of a function. To effectively manage supply chain costs, performance measures must support cost management efforts that extend outside the functional area, and even outside the organization. Appropriate measures should exert the right type of pressure to reduce costs throughout the internal and external supply chain.

Performance measures should increasingly focus on information that helps manage supply chain processes across functions and organizations. Measures cannot stop at departmental, functional, or even organizational boundaries. If they do, suboptimization typically results. Lean organizations are process oriented and focus on customers and suppliers (internal and external). Performance measures need to reward cooperation and long-term decision making. They should reward actions that help identify root causes and implement solutions to problems. Partnering with other parts of the supply chain is essential to remove waste, increase flexibility, and become more responsive. Work is being done in teams and performance measures must find ways to reward teams, not individuals. There is a need to benchmark activities and link the results to performance evaluation.

LINKING SUPPLY CHAIN COSTING TO PERFORMANCE MEASUREMENT

Supply chain costing provides both a cost and performance view of the processes and activities comprising the supply chain. Processes affected by supply chain initiatives can be mapped to identify the activities and corresponding cost drivers. After identifying these activities, supply chain costing determines the activity costs based on the resources consumed from each trading partner (see Exhibit 12.2). The use of multiple cost drivers supports a more accurate determination of costs and assignment to products, customers, or supply chains.

EXHIBIT 12.2 Supply Chain Costing—Cost Assignment and Identification of Activity Cost Drivers

The flow of costs traced to cost objects provides the footing for decisions and analyses

	Resources consumed: direct and indirect

Supply chain activities	Source and acquire materials	Store materials/ components	Schedule production	Setup/ Changeover production line	Manufacture product	Handle & store product	Deliver product
Activity driver	$/order or $/receipt	$/product move	$/production run	$/Setup or changeover	$/product	$/order pick	$/type of order
Cost object	Product/project Customer/supplier Supply chain process	Product/project Customer/supplier Supply chain process	Product/project Customer/supplier Supply chain process	Product/project Customer/supplier Supply chain process	Product/project Customer/supplier Supply chain process	Product/project Customer/supplier Supply chain process	Product/project Customer/supplier Supply chain process

Profitability by product, customer, or supplier determined by how they place demand on work activities

Using cost drivers, supply chain costing establishes a cause-and-effect relationship between the activities and the factors driving activity costs and performance outcomes (see Exhibit 12.3). Managers can identify how supply chain initiatives affect activities across the supply chain. They can target those factors driving cost and performance and take action to achieve the desired outcome. By expanding this view across the supply chain, each trading partner can develop and align performance measures that are consistent with the overall supply chain process objectives. Supply chain costing increases management's understanding of how the interactions occurring between trading partners affect overall performance by breaking down the process in measurable activities, developing performance measures, and identifying what actually drives performance and cost.

The combination of supply chain cost and performance information can directly support management decision making. The information visibility permits a supply chain–wide assessment of how activities performed by multiple trading partners interact to affect cost and performance. Managers can employ new strategies by reconfiguring processes to drive changes in the activities and how they are performed within each firm. Supply chain costing captures the effect of these changes on performance, translates the changes into costs, and, when coupled with economic value added (EVA), updates the changes into financial performance.

EXHIBIT 12.3 Using Cost Drivers to Develop Supply Chain Process Performance Measures

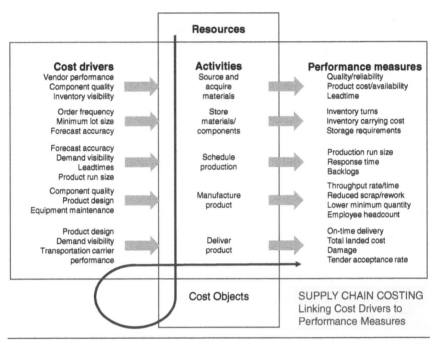

Cost drivers	Activities	Performance measures
Vendor performance Component quality Inventory visibility	Source and acquire materials	Quality/reliability Product cost/availability Leadtime
Order frequency Minimum lot size Forecast accuracy	Store materials/ components	Inventory turns Inventory carrying cost Storage requirements
Forecast accuracy Demand visibility Leadtimes Product run size	Schedule production	Production run size Response time Backlogs
Component quality Product design Equipment maintenance	Manufacture product	Throughput rate/time Reduced scrap/rework Lower minimum quantity Employee headcount
Product design Demand visibility Transportation carrier performance	Deliver product	On-time delivery Total landed cost Damage Tender acceptance rate

Resources

Cost Objects

SUPPLY CHAIN COSTING
Linking Cost Drivers to
Performance Measures

Source: Adapted from Gary Cokins, *Activity-Based Cost Management: An Executive's Guide* (John Wiley & Sons, 2001), Figure 2.17, p. 67.

USING THE SUPPLY CHAIN COSTING FRAMEWORK TO TRANSLATE SUPPLY CHAIN PERFORMANCE INTO FINANCIAL PERFORMANCE

Combining supply chain costing with an economic value added (EVA) model provides a mechanism to convert supply chain performance into financial performance. Supply chain costing is used to examine the interdependence of supply chain activities and, using cost drivers, to quantify performance into specific activity costs and measures. The EVA model incorporates these cost changes with changes in sales, costs, and assets to determine the effect on value creation in the firm and in trading partners across the supply chain. A positive EVA indicates management created value for the firm by generating profits in excess of the cost of assets employed. A negative EVA suggests managers destroyed value since profits did not cover the cost of assets.

Larger firms often have cost systems capable of tracing costs to activities and processes and use EVA to determine the value created in their firms. Limited visibility regarding their trading partners' costs and financials result in these firms not using EVA to measure value creation outside the firm. However, supply chain managers increasingly recognize that they need to be able to measure and sell the value created through supply chain initiatives, not only to their leadership team but also as a means to develop a compelling argument for their trading partners to collaborate.

Supply-Side Value Analysis

A value-added analysis can be extended to integrate the cost and performance information obtained through supply chain costing into a single framework. Exhibit 12.4 shows the supply side of this extension. The model on the left is shown from the supplier's perspective and is linked with value drivers and aligned performance measures.

Value drivers link to each of the major components of the EVA equation. The sales value drivers identify how changes in supply chain processes affect revenue growth through better understanding end-user requirements, aligning performance and resources more closely with strategy and target markets, and collaborating with downstream trading partners to reduce their costs.

The cost of goods sold (COGS) can be impacted through kaizen costing and value engineering to reduce costs internally, while target costing can drive cost reductions during product design and development with upstream suppliers. Expense value drivers address many of the inbound and outbound costs captured in landed cost or customer profitability analyses. For example, by improving the order fulfillment process or optimizing the transportation network, supply chain professionals would reduce costs for the firm and have a direct effect on EVA.

The supply chain can affect the firm's charge for assets by reducing average inventory levels, accelerating payments, and improving asset utilization through improved demand visibility and the sharing of marketing, production, and product development information among trading partners.

The linkage demonstrates how improved supply chain performance at the activity level affects the corresponding value driver and leads to value creation and increased profitability within the firm. Managers can develop performance measures at the operational level that align behavior with the value drivers.

EXHIBIT 12.4 Developing and Aligning Corporate Performance Measures with Supplier Value Drivers and Supply Chain Objectives

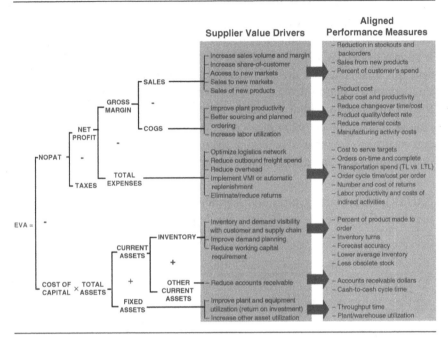

Source: Adapted from Douglas M. Lambert and Terrance L. Pohlen, "Supply Chain Metrics," *The International Journal of Logistics Management* 12, no. 1 (2001), p. 14, © Copyright Douglas M. Lambert. Used with permission. For more information about the SCM Framework see drdouglaslambert.com.

Customer-Side Value Analysis

An analysis from the customer's perspective provides the mirror image of how collaborative action drives value for downstream trading partners in the supply chain (see Exhibit 12.5). Revenue value drivers include increased sales generated through lower prices, increased product availability, the introduction of new technology, the codevelopment of new products with the supplier, and improved customer service. Price reductions in COGS may occur as the supplier passes along a lower price reflecting the reduced costs of doing business with the customer. Expense value drivers reflect several cost trade-offs. For example, customers may order and receive products more frequently, decreasing storage, order placement, and inspection costs. Current assets decrease as the supplier assumes greater responsibility for inventory management and replenishment. Optimization of the distribution network may reduce fixed assets by eliminating distribution centers or increasing asset productivity.

An extended framework results when this type of analysis is extended to include other trading partners. The customer side of the integrated approach is shown in Exhibit 12.5. Placed side by side, Exhibits 12.4 and 12.5 represent this linkage across the value chain. The extended framework promotes more effective communication by identifying exactly what needs to occur at the activity level to achieve corporate and supply chain objectives. As process changes occur, the financial implications can be identified so that managers can ensure an equitable allocation of the resulting benefits and burdens based on the costs, asset investments, and risk incurred.

EXHIBIT 12.5   Developing and Aligning Corporate Performance Measures with Customer Value Drivers and Supply Chain Objectives

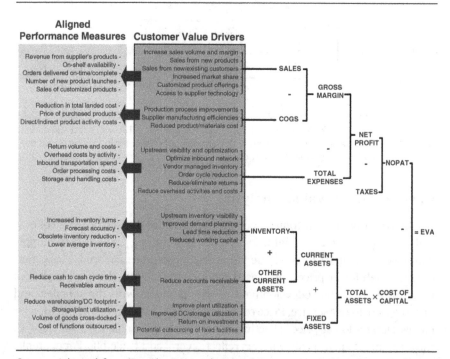

Source: Adapted from Douglas M. Lambert and Terrance L. Pohlen, "Supply Chain Metrics," *The International Journal of Logistics Management* 12, no. 1 (2001), p. 14, © Copyright Douglas M. Lambert. Used with permission. For more information about the SCM Framework see drdouglaslambert.com.

In many instances, the resulting performance measures may appear similar to those previously used by the different trading partners. However, there are key differences. Value and performance are measured by specific customers or suppliers—customer and supplier profitability analyses are essential. Measures such as on-time delivery, returns, or perfect orders continue to be tracked, but the focus shifts to how the entire supply chain performs and how each enterprise contributes to overall supply chain performance. Measures focus on achieving overall supply chain objectives, as opposed to corporate objectives. Existing metrics will need to be adapted to capture differences driven by customer, supplier, or supply chain.

An analysis from the supplier's and customer's perspectives enables management to obtain a complete assessment of how value is created by incorporating all the components of the shareholder value equation. From the supplier's perspective, the analysis can be used to demonstrate the value created with a specific customer or in an entire supply chain. For example, the analysis can be used to demonstrate the value created by working with a trading partner by including only the revenues generated in the relationship, the costs directly attributable to conducting business with the customer, and any directly traceable asset charges, including inventory carrying costs, accounts receivable, and equipment utilization. The supplier can benchmark the value achieved by working with a specific trading partner to the value obtained by selling to other customers using different supply chain strategies. Downstream trading partners can use the analysis to obtain similar capabilities. The customer can identify the revenue generated from selling the supplier's products, the cost of doing business with the supplier, and charges for asset use. A combined analysis from the supplier's and customer's perspectives helps managers evaluate how their performance will drive changes in shareholder value simultaneously in both firms.

Supply chain executives can apply the combined analysis even when one of the supplier or customer firms does not currently use profitability or value analysis. In these instances, management can use cost estimation models and, with a reasonable degree of accuracy, estimate the sales, expenses, costs, and assets by using information from other firms in the supply chain. Although cost estimation models do not provide exact calculations of cost changes, they do provide useful indications of expected changes in the value created. These estimates are useful for demonstrating how changes in the value drivers will affect value creation in other trading partners. This approach proves especially useful when attempting to sell process changes to managers who currently lack this information. Without the analysis, managers tend to focus strictly on the added costs and investment and may perceive an inequitable distribution of resulting benefits and burdens between the supplier and customer; however, an EVA analysis expands the discussion to include revenue and asset value drivers, such as inventory carrying costs.

 ## INTEGRATING SUPPLY CHAIN COSTING INTO A BALANCED SCORECARD

Integrating supply chain costing with the balanced scorecard will help ensure that a more complete set of performance measures is used. A strategy map and its associated balanced scorecard (BSC), popularized by Harvard Business School's Robert S. Kaplan and Dr. David Norton,[1] has several measurement perspectives that make it richer than exclusively financial performance measurement models. A strategy map incorporates four perspectives: financial, customer, internal business processes, and learning, innovation, and growth. Collectively, supply chain costing with a strategy map and its associated balanced scorecard provide comprehensive reporting of current operating performance and insights into what to change going forward to manage future performance.

There is also a lack of consensus as to what a balanced scorecard is. To complicate matters, many organizations initially start developing a balanced scorecard without first developing its companion, and arguably more important, strategy map, from which the balanced scorecard's key performance indicators (KPIs) should be derived. Further complicating matters, organizations confuse strategic KPIs that belong in a balanced scorecard with operational performance indicators (OPIs) that belong in a dashboard.

Kaplan and Norton recognized the shortcoming of executive managements' excessive emphasis on after-the-fact, short-term financial results. A balanced scorecard resolves this myopia and improves organizational performance by shifting attention from financial measures and managing nonfinancial operational measures related to customers, internal processes, and employee innovation, learning, and growth. These influencing measures are reported *during* the period so reactions can occur sooner. This in turn leads to better financial results.

There is additional confusion about the purpose of a balanced scorecard. Some executives say they have successfully transferred their old columnar management reports into visual dashboards with flashing red and green lights and directional arrows. A balanced scorecard is much more than that.

One problem is how anyone knows if those measures—the so-called key performance indicators (KPIs)—support the strategic intent of the executive team. Are the selected measures the *right* measures? Or, are they what you *can* measure rather than what you *should* measure? Is the purpose of the balanced scorecard really only to better *monitor* the dials against targets rather than facilitate the employee actions needed to *move* the dials?

Organizations need to think deeper about what measures drive value and reflect achieving the direction-setting strategic objectives defined by their executive team. With the correct strategic KPIs, organizations should strive toward optimizing these measures, and ideally be continuously forecasting their expected results.

The Mistake of Implementing a Balanced Scorecard without Its Strategy Map

Why are so many managers familiar with the term *balanced scorecard* but so few familiar with the term *strategy map*? The strategy map is orders of magnitude more important than the balanced scorecard, which is merely a feedback mechanism. Why do executives want to implement a balanced scorecard without a strategy map? One possible explanation is the mistaken belief that those vital few strategic KPI measures, rather than the trivial many measures, can be derived without first requiring employee teams and managers to understand the answer to a key question: "Where does the executive team want the organization to go?" This question is best answered by the executive team's vision and mission—and they must point to the direction they want the organization to follow them to. That is the executive team's primary job—setting direction. The strategy map and its companion balanced scorecard are both important, but their combination answers a different question: "How will we get there?"

Exhibit 12.6 illustrates a generic strategy map with its four stacked popular perspectives. Each rectangle in the strategy map represents a strategic objective and its associated projects or competencies to excel at plus their appropriate performance indicator measures and targets.

EXHIBIT 12.6 Generic Strategy Map

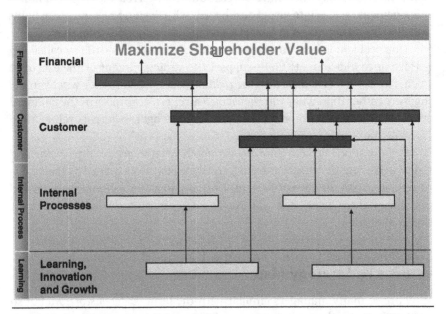

Source: Adapted from Gary Cokins, *Performance Management: Integrating Strategy Execution, Methodologies, Risk, and Analytics* (New York: John Wiley & Sons, 2001), p. 95. Copyright Gary Cokins. Used with permission of the author.

Note that in the exhibit there are dependency linkages in a strategy map with an upward direction of cumulating effects of contributions from accomplishing the strategic objectives. The derived strategic KPIs are not created in isolation but rather have context to the executive's mission and vision. To summarize, a strategy map causally links the strategic objectives from the bottom perspective upward:

▪ Accomplishing the employee innovation, learning, and growth objectives contributes to the internal process improvement objectives.
▪ Accomplishing the internal process objectives contributes to the customer satisfaction, retention, and growth objectives.
▪ Accomplishing the customer-related objectives results in achieving the financial objectives, typically a combination of revenue growth and cost management objectives.

A strategy map is like a force field in physics, as with magnetism, where the energy, priorities, and actions of managers and employee teams are mobilized, aligned, and focused. At the top of the map, maximizing shareholder wealth (or, for public sector organizations, maximizing community and citizen value) is *not* really a goal—it is a result. It is a result from accomplishing all of the linked strategic objectives with cause-and-effect relationships.

One peril that threatens the success of this methodology is executive teams that are anxious to assign performance indicator measures with targets to employees and hold them accountable. Executives typically skip two critical steps of involving the employees to gain their buy-in as well as their commitment to the measures. The first is ensuring that they understand the executive team's strategy, and the second, more critical, prior step is identifying the mission-essential projects and initiatives that will achieve the strategic objectives. The presence of enabling projects and initiatives goes to the heart of what distinguishes a strategic objective from just getting better at what you are already doing.

A strategy map and its derived balanced scorecard are navigational tools to guide the organization to *execute* the strategy, not necessarily to formulate the strategy. Executive teams are capable with defining strategy, but a high involuntary chief executive officer (CEO) turnover rate and the increasingly shorter tenure of CEOs are evidence of their failure to fully, and successfully, implement their strategy.

There is a wide variety of measures that could be part of each of the four segments of the balanced scorecard. Financial perspective measures might include revenue growth, operating income, and change in return on investment. Customer perspective measures may emphasize the number of new customers, market share in a distribution channel, and customer service ratings. On-time delivery, service response time, and order delivery time are examples of internal perspective measures. The learning and growth perspective measures include increase in employees trained in process management, percentage of delivery systems with real time measures, and the percentage of cross-trained employees.

Each organization can customize the scorecard measures to fit its situations. Various authors who have written about the balanced scorecard include lists illustrating the types of measures that fall under each of the scorecard's categories. Authors such as Bhagwat and Sharma,[2] Gunasekaran, Patel, and Tirtiroglu[3] provide lists specifically related to supply chain processes.

Measurements Are Far More a Social System Than a Technical One

Selecting and measuring strategic KPIs is critical. You get what you measure, and a strategy map with its associated balanced scorecard serves a greater social purpose than a technical one (although information technology and software are essential enablers). *Performance measures motivate people and focus them on what matters most. Therefore, having appropriate performance measures matters!*

Imagine if, every day, every employee in an organization, from the cleaning person or janitor to the CEO or managing director, could answer this single question: "How am I doing on what is important?" The first half of the question can be easily displayed on a dial with a target; it is reported in a balanced scorecard. But it is the second half of the question—"on what is important"—that is the key, and that is defined in the strategy map.

The following provides an example from an unnamed company that recognized and acted on these questions many years ago.

A computer equipment manufacturer in the Midwestern United States prided itself on communicating its strategies so that every employee at every level of the organization was aware of the company goals. Some skeptical outsiders visiting the plant decided to test this claim. They asked a janitor sweeping the factory loading dock how his job related to the goals of the company. The janitor replied as follows. "My company's goal is to reduce the cost of its products. A major cost for us is inventory. We recently shifted to just-in-time production to reduce inventory stocking cost. This means that our suppliers deliver products to us every two hours. If I do not clean this loading dock before the next load arrives, we are unable to accept delivery. This would set back the production schedule in the plant and increase the cost of production. We would also have the added cost of returning the materials to the supplier."[4]

The balanced scorecard involves identifying and integrating appropriate cause-and-effect linkages of strategic objectives that are each supported by the vital few key measures, and then subsequently cascading the KPIs down through the organization. KPIs ultimately extend into the operational performance indicators (OPIs) that employees can relate to and directly affect.

The primary task of a strategy map and its companion balanced scorecard is to align employees' work, actions, and priorities with multiple strategic objectives that, if accomplished, will achieve implementing the executives' strategy and consequently realize the end game of maximizing shareholder wealth (or maximizing citizen value). The strategic objectives are in the strategy map, not in the balanced scorecard. The strategic KPIs in the balanced scorecard reflect the strategic objectives in the strategy map.

The primary purpose of a strategy map is to communicate the executive team's strategy to employees in a way they can understand it, and to report the impact of their contribution to attaining it. Starting with KPI definitions without context to the executive's mission and vision denies this important step.

An Automobile GPS Navigator Analogy for an Organization

A strategy map and its companion balanced scorecard are similar to an automobile's GPS route navigator for organizations. For organizations, the destination input into the GPS is the executive team's formulated strategy. The executive team's primary job is to set strategic direction, and the top of their strategy map is their destination. However, unlike a GPS's knowledge of roads and algorithms to determine the best route, managers and employee teams must "map" which projects, initiatives, and business process improvements are best to arrive at the destination (realizing the strategy).

A strategy is never static; it is dynamic and needs to be constantly adjusted. This means that the destination input to the GPS navigator is constantly changing, placing increasing importance on predictive analytics to determine the best destination for stakeholders.

How Are Balanced Scorecards and Dashboards Different?

There is confusion about the difference between a balanced scorecard and a dashboard. There is similar confusion differentiating key performance indicators (KPIs) from normal and routine measures that are the operational performance indicators (OPIs). The adjective "key" of a KPI is important. An organization has limited resources or energy. To use a radio analogy, KPIs are what distinguish the signal from the noise—the measures of progress toward strategy execution. A negative result of this confusion is that organizations typically include too many KPIs in their balanced scorecard system, which should be restricted to strategic KPIs.

A strategy map design is first completed, and then the firm's strategic KPIs are selected and target levels for each are identified. With this understanding, it becomes apparent that the strategy map's companion balanced scorecard, on its surface, serves more as the feedback mechanism. It allows everyone in the organization, from front-line workers to the executive team, to answer the question: "How are we, not just me, doing on what is important?" More importantly, the scorecard should facilitate analysis to also know why. The idea is not to just *monitor* the dials but to *move* the dials.

A Balanced Scorecard and Dashboards Serve Different Purposes

The two terms—*balanced scorecard* and *dashboards*—have the tendency to be confused and used interchangeably, when each brings a different set of capabilities. The sources of the confusion are:

■ Both represent a way to track results.
■ Both make use of traffic lights, dials, sliders, and other visual aids.
■ Both can have targets, thresholds, and alert messages.
■ Both can provide drill-down to other metrics and reports.

Exhibit 12.7 illustrates the difference between a balanced scorecard and dashboards using a taxonomy starting with all measurements in general at the top. A balanced scorecard and dashboards are not contradictory; they are used for different purposes.

At the top portion of the exhibit is the realm of the balanced scorecard. A *balanced scorecard* is intended to be *strategic*. It serves to align the behavior of managers and employees with the strategic objectives formulated by the executive team. In contrast, *dashboards*, at the bottom portion of the exhibit, are intended to be *operational*.

EXHIBIT 12.7   Balanced Scorecard versus Dashboard

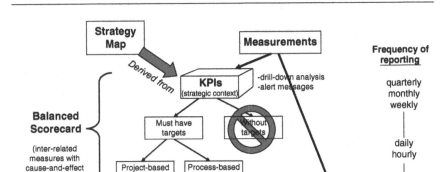

Source: Adapted from Gary Cokins, *Performance Management: Integrating Strategy Execution, Methodologies, Risk, and Analytics* (New York: John Wiley & Sons, 2001), p. 105. Copyright Gary Cokins. Used with permission of the author.

A balanced scorecard provides information that is lacking in dashboards. It answers questions by providing deeper analysis, drill-down capabilities, traffic-light-alert messaging, and pursuing inferences of performance improvement potential to determine motivational targets. A balanced scorecard does not start with the existing data, but rather it begins with identifying what strategic projects to complete and core processes to improve and excel in to accomplish the strategic objectives.

Here are some guidelines for understanding the differences:

▪ **Balanced scorecards chart progress toward accomplishing strategic objectives.** A balanced scorecard reports performance associated with an organization's strategic objectives and plans.

There are two key distinctions of a balanced scorecard: (1) each KPI *must* require a predefined target measure; and (2) KPIs should be made up of both project-based KPIs (e.g., milestones, progress percentage of completion, degree of planned versus accomplished outcome) and process-based KPIs (e.g., percent on-time delivery against customer promise dates). A scorecard comprised mainly or exclusively by process-based KPIs is not an efficient engine of change; it merely monitors whether progress from the traditional drivers of improvement, such as quality or cycle-time improvement, is occurring. Process improvement is important, but innovation and change are even more important.

■ **Dashboards monitor and measure processes.** A dashboard, however, is operational and its OPIs report information more frequently than those in the balanced scorecard. Each dashboard measure is reported with little regard to its relationship to other dashboard measures. Dashboard measures do not directly reflect the context of strategic objectives.

This information can be more real-time in nature, like an automobile dashboard that lets drivers check, at a glance, their current speed, fuel level, and engine temperature. It follows that a dashboard should ideally be linked directly to systems that capture events as they happen, and it should warn users through alerts or exception notifications when performance against any number of metrics deviates from the norm or what is expected.

A balanced scorecard should include (1) the linkage of strategic KPIs to the strategy map and the fiscal budget (as well as rolling financial forecasts); and (2) the linkage of dashboard operational OPIs selected to influence behavior that will ultimately result in achieving or exceeding the strategic KPI targets. In Exhibit 12.7 the strategy map is located in the upper left and the budget and resource planning at the bottom.

Scorecards Link the Executives' Strategy to Operations and to the Budget

A strategy map is in the upper left of Exhibit 12.7. The exhibit denotes that KPIs should be *derived from* the executives' strategic objectives and plans. If KPIs are selected independent of the strategy, then they will likely report only what *can* be measured as opposed to what *should* be measured. Failure to execute a strategy is one of a CEO's major concerns, and therefore KPIs should reflect either mission-critical projects and initiatives or core business processes that must be excelled at. Hence there is the need for both project-based and process-based KPIs.

The budget (and increasingly rolling financial forecasts) should be derived from the required funding of the projects (e.g., the nonrecurring strategy expenses and capital investments) and of the operational processes (e.g., the recurring operational capacity-related expenses that vary with driver volumes, such as customer demand).

Dashboards Move the Scorecard's Dials

The organization's traction and torque are reflected in the OPI measures—the more frequently reported operational measures. Although some OPIs may have predefined targets, they do not need to have them. OPIs serve more to monitor trends across time or results against upper or lower threshold limits. As OPIs are monitored and responded to, the corrective actions will contribute to achieving the strategic KPI target levels with actual results.

Cause-and-effect relationships between and among measures underlie the entire approach to integrating a strategy map (formulation), balanced scorecard (appraisal), dashboards (execution), and fiscal budgets (the fuel).

Many organizations overplan and underexecute. With regard to KPI and OPI selection, first learn the principles, and then apply them through selecting, monitoring, and refining the KPIs. Designing a strategy map and its associated balanced scorecard is a craft, not a science.

 INTEGRATING COSTING WITH STRATEGY, CUSTOMERS, PROCESSES, MEASURES, AND SHAREHOLDERS

Exhibit 12.8 expands the CAM-I ABC cross in Exhibit 7.2 to include customers, strategy, and performance measures. In the upper-left box is where the executives formulate their strategy, based primarily on customer needs and preferences. The supply chain costing is in the middle. Performance is in the bottom right box. Note that the performance box has inputs from the processes (e.g., productivity) and from the final cost objects (e.g., profits with profit margins).

Also note that customers are bidirectionally connected to performance. As mentioned in Chapter 9, customers are the source of financial value creation for shareholders and owners.

Exhibit 12.9 decomposes Exhibit 12.8 into more detail. In the upper left is the zone of the customer-based strategy map and its associated balanced scorecard with KPIs. At the far right are examples of operational performance enabled from the process view of costs. At the bottom, note that revenues are coupled with the strategic cost information, primarily from activity-based costing (ABC), to calculate profits. The profit levels in turn impact the shareholders' and owners' financial wealth creation. The upward arrow from the final cost objects into the activities and ultimately into the resource capacity expenses reflects driver-based budgeting and rolling financial forecasts, described in Chapter 11. The performance measurement in the lower right is bidirectionally connected to the strategy realization with variance analysis of the planned versus actual results.

EXHIBIT 12.8 CAM-I ABC Cross Expanded

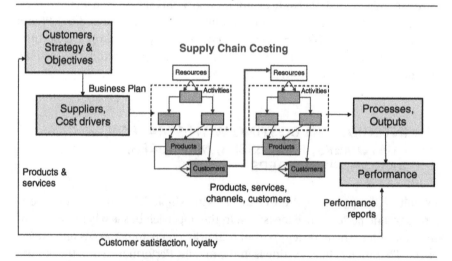

EXHIBIT 12.9 CAM-I ABC Cross Expanded and Decomposed

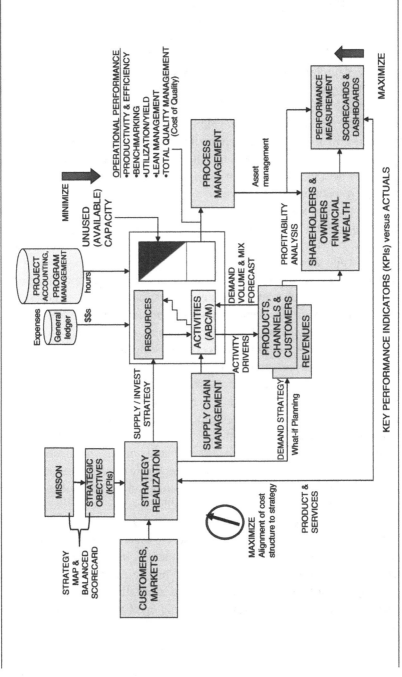

Source: Adapted from Gary Cokins, *Activity-Based Cost Management: An Executive's Guide* (New York: John Wiley & Sons, 2001), p. 200. Used with permission of the author.

ADDING VALUE THROUGH LINKAGES

The increased cost visibility made available by supply chain costing has far-reaching implications for supply chain management. Value creation will drive strategic decisions regarding the composition and structure of the supply chain. The linking of supply chain strategy to activity costs and nonfinancial performance measures will change the firm's evaluation of carriers, vendors, and trading partners' performance while providing a greater degree of influence over changes occurring in the supply chain. Restructuring the supply chain to make the most of efficiencies or seize competitive advantages will further emphasize the requirement for a mechanism capable of equitably allocating cost benefits and burdens between trading partners.

Managers can use supply chain costing as a strategic tool for restructuring relationships within their supply chains. Traditional cost management systems bury many supply chain–related costs in indirect or "overhead" accounts (e.g., SG&A) and allocate these costs based on sales or volume shipped. Supply chain managers consequently have had little insight regarding how their actions drive costs within each trading partner or drive value for the end user. Supply chain costing supports strategic supply chain management by displaying these costs and accurately tracing them to the products, customers, or supply chains based on actual consumption. Supply chain costing facilitates the construction of product, customer, or supply chain profit-and-loss statements. These documents help managers better understand what drives costs and profitability, not only in their firm but within and across relationships in the supply chain. Managers can use this newfound intelligence to target supply chain relationships yielding the greatest value for strategic alliances or partnerships while taking action to reduce or eliminate high-cost/low-value-added relationships.

Supply chain costing can play an integral role in allocating benefits and burdens within the channel. It lays the foundation for an allocation mechanism by accurately tracing costs to the specific resources contributed and the gains each partner will receive. Firms can then use this information to identify discrepancies and negotiate mechanisms to overcome perceived inequities. The information can also be used to determine how best to share any resulting savings across the supply chain. Allocation mechanisms that fairly distribute the savings according to contribution will increase the commitment to change within the supply chain and toward the building of a sustainable competitive advantage.

NOTES

1. R. Kaplan and D. Norton, "The Balanced Scorecard: Measures That Drive Performance," *Harvard Business Review* 70, no. 1 (1992): 71–99.
2. Rajat Bhagwat and Milind Kumar Sharma, "Performance Measurement of Supply Chain Management: A Balanced Scorecard Approach," *Computers & Industrial Engineering* 53, no. 1 (2007): 43–62.
3. A. Gunasekaran, C. Patel, and E. Tirtiroglu, "Performance Measures and Metrics in a Supply Chain Environment," *International Journal of Operations and Production Management* 21, no. 1/2 (2001): 71–83.
4. Shahid Ansari, Jan Bell, and Thomas Klammer, "Strategy and Management Accounting," in the modular series *Management Accounting: A Strategic Focus* (Ansari, Bell, Klammer; Lulu.com)

CHAPTER 13

Accept the Challenge of Improving Supply Chain Costing

T HE CONCEPT OF COST visibility across an entire supply chain has considerable intuitive appeal for most managers. Conceptually, few would argue against having a better understanding of what drives supply chain costs and better cost visibility with reasonable cost accuracy by not applying cost allocations that violate costing's causality principle. If this is indeed true, then why have not more managers and firms made significant progress toward implementing supply chain costing? A straightforward answer is that implementing supply chain costing is difficult and poses significant challenges. A less direct answer is that managers will have to employ multiple strategies to overcome the many challenges encountered during implementation.

Some of the challenges are primarily technical and include failures to define or capture needed information or an inability to make reasonable cost estimates. Although significant, supply chain managers can overcome these challenges by applying the costing strategies and tools leading-edge firms already successfully use internally to implement supply chain costing. These internal implementations represent a significant challenge, but an even larger challenge lies in the ability to distribute these improved technical skills throughout the remainder of the supply chain.

The most daunting challenges to improving supply chain costing are related to the organization's behavior and culture environment. These challenges are rooted in many firms' ingrained unwillingness to share sensitive cost information, the fear of an inequitable allocation of the resulting benefits and burdens from such sharing, and a basic lack of trust in the behavior of trading partners. These attitudes also may exist internally among business segments or functions as well as between the firm and its external trading partners throughout the supply chain. Movement toward achieving cost transparency across trading partners is likely to be painfully difficult.

Additional barriers slowing the adoption rate of supply chain costing are the human nature of resistance to change (e.g., many prefer the status quo), fear of being measured, fear of being held accountable, and fear of others knowing the truth about one's costs. Note that none of these barriers involve technology, software, or methods. They are all about people and behavior.

In considering these challenges, recall the definitions of supply chain and supply chain management presented earlier in this book. Supply chain management requires a much different perspective of cost management than what currently exists in most firms. The focus shifts from determining and analyzing the costs incurred within a single firm to one of managing the costs incurred by an entire supply chain in providing the final product or service to the end customer. Supply chain managers must look across the entire supply chain for new ways to enhance product or service quality while reducing costs. The definition of supply chain costing reflects this broader perspective:

> Supply chain costing is the collection, expense assignment, and analysis of cost information across all of the work activities comprising a supply chain for the purpose of identifying opportunities to obtain a competitive advantage through a combination of reduced costs or improved performance.

Supply chain managers require a broader view of costs because many of the costs incurred by a firm are driven by activities and processes performed by external trading partners. Supply chain managers require visibility of costs, and what causes costs, "dirt-to-dirt," to have the ability to control the final cost experienced by the end user. Without this visibility, managers will miss opportunities to reduce costs or the ability to optimize costs at a more strategic level through interfirm cost trade-offs.

This chapter identifies and describes the key challenges supply chain professionals need to overcome during the journey to supply chain costing. It begins by describing the challenges and their significance to supply chain costing. The remainder of the chapter presents the strategies used by leading-edge firms to address these challenges. The obstacles encountered during supply chain costing implementation range from a lack of trust between trading partners to accounting systems failing to capture needed information. These obstacles can be overcome because supply chain managers can apply strategies employed by other firms that have successfully overcome these challenges and thus make major strides forward along their journey.

 ## BEHAVIORAL CHALLENGES

A major component of supply chain costing is the exchange of information, including cost information. Management frequently has misgivings about whether the potential benefits of exchanging sensitive, proprietary cost information with trading partners sufficiently outweigh the potential risks. Overcoming these misgivings and fundamentally changing the exchange and use of costs within a supply chain requires major behavioral and cultural attitude shifts. Managers consistently indicate that this process is often far more challenging than addressing the technical changes in measuring or estimating costs.

Lack of Trust

A significant lack of trust continues to exist in most supply chains and precludes the free exchange of cost information. Many managers believe their trading partners will act opportunistically if granted access to their cost information. Instead of focusing on jointly reducing costs with mutually beneficial results, they contend that their trading partners may use the cost information to increase profitability at the expense of other firms in the supply chain. As a result, exchanging cost information remains an extremely sensitive topic and senior managers are often currently unwilling to exchange any cost information.

Suppliers have major reservations regarding the sharing of cost and operational data with their trading partners. They contend that their customers will use the information to extract price concessions during future negotiations. As the customer acquires more knowledge about the supplier's processes, the customer has less difficulty in developing new sources or exchanging the information with competitive suppliers to obtain lower costs (prices). Some suppliers face the possibility that their customer may decide to vertically integrate to avoid paying the profit margin now earned by the supplier.

Downstream customers have similar concerns regarding the potential loss of competitive advantage. Customers may have devised unique ways to use a supplier's product to achieve lower costs or higher performance than their competitors. Managers in these firms believe that their suppliers may seek this information to obtain a competitive advantage for themselves. The supplier can use this information to show other customers how to better use the product or service. Any advantage the customer held evaporates as competitors adopt the same practices.

Trust appears to be a more significant hurdle to overcome in existing relationships than in new or potential relationships with other trading partners. These relationships are often marked by previous adversarial practices, and managers are very suspicious of any actions that could result in profit margin erosion or the release of competitive information. Large suppliers, and especially those that have successfully cultivated high profit margin business, simply refuse to disclose any cost data or collaborate with their trading partners in any way. Managers typically report that they can more easily obtain cost information from new, or potential, trading partners than from their existing trading relationships. The new trading partners have a "whatever it takes" attitude to establish a foothold or develop the relationship. This attitude often extends to being more willing to share cost information.

Limited Two-Way Sharing of Cost Information

Due to management concerns about sharing cost information, few, if any, situations exist where all firms across an entire supply chain exchange their costs and management has complete cost visibility. In fact, few instances of bidirectional cost flow between firms have been identified and these exchanges are far from totally cost transparent. These firms exchange only information on the direct costs associated with a proposed process change and do not disclose any data on indirect costs or the costs of performing any other processes or activities.

Research shows that cost information flows primarily in one direction, from supplier to customer, and typically occurs during purchase negotiations. Large buyers require their suppliers to provide a detailed breakout of their costs. The breakout is used to determine whether the price is reasonable based on the supplier's labor, material, operating, and overhead costs. The information provided by the supplier rarely breaks out costs by process or activity. The fact that the information is "required" often increases the level of the supplier's mistrust.

The quality of information provided, even within the limited context of traditional labor, material, and overhead costs, varies by supplier. Some suppliers intentionally distort the cost information required by their customers because they fear it may be misused. Small suppliers often do not provide accurate cost information because they do not understand their costs. In some instances, customers report having a better understanding of their suppliers' costs than do the suppliers. Managers have cited instances where their suppliers bid well below the total cost the customer estimated was necessary to manufacture and deliver the product. The lack of cost knowledge within the supply chain remains one of the technical challenges of supply chain costing.

In many relationships, no cost information is exchanged. Some suppliers refuse to provide cost information even when required by the customer. Those that are in a strong market position due to their market dominance, specialized capabilities, or quality have no incentive to provide cost information that may only be used against them in price negotiations. Customers generally do not provide cost information when acquiring materials or services. They provide limited cost information only when the focus is on reducing their costs through a process improvement.

The lack of a two-way flow of cost information presents an obstacle to supply chain costing. Ideas and suggestions largely flow in only one direction and suppliers lack the information needed to improve supply chain performance. Greater information visibility would provide more opportunities for the supplier to understand how their product or service is used and how changes in design or performance could create additional value downstream. When information is not shared, the supplier must rely entirely on the customer to identify these opportunities. This one-way flow may result in missed opportunities and does not motivate the supplier to go beyond the minimum required to maintain the customer's business.

The current one-way exchange of cost information is a major factor that fosters distrust in a supply chain. The supplier risks the customer's using the information to develop new sources or products—which customers frequently admit to doing. Upstream trading partners are reluctant to share cost information because they perceive that their customers will receive all the benefits while they incur all the burdens. The profitability of channel partners can be significantly affected by shifting functions from one trading partner to another in the supply chain. Changes in sales volume, product mix, or services offered can reduce revenues or increase costs at any point in the supply chain. Suppliers frequently experience the brunt of changes in the supply chain. They contend that their customers simply push inventory backwards in the supply chain and demand frequent and rapid replenishment without pursuing any initiatives to obtain offsetting cost reductions in other areas. As a result, the customer obtains the benefits of lower inventories and higher service levels while the supplier is left "holding the bag" with higher inventory levels, transportation costs, and greater risk.

Suppliers also contend that customers will use cost information to extract greater concessions. In some supply chains, customers require their suppliers to provide cost information to establish the prices they will pay. Customers expect the supplier to reduce costs (price) by a stated percentage each year. Suppliers generally receive little benefit in exchange for the additional burden imposed on them.

Inequitable Allocation of Resulting Benefits and Burdens

The perception of an inequitable allocation of benefits and burdens in the supply chain partially stems from the lack of a two-way flow of cost information. Since the customer provides no visibility of downstream costs, the supplier assumes the worst—that the customer is hoarding any cost savings. The supplier cannot determine whether any cost savings have been passed downstream or whether future sales will increase due to the additional value created for the end user. The supplier's efforts to obtain additional cost reductions are stymied as well. The supplier cannot identify where offsetting cost reductions could be obtained in other processes or activities through collaboration with the customer.

Any alteration to a supply chain process will affect firms differently and may further contribute to perceptions of an inequitable allocation of benefits and burdens. For example, the adoption of a continual replenishment strategy generally provides greater benefits for downstream trading partners. Despite higher transaction costs due to more frequent ordering and receipts, they obtain even greater offsetting cost savings through higher inventory turns and fewer lost sales. Upstream trading partners achieve an overall cost reduction by trading off higher transportation and order fulfillment costs for lower inventory and production costs, made possible through more accurate demand information and forecasting. Although costs have decreased in both firms, the downstream trading partner generally obtains a greater benefit. Inventory, labor, and facility costs are higher downstream and the potential for savings can be much greater. These differences can create perceptions of inequity, especially when the level of investment or effort varies considerably between firms.

An equitable sharing of benefits and burdens does not necessarily imply an equal sharing. Suppliers have little motivation to exchange cost information if they are forced to reduce margins and incur additional costs and risk. Manufacturers tend to have higher margins than their suppliers or customers due to their large capital investment and the risks incurred. Their return on investment must cover product development and commercialization as well as the associated risk. Other trading partners may perceive an inequitable allocation when the manufacturer obtains higher margins. Complete cost transparency would reveal that the manufacturer incurred a substantial amount of the burdens to obtain a larger share of the benefits; however, few firms would be willing to provide this level of cost visibility or access in areas considered a core competency or source of competitive advantage.

 TECHNICAL CHALLENGES

Cost knowledge refers to a firm's capability to provide cost information in a form that supports management decision making. The level of cost knowledge directly affects managers' ability to understand and identify key cost drivers within their firm and in key trading partners. Cost knowledge has multiple dimensions that correspond to the different views of cost discussed previously in this book. These dimensions include the cost to serve customers or market segments, costs portrayed by product or division, and the costs required to support different supply chains or distribution channels.

Limited Cost Knowledge

Limited cost knowledge pervades most supply chains. Supply chain managers note that the majority of their trading partners do not have sufficient cost knowledge to integrate supply chain processes. These trading partners do not understand their key cost drivers, and the vast majority have little understanding of how their business practices drive costs elsewhere in the supply chain. There are numerous examples of suppliers quoting prices substantially below actual material and production costs.

Many managers report that their firm continues to rely on traditional costing approaches, and their cost systems provide little insight regarding the costs to support key processes or perform specific activities. As a result, these managers rely on surrogate nonfinancial measures to direct activities within their firms. Based on their experience and intuition, managers focus on a few indicators that they believe drive most of their costs and have the greatest effect on financial performance.

The lack of cost knowledge poses a significant challenge to implementing supply chain costing. Managers with limited cost knowledge refuse to exchange cost information to prevent exposing this potential weakness to their trading partners. If an exchange occurs, the information shared does not provide the insight or the accuracy necessary for supporting supply chain decision making. Differences in the level of cost knowledge across firms and functions make communication difficult and lead to adverse relationships in the supply chain. Limited cost knowledge prevents managers from understanding how process changes affect the firm's total costs. Managers frequently attempt to reduce costs within their firm at the expense of their trading partners—a situation leading to substantial suboptimization and higher costs and lower performance to the end user. If costs rise in their responsibility center, they are likely to refuse to participate in collaborative supply chain initiatives, despite lower overall total costs to their firm. When managers have limited cost knowledge, they are unable to determine how the firm is affected except in their individual areas.

Inadequate cost knowledge has serious implications for supply chain management. The end user incurs higher costs since the upstream channel members are unable to identify and exploit cost reduction opportunities. The channel members may become less competitive if alternative, lower-cost channels emerge. Without sufficient cost knowledge, managers are unable to accurately measure and sell the benefits of supply chain management. They do not possess the cost information to demonstrate how process changes will affect costs, which firms will be impacted, and how to fairly allocate the resulting benefits and burdens. Within the firm, managers lack the capability to translate changes in nonfinancial performance into financial performance. Any improvements requiring investment or additional expenses are consequently difficult to sell to other trading partners.

Lack of Cost Estimation Capability

Customers frequently lack the capability to perform cost estimation or "should cost" analyses for their acquisitions. A cost estimation analysis requires the capability to reverse engineer the products and then determine the supplier's costs and how these products can be most efficiently purchased, manufactured, and distributed. Although the manufacturer may have designed the part, employees may not understand the manufacturing costs.

Several factors may contribute to the lack of cost estimation capability. The customer may lack the technical or engineering expertise associated with the product or service the supplier provides. The customer may not have sufficient manpower to perform this function in-house. Cost estimation requires expertise regarding the cost structure of suppliers and may not have the costing expertise to understand how process changes affect costs. Lastly, management may not perceive the value of cost estimation analyses, especially when competitive bids mask opportunities for cost reduction and management assumes that a competitively obtained price represents the lowest cost to the firm.

The absence of an accurate cost estimation capability can seriously affect implementation of supply chain costing. Cost estimation provides the capability to develop process and activity costs for the entire supply chain, even when the trading partners do not exchange costs or possess sufficient cost knowledge. Without a cost estimation capability, supply chain managers have only isolated snapshots of their trading partners' costs. They are unable to determine what is driving their trading partners' costs and performance. The lack of cost estimation capability keeps managers from identifying potential cost reduction opportunities in their supply chains. Instead, their attention focuses primarily on high-price items where competitive bidding has revealed a wide disparity in costs/margins or instances when the price obviously warrants attention.

An improved cost estimation capability would promote the exchange of interfirm cost information. Greater cost intelligence enables the customer to challenge supplier pricing more effectively. These price challenges can include a detailed analysis of what the product should cost. The customer can use this intelligence to suggest opportunities where the supplier can reduce costs. In instances where the supplier lacks sufficient expertise to effect the improvement, the customer can provide assistance, thereby promoting collaboration and the exchange of additional information. A key ingredient to the success of this approach will be how the customer agrees to share any benefits and how the supplier's margin will be affected.

Inconsistent Definition and Calculation of Cost across the Supply Chain

Cost can be defined in many different ways, and the lack of clear and consistent usage jeopardizes actions to implement supply chain costing. Management accountants across a supply chain may assign costs in different manners depending on the focus of their costing efforts. For example, a product-oriented costing approach produces different results from a customer-oriented costing approach. A firm using standard costs may assign only direct costs and use an arbitrary scheme for assigning indirect costs. Another firm in the supply chain may use an activity-based costing (ABC) approach that more accurately calculates costs.

Inconsistent definitions in calculating costs also obstructs benchmarking within an organization, resulting in comparisons of apples to oranges rather than apples to apples for comparative analysis.

The lack of clear cost definitions makes communication and collaboration extremely challenging. For example, most managers believe that their financial systems can provide expenses at a very precise and detailed level. Further investigation reveals that although managers may have detailed cost information regarding their labor, material, and other expenses, they more often than not lack information regarding costs to perform specific activities or processes or their cost-to-serve different customers. Even firms with intricate standard cost systems have difficulty determining exactly what a product costs to make.

Senior managers find this situation frustrating but, in many instances, understandable. They frequently distrust the cost information in the accounting system due the lack of adequate cost drivers, different reporting mechanisms, or time lag. They tend to question the results of cost study teams due to the many assumptions made to derive costs and the inability to reconcile these special studies with the corporation's external financial reporting for government regulatory agencies. In some instances, they require that all cost studies be coordinated with the CFO to ensure some degree of consistency. As a result, managers find it difficult to communicate in cost-based terms with their trading partners.

STRATEGIES SUPPLY CHAIN COST LEADERS USE FOR OVERCOMING THE CHALLENGES

Finding ways to overcome the challenges associated with completing the supply chain costing journey remains an elusive objective. There are several strategies that leaders in the supply chain costing area are employing to cut across internal and external barriers and establish communication and information links across trading partners. These strategies focus on enabling managers to demonstrate how the exchange of cost information can produce a competitive advantage for the supply chain by eliminating waste, aligning performance, and leveraging the unique competencies within each of the participating trading partners.

These thought leaders are aware of the need to address the technical costing issues and cognizant of the behavioral and cultural challenges that exist. Such awareness is an essential starting point for dealing with these challenges. On the technical side, the examples and explanations of the types of foundational knowledge and ways to use various costing tools described throughout the book provide an underpinning for helping to educate internal and external managers about the value of more cooperative supply chain costing efforts. Firms that are serious about improving their ability to manage supply chain costs will need to focus resources on educating supply chain partners on the nuances of supply chain costing.

Leading firms are leveraging their cost knowledge and market position in several ways that collectively provide a template for improving cost knowledge throughout the supply chain and demonstrate the potential benefits of increased levels of trust about sharing cost information.

Cost Estimation

Some firms have developed sophisticated cost estimation tools that allow them to model and estimate the costs of other trading partners. This tool uses publicly available information and the firm's knowledge of their trading partner's processes, business strategies, and technology. Estimates can be developed independently, so collaborative relationships are not required to obtain costs. The experience gained in developing costs for immediate upstream or downstream trading partners enables firms using the most advanced applications of cost estimation tools to determine how process changes will affect costs throughout the supply chain.

These highly proprietary tools are used primarily for the firm's own benefit, but these tools can provide opportunities to leverage the value-adding efforts of each trading partner. Some firms use cost estimation to identify where eliminating unnecessary steps and waste from the supply chain could lead to cost reductions and shorter lead times or create opportunities to develop more effective strategies based on all of the trading partners' costs and capabilities. Cost estimation tools can be used to demonstrate the cost and revenue implications of a new product or service. The analysis helps identify the process steps, required capability, and associated costs. Suppliers can more easily assess whether their current processes can accommodate a certain new product or service. The customer can provide additional information such as price, volume, and forecasts to assist the supplier in making the decision whether to produce this product or provide this service.

Cost estimation models can simulate the causal effect between end-user demand and trading partners' costs and performance across the entire supply chain. The ability to simulate process changes is one of the most significant capabilities offered by supply chain costing and cost estimation. Managers can simulate whether changes in flexibility, cost, quality, and time produce a competitive advantage at the end-user level. The simulation enables an assessment of the contribution of each trading partner and how they affect value creation in the supply chain. Based on the analysis, specific trading partners can be targeted for collaborative efforts or alternative providers. Instead of focusing on internal improvement, managers use cost and performance information to influence external behavior.

Leveraging Information-Sharing Requirements

Many customers leverage their purchasing power to compel their suppliers to provide cost information. While this is a common strategy, if used inappropriately, it can simply exacerbate the trust issue. Some executives recognize this issue and have initiated efforts to work carefully with trading partners to pursue mutually beneficial improvements. Others have started by pursuing operational improvement opportunities or sharing expertise related to measuring and using supply chain cost data. They further foster trust by exchanging selected information with cooperating suppliers to collectively identify, simulate, and test the effects of proposed changes on overall supply chain costs.

The following examples show how firms can apply this strategy. Firms may require suppliers to submit their production-related costs with their response to the customer's request for bids. The cost submissions follow a standardized reporting format that breaks out costs by labor, materials, other direct costs, equipment depreciation, and overhead. In a few firms, more sophisticated reporting requirements ask the supplier to map their process and identify their costs to perform each step with indirect cost allocations explained and justified. Buyers then circulate this information to internal technical experts and cost estimation analysts to validate the accuracy of the reported costs. A report with questionable data, either high or low, is discussed with the supplier.

Suppliers with long standing relationships or participating in a preferred-supplier program may report their information through a more formal and ongoing process. Online reporting systems are used for suppliers to report their costs for components, services, or products provided to the customer. These costs are jointly reviewed by the trading partners to confirm their validity and to target areas where cost reductions or other improvements can most likely be obtained. In some instances, this reporting is tied to a cost reduction program. By participating, the supplier agrees to propose actions yielding a specified cost reduction each year. Cost reductions can occur within the supplier, customer, or in activities spanning the firms. These proposals must generate "hard savings," producing quantifiable reductions in expenses or bottom-line improvements. The standardized format associated with the supplier program provides a means for both trading partners to readily evaluate the initiative, check key assumptions, revise cost estimates, validate savings, and approve actions.

With their knowledge of supply costs, downstream trading partners have been able to assume a leadership role in improving the supply chain process. Joint supplier-customer teams have used this information to conduct kaizen events to obtain cost savings by improving productivity, increasing quality, or eliminating waste and redundancies across the firms. Customers have identified where multiple tier one and two suppliers purchase the same commodities or components, and they use this knowledge to negotiate a single contract to leverage their combined purchasing power to obtain lower costs. Other analyses have demonstrated where customer investments in new supplier equipment can increase capacity, eliminate bottlenecks, or provide greater flexibility upstream to produce substantial cost reductions. By providing engineering and technical support, the customer can streamline and improve the productivity of the supplier's operations. The customer's marketing staff can assist the supplier in identifying noncompetitive markets for related products to generate additional contributions toward fixed costs and profit.

Suppliers can receive similar benefits through the resulting exchange of cost and process information. They obtain a better understanding of how their behavior and capabilities drive downstream costs. Suppliers can combine this understanding with their unique competencies to assist their customers in resolving a wide variety of issues ranging from manufacturing to product development. Customers frequently turn to their suppliers for assistance in reducing design complexity, such as combining several components to complete an assembly, or to perform a needed function. Suppliers may possess greater flexibility than their customers, and they can use this flexibility to efficiently produce in smaller lot sizes or to custom manufacture to end-user specifications. They may possess a competency or technology their customers do not have, which can lead to new innovations within shorter time spans. Their increased knowledge and understanding of costs make them a more effective trading partner, capable of generating more value to their customers and the downstream supply chain.

This strategy initially makes the exchange of cost information an awkward and sometimes adversarial experience. The profit motive naturally causes each firm to concentrate on how any changes will affect them, and they will use the information to support incremental price and cost trade-off analyses.[1] By taking a leading role in collecting and exchanging cost information, the customer can move supply chain costing forward. As the exchange of cost and process develops, this strategy can overcome the major challenges posed by attempting to manage costs across multiple trading partners. This strategy provides several benefits that are inherent to resolving existing supply chain costing issues.

The use of a standardized format helps ensure consistency in how costs are defined, assigned, and reported across firms. Accurate and consistently developed cost data is important for understanding what is driving costs today and for determining how to drive future profits and new strategies within the supply chain.

Managers use the reporting process to determine their trading partners' level of cost knowledge and to educate their upstream trading partners. Many suppliers do not have a thorough understanding of their costs and cost drivers. Managers can easily discern the level of cost knowledge by the information reported and the level of detail. By improving the suppliers' cost knowledge, the trading partners can enter into a more productive dialogue regarding how the demands placed on them by other trading partners drive their costs.

The subsequent cost exchange will encourage collaboration within the supply chain. One way to foster collaboration between trading partners is for them to understand how they affect each other's costs. Collaboration will grow in importance as the trading partners can credibly measure the cost impact that they create among themselves. Reliable cost and performance measures foster better communications, analysis, and understanding of how trading partners might collectively reduce costs.

In many instances, cost reporting identifies previously unknown competencies and knowledge resident in the upstream trading partners. This new knowledge enables the firm to seek opportunities to lower costs, increase customer service, obtain new services, achieve greater flexibility, and more quickly introduce new products and innovations. A cost reporting strategy increases cost visibility. Cost information is needed to see and understand the trading partners' cost structure both upstream and downstream. Without this information, managers within the supply chain will miss the opportunities for making effective cost trade-offs. Cost visibility enables firms to eliminate excess costs all the way through to the end user. Lower costs and improved performance increase overall product demand and profitability for the entire supply chain.

Pilot Projects

Using pilot projects for overcoming the challenges associated with supply chain costing is a useful methodology. The initial sharing of a limited amount of cost information provides the catalyst for fostering collaboration and trust between trading partners. Successful pilot projects have led to a greater two-way exchange of cost information as the trading partners attempt to broaden the scope of cost reduction opportunities. A limited test enables the participating firms to work out a method for ensuring the equitable allocation of the resulting burdens and benefits. Managers can use the pilot to increase their trading partners' level of cost knowledge while enhancing their cost estimation capabilities. During the pilot project, the trading partners can resolve any differences regarding cost definitions or allocations.

Revisit Chapter 10 and its section describing the rapid prototyping with iterative remodeling approach to implement activity-based costing (ABC). This approach arrives at a permanent, repeatable, and reliable ABC production system in weeks, not in months. Its additional benefits are that it accelerates the learning and understanding of managers on how to calculate costs, gets buy-in from those who are reluctant to use ABC, and stimulates the thinking of managers on how they will use the ABC information to make better decisions.

Managers should carefully pursue pilot projects for supply chain costing. Selection of an inappropriate pilot or partner may alienate rather than integrate the participating firms. Major factors that managers should consider when selecting a pilot study and partner are listed in Exhibit 13.1.

One example of a successful pilot project was the cooperative process used to reach a mutually beneficial delivery process change between a supplier and a major retailer (described in Chapter 2). Pilot projects such as this provide a quantitative understanding of the relationship. The use of costs enables managers to translate nonfinancial performance (such as dwell time and dock-to-stock time) into financial measures. To fully understand the cost trade-offs being made, costs need to be made visible to management. When the trade-offs occur across firms, management needs to have cost transparency regarding the complete process.

Pilot studies can provide several additional benefits that go beyond the sharing of cost information and obtaining process improvements. Managers can use the pilot as an opening to address a large number of disparate problems associated with restructuring supply chain processes.[2] These potential problems include the handling and ownership of any intellectual property resulting from the development of new services or products; information disclosure between the firms regarding demand forecasts, production levels, new product deployments, and sales promotions; and release of any information to other trading partners to obtain further improvements across the supply chain.

EXHIBIT 13.1 Selecting Pilot Projects and Partners

Factor	Explanation
Limited scope	The pilot scope should be large enough to permit a sufficient demonstration of the benefits of supply chain costing. Managers need to limit the scope to ensure a quick success without being encumbered by excessive detail or too broad an analysis. A short timeframe will ensure commitment of sufficient resources and continued management attention.
High probability of success	The pilot must have the capability to yield a noticeable cost reduction or performance improvement for the trading partners. Pilot selection should address a known problem capable of being fixed through collaborative effort.
Cost and performance data readily accessible	The cost and performance data needed to assess the pilot study should be easily accessible and not require the development and processing of specialized reports or data inquiries. Pilot selection should avoid situations where performance measures cannot be easily captured or where the costs are not directly assignable to the activities or processes under study.
Proprietary or sensitive information	The pilot should not require access to any sensitive or proprietary information from either trading partners. A key objective is to build trust, and the exchange of non-sensitive information will go a long way in developing open communication channels between the firms.
Sustainability	Changes resulting from the project should be sustainable over time. Process change should not be expensive or capital intensive and not require on going expenses or maintenance.
Education	The pilot should provide a chance for the trading partners to learn about each other and serve as a foundation for future collaboration. The project can serve as a classroom for educating the trading partners on costing techniques and the benefits of supply chain costing.
Simple design	The pilot should be easy to implement and understand. Value creation within the supply chain does not necessarily require radical reengineering of processes or relationships. The emphasis is on building rust, working toward common objectives, implementing innovative solutions, and creating value for both firms.

Despite the benefits, managers need to proceed with caution when pursuing supply chain costing initiatives. They need to ensure that their organization has developed a strong in-house costing capability and tackled internal cost reduction initiatives before seeking external improvements. Otherwise, the firm will create a perception that the burden for improving supply chain performance is simply being shifted onto the shoulders of other trading partners. Any decision to expand the scope or span of the pilot project should be based on a careful assessment of the costs and resources consumed by processes and the benefits they will produce. The decision by multiple trading partners to integrate their supply chain processes requires these trading partners to weigh increased output performance against the costs of resources used in the process. Adding more processes to the integration initiative will increase the resources consumed and outputs produced and further complicate the task of supply chain costing.

New Trading Partners

Many firms initiate supply chain costing with new trading partners to increase their chances for success. New trading partners are more receptive to exchanging cost information. These firms focus on gaining market share and expanding the relationship more than on preserving margin. They are much more willing to exchange and use cost information as a way to create additional value and solidify the relationship. Established trading partners, on the other hand, are often reluctant to exchange cost information. They have built up their margins over time through internal efficiencies or by advancing along the learning curve. The exchange of cost information will reveal these higher margins. They fear future negotiations will erode these margins and the advantage they hold.

Initiating supply chain costing with a new trading partner provides a means to establish trust between firms. Trust develops from the working relationships established at multiple levels and on how the firms handle and safeguard the exchanged information. The ability to create value for both firms through the exchange of cost information and shift functions builds a solid foundation for a strong alliance and a trusting relationship. As trust develops, management can focus their collective efforts on other areas likely to yield high payoffs. The greater the degree of trust, the more the trading partners can exchange detailed information to better understand their costs and the factors driving these costs.

On the surface, this strategy may appear overly simplistic. However, the exchange of cost information occurs more frequently with new trading partners than in well-established relationships. Managers should carefully consider how to best use these relationships to create mutually beneficial processes that can lead to creative approaches for value creation. A focus on attempting to collaborate with long standing trading partners may result in missing opportunities with new relationships.

The ability to exchange cost information with new trading partners provides a distinct advantage over other existing trading partner relationships. Management can more accurately determine how current processes between companies are performing, and improvements can be targeted where they will have the greatest effect. A free, cross-boundary sharing of information fosters team problem solving, and management can engrain this culture and action within the new relationship from the very start.[3] The exchange of cost and performance information supports the development of a common vision and strategy with the ability to accurately assess performance and profitability for each firm and the supply chain.

Value-Based Strategy

A value-based strategy provides a powerful tool for measuring and selling the value of supply chain costing to other trading partners. As managers make cost trade-offs across the supply chain, costs will go up for some trading partners and go down for others. Focusing too narrowly on costs produces a "you win, I lose" scenario and means managers will miss opportunities for creating value for themselves, other trading partners, and the end user in the supply chain. By considering how these trade-offs affect value creation, managers can more effectively demonstrate that sound business decisions targeted at improving process performance more often than not produce a win-win for collaborating trading partners.

Tools such as EVA and the balanced scorecard (see Chapter 12) represent good examples of a value-based approach that combines supply chain costing with other collaborative initiatives. Since many supply chain initiatives are focused on improving performance rather than on reducing costs, to obtain a competitive advantage, the ability to determine the effect on assets, costs, and revenue is extremely important to supply chain managers. Value-based measures incorporate multiple views of financial and nonfinancial information.

 WHAT STILL NEEDS TO BE DONE AS THE SUPPLY CHAIN COSTING JOURNEY CONTINUES

Expanding on what is already being done in the supply chain costing area will help organizations address the technical challenges inherent in implementing supply chain costing. This book might be characterized as a roadmap for dealing with many of the technical aspects of supply chain costing. It is clear that increasing the level of cost knowledge across the supply chain is essential for moving supply chain management to the next plateau of performance and value creation. Firms must increase the level of cost knowledge of managers across trading partners. Leading-edge companies need to be proactive in educating their trading partners inside and outside the organization. This process often needs to start with modifying the individual's view of the supply chain, supply chain processes, supply chain management, and supply chain costing itself.

Existing costing systems, particularly those designed to support external financial reporting needs, do not provide the support data needed for supply chain costing. How costs are defined, classified, and measured has major implications for how the cost information can be used. Organizations first need to be certain that their own costing house is in order and what type of cost[4] information is required, how measurement should occur, and what type of analysis is needed in different situations. Common definitions and measurement approaches are essential. Top managers may need to be convinced that there is value in putting additional resources into forward-looking supply chain costing efforts and less into assigning responsibility for past costs.

In evaluating the incurred costs, management needs to carefully consider whether sufficient attention has been placed on finding the underlying causes of cost, making the necessary adjustments to products or processes, and emphasizing future cost improvement. Many firms are not making enough use of key tools such as activity analysis, value chain costing, and customer profitability analysis. There is also a need to work on improving cost estimation within the context of budgeting, capital projects, and capacity—and on evaluating which additional costing tools are most appropriate.

Supply chain costing involves the entire value chain, and the challenge of having appropriate understandings of cost and cost tools exponentially compounds the complexity of the costing effort. As the focus turns to external trading partners, managers should document their interactions with their trading partners, paying special attention to how activities and changes in activities influence supplier and customer costs. Documentation will facilitate the improvement of technical costing efforts and establish a basis for more effective cost sharing. When cost sharing begins, trading partners need to reach agreements on the types of costs that will be included in the information exchange and on how that information may be used. By starting with a solid cost structure, they will have laid the groundwork for why cost sharing should occur.

Lack of trust is a major impediment to achieving the type of cost transparency capable of reducing overall supply chain costs and improving supply chain management. Management must recognize that their organization's unwillingness to share cost data may be a primary cause of this mistrust. Convincing top management to embrace cost transparency may be the biggest challenge facing even the most progressive supply chain manager. Cost transparency is a concept foreign to almost every manager. That "knowledge is power" is part of the business DNA. Breaking down the cultural and behavioral barriers that limit trust and inhibit sharing information, particularly cost information, will be a long-term process.

Trust is earned slowly and can be lost instantly. Many actions can be taken to help build trust. Managers must consciously focus on identifying ways to improve (and not reduce) the level of trust between organizations and functions. They must avoid taking actions that benefit (or are perceived to benefit) only one party. The exchange of cost information requires careful communication to overcome suspicion and foster greater trust. Operational information is more readily shared than financial information. Managers need to carefully explain why certain cost information is needed, how it will be used, and how it *will not* be used. Trading partners should look for opportunities to create win-win situations by sharing operational or only limited amounts or types of cost data. The ability to demonstrate how expanding cost sharing to additional cost areas would be mutually beneficial opens the door for further collaboration. Managers should use the cost lessons from their organizations to help improve process or reduce costs of trading partners. Due to the complexity of supply chain costing and cost assignments, the approach should progress slowly in adding to the level of information sharing.

Improved cost information can help your organization sell the benefits of supply chain costing to trading partners by creating situations beneficial to both parties. Managers should establish the importance of having quality cost information. They should use success stories from working with new trading partners to sell benefits of more information sharing with existing partners and demonstrate the benefits both sides derived from information-sharing arrangements. Firms should establish long-term relationships that entail communication about upcoming product or service changes, volumes, influence of environmental, strategy, or production shifts. Managers should reach and respect agreements to keep shared information confidential. They should acknowledge the effect of process changes and share the benefits. Documenting clear cases of win-win results from shared cost information is the most effective way to convince both internal and external managers that there is value to cost sharing. Overall, it is critical to sell the benefits of better supply chain costing.

 ## OVERALL CONCLUSIONS

Supply chain costing is still in its infancy, and firms that move out aggressively have a major opportunity. Leading firms already do many things right. There are opportunities to learn from their experiences using the examples and exhibits embedded throughout the book. Here are some parting observations for those taking the journey to improve supply chain costing.

- The low-hanging cost reduction fruit within the firm has largely been picked. Firms must look for new opportunities outside the firm, but this will require a broader vision of costs and an additional level of effort.
- Rising transportation prices, globalization challenges, and supply chain disruptions (such as those related to the COVID-19 pandemic) will intensify the focus on managing supply chain costs. Supply chain costing will be the platform for the future; major breakthroughs in supply chain management can identify the opportunities, determine the value created, and sell new initiatives.
- The value of cost knowledge is not understood by many managers within the firm. There is a culture of not looking outside the firm for opportunities to drive cost reductions or improve performance. The value of supply chain management is not currently measured and sold due to the inability to capture costs across trading partners.
- Supply chain management is not as well understood as many believe, especially when dealing with smaller customers or suppliers in many supply chains.
- Common definitions of the supply chain and supply chain costing are essential. Managers must have a solid understanding of the environment, organizational strategies, and types of production processes being used.
- Managers need to instill a cost-conscious culture in their firms. Costing is a core competency that can yield competitive advantage. Cost information

must take many forms to be useful for decision making. There must be a focus on both direct and indirect costs.

■ Supply chain costing is not a single costing technique. Like supply chain management, it is a broad term that encompasses many different costing techniques for expanding cost visibility across the supply chain.

■ Supply chain costing requires a major investment to do it right, but this investment provides a platform to make the leap to the next plateau in supply chain management.

■ The cost knowledge required to truly manage the supply chain, using operational and surrogate measures, can move the firm only so far ahead. Better cost information, within and between firms, is needed to make major strides forward. Trust and dependency are critical in determining whether cost data will be exchanged across firms.

■ Much of the cost data that is needed may not be as sensitive as managers currently perceive—cost and performance data is specific to the activities, process, and strategies being employed by the firm and its trading partners. The ability to exactly replicate these strategies and business practices, especially when involving multiple trading partners, is highly unlikely.

■ Supply chain costing is a strategic, competitive weapon that can also be used to support tactical and operational decisions once in place. To be effective, performance measures must be aligned with supply chain costing.

There are major challenges that are part of the supply chain costing journey, but taking the time to meet and overcome these challenges should be worthwhile for most organizations.

John Nash, the great Princeton University mathematician and Nobel Prize winner profiled in the Academy Award–winning movie *A Beautiful Mind*, with the actor Russell Crowe playing Nash, researched how rational people behave when faced with conflicts. Nash says in the movie:

> I like numbers because with numbers, truth and beauty are the same thing. You know you are getting somewhere when the equations start looking beautiful. And you know that the numbers are taking you closer to the secret of how things are.

For successful supply chain costing, it is essential to have effective methods and tools to provide managers insights, reduce internal debates, make better decisions, and improve an organization's performance.

NOTES

1. Gary Cokins, "Measuring Profits and Costs Across the Supply Chain for Collaboration," *Cost Management* 17, no. 5 (2003): 22–29.

2. Arthur Andersen LLC and C.J. McNair, *Tools and Techniques for Implementing Integrated Supply Chain Management* (Montvale, NJ: Institute of Management Accountants, 1999).

3. Ibid.

4. Cost information is defined as including revenue, cash flow, and any other type of financial data that the firm may find useful.

Appendix: Additional Process and Productivity Tools for Supply Chain Costing

A T THE OPERATIONAL LEVEL, organizational managers often focus primarily on reducing costs and on avoiding future costs. These managers are interested in understanding what can be changed, how to identify opportunities, and how to compare and differentiate high-impact opportunities from nominal ones. Tasked with productivity improvement challenges, they typically focus on streamlining processes, on reducing waste and low value-added work activities, and on increasing asset utilization. Tools that fall into this area include Six Sigma quality initiatives, lean management principles, and just-in-time (JIT) scheduling techniques. Each of these tools is a useful adjunct for improving supply chain costing throughout the value chain.

Operations managers and employee teams ideally should achieve a mastery of (or at least reasonable proficiency in) understanding the properties applied in assigning their department's expenses (e.g., general ledger accumulations of spending) into their calculated costs—the uses of the spending of resources needed for processes and their outputs. In short, costing is modeling. It models how the demands on work and resources are uniquely consumed and reported. Costs measure effects. Using this knowledge, operational employee teams can use managerial costing for productivity and process improvement.

What follows is a brief introduction to several additional tools that may be useful for the supply chain costing toolbox.

UNIT COSTS OF OUTPUTS AND BENCHMARKING

Operating managers should know the cost of processing various types of engineering changes in a manufacturing environment. Assume an analysis shows that it would cost $740 to make a product design change and $1,240 to complete a customer-requested product change. To determine these costs, managers need information on the individual unit costs of the work activities that are needed to determine the cost of each change. When employee teams are equipped with this type of unit cost of outputs data, they can ask better questions regarding the magnitude of costs constituting a process and what may be causing the cost to exist or fluctuate up or down. In addition to knowing what causes costs, organizations can compare the unit output costs of different divisions or departments that perform similar processes and use this as a form of internal benchmarking to promote the pursuit of best practices.

COST OF QUALITY (COQ)

For each work activity in a process, the Six Sigma and quality management community can use "attributes," ideally from an activity-based costing system, to calculate the cost of quality (COQ).

Exhibit A.1 illustrates how quality attributes for COQ categories can be tagged or scored into increasingly finer segments of error-free costs and the two primary COQ segments: (1) costs of conformance, and (2) costs of non-conformance. The former has two branches: prevention and appraisal. The latter's branches are internal failure and external failure. Each branch can be further segmented into the COQ types within them. A coding scheme is created for the branches.

Using the coding scheme, the code numbers are tagged to the individual work activities that belong to the various processes. These costs have already been calculated using activity-based costing (ABC). So, think of ABC's attributes as an additional dimension of costs. Because all the resource expenses can be assigned to the activity costs, 100% of the activities can be tagged with one of the COQ code scheme attributes. Summary rollups of COQ costs can be reported.

In the "error-free" category, a good and stable process exists. The "conformance-related work" category has quality-related costs because the process is not sufficiently stable to trust, so inspecting and testing are required. The "nonconformance-related work" category also has quality-related costs because something is already defective or has not conformed to specifications defined by the service recipient.

With costing rigor like this, quality teams can pursue stronger improvement programs and shift their time and emphasis away from documentation and reporting to taking corrective actions. Multiple activities can be simultaneously tagged with these grades and, of course, the money amount trails along, first at the work activity level and then into the cost objects (e.g., services).

EXHIBIT A.1 Cost of Quality Work Activities—Attributes can *Score* and *Tag* Costs

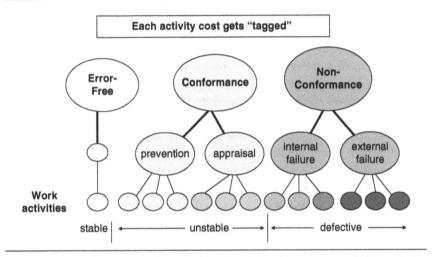

Source: Adapted from Gary Cokins, Activity-Based Cost Management: An Executive's Guide (New York: John Wiley & Sons, 2001), p. 88. Used with permission of the author.

When attributes are tagged to activities, each cost object will consume multiple grades of a select attribute and, as a result, will reflect different blends of the category costs. An analogy would be the different gallons (cost amount) of distinctively colored paint (an attribute's different score) being poured (activity driver) into an empty paint can (cost object). As each empty can is filled, the color of the paint will be different, even if the cans are filled to comparable levels (same amount of cost). Hence, you can see the colors of money.

Other popular ways exist to tag attributes. One is to tag activities along a scale of their contribution to profits or satisfying customers. An example of this would be to use these four attributes of work activities in a process: high value-adding, medium value-adding, low value-adding, and no value-add.

For COQ and other attribute cost measures, the financial accounting system requires enhancement. Without an activity-based costing system to tag individual activity costs, the COQ categories and attributes cannot be isolated and scored.

 ## TIME-DRIVEN ACTIVITY-BASED COSTING (TDABC)[1]

A more granular ABC modeling technique calculates potential unused capacity. It uses activity drivers only of time duration (e.g., number of minutes) rather than of transactions (e.g., number of events). Recall that base-level ABC traces resource expenses to work activities and ultimately into their outputs (e.g., product, SKU, route) without capacity sensitivity. Any idle capacity expenses, which may include safety or buffer capacity, are included in the output costs as a business sustaining category, as described in Exhibit 10.3.

For conditions where unused capacity is suspected to be more than negligible, it can be made visible using TDABC's industrial engineering, time-standards approach. Each step in a process is measured in minutes for an individual unit processed. Next, the quantity of output units processed is multiplied by each step's per-unit minutes. Then the step's cost is calculated based on the expense per minute of the resources *supplied* and contributing to the process. All of the steps are then summed. This total calculates the resource expenses *used* assuming standard unit-level duration times. The *used* expenses (at standard) are subtracted from the expenses *supplied*, the difference being the unused capacity.

TDABC is a "pull" costing model that starts at the "bottom" of the cost assignment network in Exhibit 10.3. It calculates the volume and quantity of the activity cost drivers multiplied by the standard time rates to solve for the expected level of resource expenses with the standard rates. In contrast, ABC is a "push" costing model that starts at the "top" of Exhibit 10.3. It traces the transformation of the resource expenses, where the capacity expenses reside, into the final cost objects.

TDABC is applicable under the special condition where management wants to precisely calculate the cost of its operations' idle and excess capacity. With traditional ABC, an estimate of the idle or excess resource expenses can be assigned to an idle activity and then further traced to a business-sustaining final cost object. This prevents overcosting products or customers with costs they did not cause. In effect, ABC is a simpler way to calculate idle and excess capacity compared to the complex TDABC.

Another shortcoming of TDABC is that it does not have a middle activity module with an explicit activity dictionary, as with ABC. Instead, as shown in Exhibit A.2, TDABC has time algorithms in the bottom final cost objects module without a middle activity module. This makes designing and maintaining a TDABC more time consuming and complex. Math majors may understand the equations, but not line managers and executives who need the ABC information about their existing costs, especially for profit margin analysis, for insights and decision making. Displaying the ABC work activities, ideally with verb-adjective-noun grammar, makes the ABC information cause-and-effect information more understandable to line managers and executives.

EXHIBIT A.2   TDABC Costing Method versus ABC

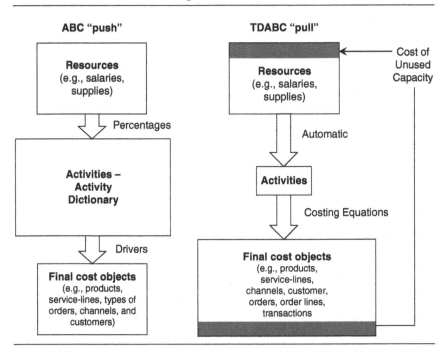

Source: Adapted from Gary Cokins and Douglas Paul, "Time-Driven or Driver Rate-Based ABC: How Do You Choose?" Strategic Finance (February 2016), p. 28, Institute of Management Accountants, Montvale NJ (www.imanet.org); Copyright Gary Cokins. Used with permission of the author and the IMA.

RESOURCE CONSUMPTION ACCOUNTING (RCA) AND GERMAN COST ACCOUNTING'S GPK

Activity-based costing *pushes* resource expenses into activity costs with assignments traced on time estimates (e.g., number of fractional hours, percentage splits of work activities during the time period). It begins with the expense data collected in the financial accounting general ledger (or its feeder subsystems, such as payroll or purchasing). An alternative method, resource consumption accounting (RCA), *pulls* the consumption of activity costs and resource expenses based on transaction activity drivers. It is similar to TDABC, but does not require each process step's minutes. RCA segments all resources into two categories: (1) fixed expenses that remain constant independent of changes in the quantity or volume of the activity driver, and (2) proportional (e.g., variable) expenses that linearly change with changes in the quantity or volume of the activity driver.

This segmentation allows for a more accurate calculation of the predictive view impact on resource expenses to enable a more reflective view of cost consumption behavior. It enables marginal cost analysis—the impact of volume and mix changes on resource capacity expenses. Similar to TDABC, RCA isolates unused capacity and includes it in outputs costs. A German costing method called GPK (for Grenzplankostenrechnung) is similar to RCA.

Both TDABC and RCA/GPK isolate some of the unused capacity, make it visible, and thus can help operations identify opportunities for productivity improvements. RCA/GPK also facilitates marginal cost analysis for the predictive view of expenses required. They do, however, required extra administrative effort to collect input information (e.g., time) and design a more robust cost model.

 ## ACCOUNTING FOR LEAN MANAGEMENT

A relatively new concept of measuring costs referred to as lean accounting is intended to support lean management principles.[2] Lean management principles advocate simplicity. Lean management is a systematic approach to identifying and eliminating waste and errors, including non-value-adding (nonproductive) work activities. Productivity increases are accomplished through continuous improvement of processes to accelerate the throughput cycle time of products or services. A popular method of visualizing and measuring processes is value stream mapping. Please refer to Exhibits 7.2, 7.3, 7.4, and 7.5 and the discussion about the vertical view (cost assignment) and horizontal view (process) of costs. Exhibit 7.5 displays a value stream map.

A value stream map consists of all the activities (e.g., steps) to create customer value for a product family or service offering.[3] It removes the barriers of functional or department silos to aid process improvement teams with better communications and decision making. A value stream map is similar to a process flowchart.

Accounting for a lean management environment developed as a result of the frustrations of managers and employee teams in operations. They disliked traditional standard cost accounting's inability to evaluate lean projects for their cost savings potential and its inability to measure incremental improvements. In addition, operations personnel questioned the worth of their daily efforts to collect transactional data, given that many operations people had found little use for actual-to-standard cost variance reporting. This frustration is understandable given what is now generally understood about deficiencies with traditional standard costing.

Accounting for a lean environment attempts to solve some of operations' immediate financial measurement problems. As operations personnel make improvements (e.g., eliminating non-value-adding costs, reducing resources, and/or increasing the rate of throughput in processes), they can financially measure productivity increases that ultimately show up on the bottom line of their company's income statement.

Lean accounting is appealing to the vast majority of employees who make daily operational decisions because they see it as a simpler and more relevant costing technique for them. However, the minority of employees who make less frequent but more important strategic decisions that may impact hundreds of day-to-day decisions need an enterprise view to understand the long-term economic consequences. Lean accounting is not the answer for these employees.

Lean accounting advocates and ABC advocates often debate which is the most appropriate costing method. There are rival camps. Some lean accounting advocates, who create and use value stream maps, criticize ABC as being too complex. Some of them fear that ABC will compete with their desire for lean accounting to be the only cost accounting method. Conversely, ABC advocates argue that ABC provides more cost driver visibility and much greater cost accuracy than the flawed and misleading costs from traditional and cost distorting cost allocation methods. Is one or the other correct?

One needs to ask a different question to resolve this dilemma. Can a company have two or more coexisting management accounting methods? The answer is that it can. There can be different costs for distinctive purposes used by different types of managers and employee teams. ABC is used strategically to understand profit margins. Lean accounting is used operationally to improve productivity.

 ## THEORY OF CONSTRAINTS THROUGHPUT ACCOUNTING

The theory of constraints (TOC) is a methodology based on the observation that a capacity constraint anywhere in a flow system will govern the entire system's rate of the final throughput of outputs. It was originally used to schedule and dispatch production orders. It observed that a quest for high-capacity utilization at any work center is suboptimal and leads to unnecessary buildup of in-process inventories—which is counter to just-in-time synchronous flow practices. A companion managerial accounting technique of TOC is called *throughput accounting*.

Throughput accounting was originally intended to support short-term production order scheduling and dispatching decisions to prioritize the sequence of products to make based on their level of profit.

However, a severe limitation of TOC's throughput accounting is that it requires the very special condition of a 365-day/24-hour physical bottleneck constraint (like a heat treat oven in a foundry). This condition is very rare. When there is not a 24-hour, 7-day, 365-day physical bottleneck, then conventional incremental and marginal expense analysis applies. This analysis considers the ease or difficulty of adjusting each resource's capacity. This type of analysis classifies each resource's capacity as sunk, fixed, step-fixed, or variable. Moreover, the classification depends on the planning time horizon. Review the discussion related to Exhibit 6.2.

TOC's throughput accounting can lead to production scheduling to maximize short-term profits. However, TOC's assumption that most expenses (i.e., capacity) are fixed obscures conclusions that some capacity is adjustable even in the short run (e.g., replacing full-time employees with temporary contractors) and all of it is adjustable in the long run.

NOTES

1. Gary Cokins and Douglas Paul, "Time Driven or Driver Rate Based ABC: How Do You Choose?" *Strategic Finance*, February 2016.

2. Gary Cokins, "Lean "Lean Accounting and Activity Based Costing: A Choice or a Blend?" *Cost Management*, January/February 2019.

3. Institute of Management Accountants, "Lean Enterprise Fundamental," *Statement of Management Accounting* (2008): 5.

Index